THE LOW APPETITE COOKBOOK

THE LOW APPETITE COOKBOOK

Over 100 nutrient-dense meals to make every bite count

Rob Hobson

Thorsons

CONTENTS

Introduction 6

Why Is Low Appetite a Problem? 10
The Key Principles of Low Appetite Eating 15
Protein and Muscle Mass 20
The Thing About Fibre 28
How Much Should You Eat When Your Appetite Is Low? 31
The Low Appetite Survival Guide 33
Understanding GLP-1 Medications 40
Five Fixes to Make Every Bite Count 50
How to Fuel Exercise with Low Appetite 56
Health Hacks for Mealtimes 61
Managing Leftovers and Getting Organised in the Kitchen 65
Building a Low Appetite Store Cupboard 71
No-cook Recipe Ideas 74

The Recipes

Breakfast 76
Lunch 90
Dinner 140
Nutrient Boosters 192
Juices, Smoothies & Warming Drinks 204
Pre- and Post-workout Snacks 210

Meal Plans 222
Appendices 228
References + Acknowledgements 234
Index 235

INTRODUCTION

What do you eat when your appetite disappears but your body still needs fuel?

Whether you're taking GLP-1 medications like Ozempic, Wegovy or Mounjaro, or finding it harder to eat due to illness, recovery, stress, hormones or emotional strain, eating well with a low appetite requires a different approach. Traditional ideas about three square meals a day, full plates and fuelling a busy lifestyle don't always fit.

These are different experiences, but they all share one important truth: when you eat less, you're at risk of becoming undernourished, especially if you're skipping meals or struggling to finish your meals. Without proper guidance, this can lead to reduced muscle mass, nutrient deficiencies and low energy.

Earlier in my career, I worked in settings where low appetite was a daily reality, supporting people who were in recovery from illness or surgery rebuilding strength after fatigue, or navigating food aversions that weren't a choice. I've also worked with older adults, picky eaters and clients for whom food simply lost its appeal. The pattern was always the same: appetite low, energy limited, and food needing to work much harder.

My work as a nutritionist has always been about helping people build positive, realistic relationships with food where nourishment, balance and enjoyment all matter. But increasingly, I've seen a quieter challenge come to the surface: how do you eat well when your appetite is low, your portions are small and eating feels like a chore?

This is becoming increasingly relevant with the rise of GLP-1 medications, which can dramatically suppress appetite, reduce interest in food and make it difficult to maintain a balanced diet. While I don't work in a clinical setting, I've supported private clients using these medications and have seen first-hand how challenging it can be to meet basic nutritional needs, let alone support muscle maintenance, exercise recovery or general wellbeing. Some struggle with nausea or early fullness, while others skip meals due to lack of hunger.

For active individuals with a low appetite this is more complex as fuelling for training, getting enough protein to repair and preserve lean mass and staying energised throughout the day require a bit of planning.

As a nutrition expert with my finger on the pulse of both research and real-world trends, I've spent time developing practical, realistic strategies to help people navigate some of these challenges and bring enjoyment and nourishment back to the table. This book brings together my experience and insights to support anyone navigating the complex challenge of eating well with a reduced appetite.

A toolkit for small appetites

You won't find rigid meal plans or unrealistic expectations here. This book is a flexible, practical guide for eating well when your appetite is low, your portions are small and your motivation to cook from scratch might be even smaller.

Whatever your health goal, the solution to eating well with a reduced appetite is the same: smaller meals, smarter nutrition and a gentler way of eating.

When you're eating less, every bite matters. That's why the focus here is on nutrient density and not portion size. You'll learn how to create satisfying meals and snacks that deliver protein, fibre, healthy fats and essential micronutrients in smaller volumes. You'll also find ideas for when cooking feels like too much, when your appetite shifts unexpectedly, or when you just need something simple to get through the day.

LOW APPETITE EATING DOESN'T JUST CHANGE HOW MUCH YOU EAT; IT CHANGES:

- How you plan and shop for meals
- How you respond to hunger (or lack of it)
- How you feel about food emotionally
- How your body absorbs and uses nutrients

Large meals can feel physically uncomfortable or emotionally off-putting, and it's easy to skip meals altogether. That's why this book offers a different model, one that's flexible, nourishing and designed to make food feel doable again.

THIS BOOK IS DESIGNED FOR ANYONE WHO:

- Is using GLP-1 medications such as Ozempic, Wegovy or Mounjaro
- Is recovering from illness, surgery or long-term treatment
- Has a naturally lower appetite due to ageing, hormones or stress
- Finds large meals uncomfortable or off-putting
- Prefers to eat light, small or frequently
- Is active, but struggles to fuel properly due to low appetite

How to use this book

This book is designed to meet you wherever you are. Some days you'll want light, simple options, but other days you might feel ready for more. Use it to guide your choices based on how you're feeling, whether your appetite is low, your energy is limited or you're aiming to rebuild strength. It's about personalising your approach, one meal at a time. That might mean eating solo and keeping things simple, or it might mean sharing a meal with others and choosing something that feels good in company, even if it's just a few bites.

INSIDE YOU'LL FIND:

- Guidance on how to eat well when appetite is reduced
- Flexible recipes tailored to different appetites, energy levels and moods
- Ideas for protein-packed snacks, no-cook meals and easy nutrient wins
- Smart food pairings to improve energy levels, support recovery and reduce pressure
- Tools for making cooking feel simpler, faster and more manageable
- Advice on structuring small meals across the day to meet your needs or busy schedule

Using the chapters before the recipes

You don't need to read this book cover to cover; you can – if you want – jump straight to the recipes. However, the first part of the book offers flexible guidance on low appetite eating, whether you're adjusting to GLP-1 medications, trying to understand how much to eat or simply navigating the ups and downs of daily appetite.

This book isn't intended to replace medical advice, nor is it a prescriptive guide to using GLP-1 medications. I'm not a doctor, and I don't prescribe or manage these drugs. Instead, my aim is to offer nutritional support and practical strategies that work alongside medical care because eating well matters just as much as the medication itself. Everyone's journey with appetite, weight and health is different, and this book is designed to support you wherever you are on that path.

Feel free to dip in and out. These chapters are here to support you, not prescribe anything. Use what's helpful, skip what's not and come back whenever you need a bit more structure or encouragement.

How the recipe chapters work

Recipes are grouped not just by mealtime, but also by mood and energy level. That way, you can find meals that:

- Deliver solid nutrition in small volumes
- Use flavour, colour and texture to help spark appetite
- Feel emotionally satisfying without being overwhelming

Each recipe is designed to support a smaller appetite so meals feel manageable, not overwhelming. You'll find straightforward methods, familiar ingredients and portions that are satisfying but not too much. Recipes make two servings so you can 'eat one and save one' for later.

Each meal section – breakfast, lunch and dinner – is also divided by how you feel and what you can manage. So you can build a nourishing day one meal at a time, based on how you feel in the moment. You'll find:

- **Light and energising** – when you need fuel without heaviness
- **Easy to digest** – when digestion feels off or your appetite is unpredictable
- **Protein packed** – when you need to get more protein without eating more food
- **Comforting and warming** – for days when you crave something soothing

You'll also find extra sections at the end of the book: Nutrient Boosters help you to add more nourishment to meals in a simple way, Juices, Smoothies & Warming Drinks are an easy nutrient fix or to pair with smaller meals, and Pre- and Post-workout Snacks support energy and recovery when your appetite is low. These can be mixed and matched to suit your needs throughout the day.

EACH RECIPE ALSO INCLUDES NOTES ON:

- Optional ingredients or additions to boost protein, calories or other nutrients like fibre, vitamins and minerals
- Which vitamins and minerals in the recipe will contribute to your recommended daily allowance
- How to store leftovers or prep ahead
- If it's suitable for next-day take-to-work lunches or meals on the go

Throughout the recipes are smart pairings to make meals more satisfying or nutritionally complete – soup with protein-rich crackers, or a handful of nuts with a smoothie.

A note on simplicity

The recipes are designed to be as simple as possible. Short ingredient lists, minimal prep and quick cooking methods mean you won't need to dig deep for motivation. These aren't elaborate, chef-style meals – because they're not supposed to be.

That said, they're still big on flavour. Every recipe is satisfying, balanced and based on real food. Whether you're craving something fresh, warming or that you can grab and plate up with no fuss, you'll find it in here.

Using cooked ingredients

Some recipes use cooked grains (like quinoa or rice) or some form of pre-cooked protein (like chicken, tofu or lentils). This isn't about making life complicated, it's about saving time and offering options on days when cooking from scratch doesn't appeal. While some ready meals and shortcuts can be helpful, many convenience products are ultra-processed, meaning they may be lower in nutrients and higher in additives. The aim here is to keep things simple without relying on UPFs. Here's how to make it work:

- Batch-cook at the start of the week
- Use shortcuts like pouches of grains, tinned beans or ready-cooked proteins
- Prefer to cook from scratch? Recipes include raw or dry weights so you can prepare what you need on the spot
- For the best flavour and texture, cook grains fresh where possible. You can still batch-cook and store them, then they're ready to go when your appetite allows

This book supports a flexible approach to eating, so there's no pressure to stick to conventional mealtimes or portion sizes. It's about giving you choices, whatever makes eating feel doable that day. Every recipe is designed with smaller appetites in mind, but most can be scaled up or paired with a simple side if your hunger increases or you're cooking for others.

The tips and tools in this book are designed to support real-life eating, when energy, appetite or motivation might be inconsistent. Use them to reduce decision fatigue and get more out of each meal.

WHY IS LOW APPETITE A PROBLEM?

This book began with a simple but urgent truth that over a prolonged period of time not eating enough can quietly sabotage your health, even if you're on a weight-loss journey.

And yet, it often flies under the radar. Many people don't realise that a low appetite isn't just inconvenient but can have serious health implications, especially if it continues over time. The effects can creep in slowly, but they're real and significant. You may feel more tired, lose strength or your immunity might be compromised.

Food isn't just fuel. It's your body's main source of raw materials to keep everything running, from your immune system and muscle mass to your brain, bones and mood. It's also about more than just biology, as eating can bring joy, connection and comfort, too, whether that's trying something new, sharing a meal or simply enjoying a favourite flavour. That's why I wrote this book, to help you nourish your body, even when eating feels like a struggle or simply slips your mind.

Why undereating is risky

When you consistently eat less than your body needs, the short-term effects can quickly snowball into something more serious if you don't keep a check on it. People with low appetites often experience:

- Loss of muscle mass, especially in midlife and older adults
- Weakened bones, especially in women in midlife and beyond, increasing the risk of fractures and falls
- Dental health issues, which can be made worse by nutrient deficiencies or changes in eating patterns
- Slower recovery from activity, illness or injury, as your body lacks the nutrients it needs to repair and rebuild
- Fatigue, poor concentration, low mood and brain fog
- Weakened immunity and getting sick more often
- Increased risk of vitamin and mineral deficiencies
- Low blood pressure, which can cause dizziness or faintness, especially if you're not eating or drinking enough
- Changes to your metabolism over time, which can affect how efficiently your body uses and stores energy

While these issues might not sound dramatic at first, they can chip away at your strength, resilience and overall quality of life. And if you're already managing a health condition, poor nutrition can make it harder to recover and stay well in the long term.

Muscle loss deserves special mention. If you're not eating enough, especially not enough protein, your body will gradually break down lean tissue, including muscle. This makes you feel weaker, reduces stamina and slows your metabolism. It also puts you at greater risk of injury and makes it harder to bounce back after being unwell. For men and women in midlife and beyond, this is a big deal because age-related muscle loss (sarcopenia) accelerates after the age of 40 and can be compounded by undereating.

Add to that the impact on bone health. Over time, a diet low in calcium, protein and vitamin D can weaken bones, increasing the risk of fractures; this is especially true for women post-menopause, when bone loss accelerates.

Appetite loss also raises the risk of deficiencies in essential nutrients like iron, B12, magnesium and vitamin D. These shortfalls can leave you feeling tired, mentally foggy and more vulnerable to falling sick, and because these symptoms are often gradual or mistaken for just 'getting older' or 'being run down', they can often go unrecognised.

Appetite, weight loss drugs and nutrient gaps

We're entering a new phase in health where increasing numbers of people are losing weight, often through the use of GLP-1 medications, but becoming more vulnerable to nutritional shortfalls in the process. These drugs work by altering gut hormones and slowing gastric emptying, often making people feel full very quickly, even after just a few bites. While they can be effective for weight loss and blood sugar control, they're not a straightforward fix. Side effects like nausea, fatigue or digestive discomfort are common, and the reduced desire to eat can make it difficult to meet even basic nutritional needs, let alone support energy, muscle repair or overall wellbeing.

While these medications have been transformational – for weight loss, for managing obesity-related health conditions like type 2 diabetes and for reducing cardiovascular risk – they also make it easier to overlook what the body still needs: protein, fibre, healthy fats, vitamins, minerals and enough energy to function well. This reduction in appetite, though helpful for weight loss, raises a nutritional red flag. If your intake drops without careful planning, it's easy to miss key nutrients.

A study published in the journal *Frontiers in Nutrition* in 2025 offers some much-needed insight into what's actually happening with diet quality when people use GLP-1 medications like semaglutide (Wegovy, Ozempic) and tirzepatide (Mounjaro).[1] While these drugs are highly effective at reducing appetite and driving weight loss, the study found they may also be leading people into quiet but significant nutrient shortfalls (although this was not covered in the study, the long-term health impacts of these nutrient gaps and of GLP-1 use more generally are still being researched).

The researchers analysed three-day food records from 69 people taking GLP-1s and compared their intake to standard recommendations. What they found was that most people weren't getting enough essential nutrients. Fibre, calcium, magnesium, iron, potassium, choline and several key vitamins including A, C, D and E, were all significantly below target. Fibre intake, for instance, was about 14g per day – less than half the recommended 30g. That's a concern not just for digestion, but for cholesterol, blood sugar and overall gut health.

Fruit and vegetable intake was also low, at less than one serving of fruit and just over one serving of veg per day on average. Interestingly, many people in the study thought they were eating better than they actually were, which shows how easy it is to misjudge your intake when you're eating less overall. A reduced appetite makes portion control easier, but it can also mean you miss out on diversity, especially across food groups, and that is where nutrient density becomes so important.

Diversity in the diet helps ensure you're getting a broader range of vitamins, minerals, fibre and beneficial plant compounds that no single food can provide on its own. It also supports a healthier gut microbiome. Research from the American Gut Project suggests aiming for around 30 different plant foods a week, including fruit, vegetables, whole grains, legumes, nuts, seeds, herbs and spices, to help nourish a wide range of beneficial gut bacteria.[2]

Protein was another area that raised flags. While intake as a percentage of calories looked okay, it fell short when measured per kilogram of body weight. This is a problem because preserving lean muscle is essential during weight loss, especially when using GLP-1s, which I will talk about in the following sections. Although the general guideline for protein is around 0.8g per kilogram of body weight per day, this is a minimum aimed at healthy adults with stable weight and average activity. For those actively losing weight, and particularly those using appetite-suppressing medications, protein needs are higher. Only a small percentage of people in the study were hitting even the lower end of the recommended 1.2–2.0g of protein per kilogram of body weight per day when losing weight.

What all this tells us is simple: just because you're eating less, doesn't mean you're eating well. And the takeaway? If you're using a GLP-1 drug, you'll likely need to be more intentional about the foods you eat.

The case for nutrient-dense meals

When your appetite is smaller or you're eating less overall, the nutritional quality of each bite becomes even more important. With fewer opportunities to meet your needs, every meal must pull more weight. While someone with a larger appetite might get away with the occasional nutrient-poor meal, that margin is much smaller for you. Every mouthful needs to count. Think of your food as your body's toolkit; if you're eating less, the kit gets smaller and your body has to do the same amount of work with fewer resources.

Vitamins and minerals support everything from energy and immunity to bones, sleep,

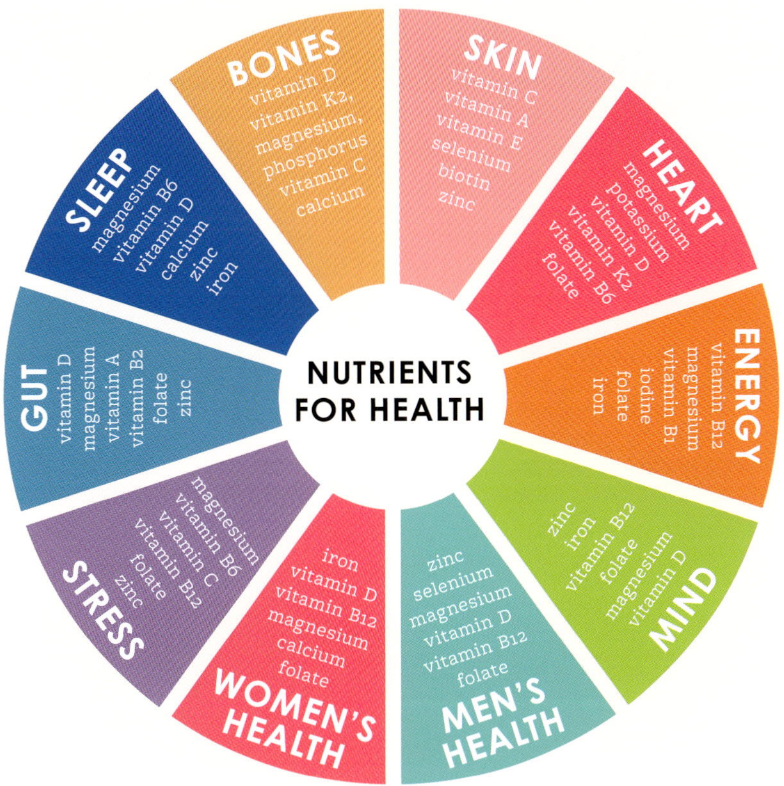

mood and skin health. The graphic above show just how many areas of your body rely on key nutrients so even a small meal can have a big impact when it's packed with the right ones.

Key nutrients to prioritise when you're eating less

All nutrients are important for health, but the ones highlighted are particularly important because they support the areas most affected by low appetite: muscle strength, bone health, energy, immunity and recovery. These are also the nutrients most often lacking when people eat less, including those using GLP-1 medications. By improving the quality of your meals, you'll naturally increase your intake of these and other important nutrients. For a full list of key vitamins and minerals, see Appendix 2 on page 232.

A low appetite can be a challenge, but learning how to eat *well* with a low appetite is the solution.

It's not about fixing your appetite, it's about feeding your body well, whatever your appetite is doing. It's a flexible, nutrient-focused approach to eating that works with your current appetite, rather than against it. For some, this means remembering to eat – and eat the right things – even when hunger is absent. For others, it means gently rebuilding interest in food and making eating feel possible again.

Nutrient	Why It Matters	Top Food Sources	Signs of Deficiency
Protein	Essential for maintaining muscle mass and supporting immune function, hormone production and tissue repair	Eggs, poultry, fish, seafood, tofu, tempeh, legumes (e.g. lentils, chickpeas), dairy and fortified plant alternatives, nuts, seeds, protein powders	Muscle wasting, reduced strength, poor wound healing, hair thinning, fatigue, slow recovery from illness, frequent infections
Calcium	Builds and maintains bones and teeth; supports nerve signalling, blood clotting and muscle contraction	Fortified plant milks and yoghurts, dairy, tofu with calcium, tinned fish with bones (e.g. sardines, salmon), kale, broccoli, almonds, sesame seeds (tahini)	Muscle cramps, brittle nails, tooth decay, numbness or tingling, low bone density, increased fracture risk
Vitamin D	Helps calcium absorption; supports immunity, muscle function and bone health	Sunlight exposure (main source), oily fish (salmon, mackerel), egg yolks, fortified foods (plant milks, cereals), mushrooms (UV-exposed), supplements	Fatigue, low mood, bone and muscle pain, frequent colds/ infections, delayed healing, muscle weakness
Iron	Carries oxygen in the blood; supports cognitive function and energy metabolism	Red meat, liver, lentils, chickpeas, tofu, quinoa, spinach, pumpkin seeds, fortified cereals, dried apricots (pair with vitamin C foods for better absorption)	Tiredness, pale skin, shortness of breath, dizziness, brittle nails, brain fog, feeling cold, frequent illness
B Vitamins (especially B6, B12, folate)	Important for energy production, red blood cell formation, brain and nerve function	Wholegrains, legumes, eggs, leafy greens, fortified cereals and nutritional yeast, meat, dairy, fish (B12 is mostly found in animal products)	Low energy, irritability, numbness or tingling in hands/feet, anaemia, poor memory, mouth ulcers
Omega-3 Fats (EPA and DHA)	Supports brain function, reduces inflammation, protects heart health, supports mood	Oily fish (salmon, mackerel, sardines), flaxseeds, chia seeds, walnuts, algae oil (vegan), hemp seeds	Dry skin, poor concentration, low mood, joint stiffness, visual disturbances, frequent inflammation
Fibre	Supports digestion and bowel health, stabilises blood sugar, feeds gut bacteria	Oats, beans, lentils, chickpeas, flaxseeds, chia seeds, wholegrains, berries, apples, carrots, broccoli	Constipation, bloating, unstable blood sugar, feeling sluggish, poor gut health, increased cholesterol
Magnesium	Regulates muscle and nerve function; supports energy production, sleep and bone health	Nuts (especially almonds, cashew nuts), seeds (pumpkin, chia), wholegrains, dark leafy greens, avocado, dark chocolate, legumes	Muscle twitches or cramps, poor sleep, fatigue, low mood, anxiety, irregular heartbeat

THE KEY PRINCIPLES OF LOW APPETITE EATING

When your appetite drops, knowing how to eat can be just as important as knowing what to eat. That's why this book is built around key principles that support eating well when your hunger signals are blunted.

The five pillars of low appetite eating

These pillars are the guiding principles that can help you navigate low appetite in a flexible, manageable way, so you can get the nutrition you need without relying on big meals or complicated plans. They underpin every recipe, strategy and suggestion in this book, offering a framework you can return to whenever eating feels difficult.

Keep these five pillars in mind as you move through the book, as they're your foundation for eating well, even when your appetite is diminished.

THE 5 PILLARS OF LOW APPETITE EATING

Nutrient Density	Appetite Stimulation	Motivation and Joy	Effortless Eating	Mood and Resilience
Focus on quality over quantity	Use flavour, smell and timing	Connect food with purpose and pleasure	Make meals easy and accessible	Support the mind-body connection

PILLAR 1: NUTRIENT DENSITY

When you're eating less overall, it's important that each bite works harder for you, so that you are packing nutrition into smaller portions. Nutrient-dense foods are those that provide a more concentrated source of vitamins, minerals, fibre, healthy fats and protein relative to their calorie content. They deliver the essential building blocks your body needs to function, repair and maintain strength without relying on large portions.

Low appetite eating isn't about volume, it's about making smart, satisfying choices that give you more nutrition in fewer bites. That's why the recipes in this book are built around nutrient-rich ingredients and clever food pairings that help you meet your needs, even if you're only eating a few times a day.

PILLAR 2: APPETITE STIMULATION

When your appetite is low, food needs to appeal to more than just hunger; it needs to appeal to all your senses. This is relevant to those on GLP-1 medication as well as those who are struggling with low appetite for other reasons. Smell, taste, texture and appearance all play important roles in triggering the desire to eat when you're not hungry or food doesn't feel appealing.

Even simple sensory cues like the aroma of something cooking or the colour and crunch of a dish can gently reignite interest in food. That's why so many recipes in this book are designed to be visually appealing, aromatic and texturally satisfying without being overwhelming.

PILLAR 3: MOTIVATION AND JOY

Reduced appetite, whether related to GLP-1 medication or other factors, can affect your motivation to cook and eat. Re-establishing a practical, positive connection with food is an important part of managing low appetite. This might involve simplifying meal preparation, returning to familiar foods or focusing on straightforward, enjoyable meals. The goal isn't to increase intake for its own sake, but to make eating more manageable and sustainable in day-to-day life. Over time, these strategies can help support a more consistent eating pattern and improve overall dietary quality.

PILLAR 4: EFFORTLESS EATING

When your appetite is low, energy levels can also take a dive. Whether you are on GLP-1 medication or need low appetite support, long cooking sessions and complicated recipes from fancy cookbooks are neither realistic nor necessary.

Low appetite eating works best when it's rooted in convenience and simplicity. That might mean cooking small portions and freezing them for easy reheating, or relying on pre-prepped staples like cooked grains, roasted veg or tinned pulses that cut kitchen time without compromising nutrition.

Some people also experience nausea or sensitivity to smells, especially during medication use or illness. In those moments, strong cooking odours or rich dishes can feel overwhelming, so this book includes light, neutral-flavoured options that are easier to tolerate, plus cold meal ideas that sidestep cooking altogether when you need it.

Eating well also shouldn't come at a high price. Many of the recipes here use budget-friendly ingredients like tinned fish, frozen vegetables and affordable plant proteins. Convenience doesn't have to mean expensive pre-packaged food: with the right approach it can be both nutrient-dense and cost-conscious.

Throughout this book, you'll find realistic, time-saving strategies woven into the recipes, so even if you're having a low energy day, eating well will still be within reach.

PILLAR 5: MOOD AND RESILIENCE

It's common for taste and texture preferences to shift, with foods you once enjoyed becoming unappealing, and unexpected cravings or aversions emerging. One moment you may want something light and sharp like avocado with lemon or a crunchy salad with tangy dressing, then the next, only something soft and warm like mashed vegetables or a mild dhal will be tolerable.

This pillar supports eating in response to what feels manageable and appealing at the

TWO MINDSETS, ONE NUTRITIONAL GOAL

Throughout this book, you'll see references to both GLP-1 medications and other causes of low appetite. These are two very different experiences, with distinct mindsets.

If you're taking GLP-1s, you may feel a deep sense of relief from the constant food chatter or 'food noise' that once shaped your eating habits. For many people, this quiet is welcome as it means less emotional eating, fewer cravings and a break from the mental load of thinking about food all the time. In this context, you may need reminders to eat and stay nourished, without feeling pressured to eat more than your body wants.

If your low appetite is caused by any other reason, then your focus may be on gently rebuilding regular eating habits, restoring strength and finding comfort in food again.

This book is designed to support both journeys. While not every section will apply to everyone, each part is rooted in the same core challenge; you're eating less, but your body still needs meaningful nutrition. As a nutritionist, I've spent years helping people find realistic, evidence-based ways to nourish themselves even when appetite is low, energy is limited, or eating feels like a chore. That's why the focus here is on essential nourishment and getting what you need in smaller, more manageable portions.

To help you navigate what's most relevant to your experience, health goals and priorities, look out for these flags throughout the book:

 GLP-1 Guidance  Low Appetite Support

These markers will help you quickly identify tips and strategies that speak directly to your needs, while still giving you the flexibility to dip into whatever feels useful.

time, not just the time of day. That's why the recipes in this book are grouped not only by meal type, but also by mood, helping you find options that align with your changing preferences and support more consistent eating habits.

The Nourishing Dozen

When your appetite is low, every bite counts, so food needs to work harder for you. That's the thinking behind the Nourishing Dozen. While there's no one-size-fits-all list, these twelve ingredients have been chosen for their high concentration of key nutrients in relatively small portions. They support muscle maintenance, bone health, energy levels, brain function and gut health – all areas that matter when you're eating less.

They're also quick to prepare, easy to find and budget-friendly. You'll find these foods throughout the recipes in this book but keeping them in mind can help guide everyday choices, especially on days when you're only managing smaller meals.

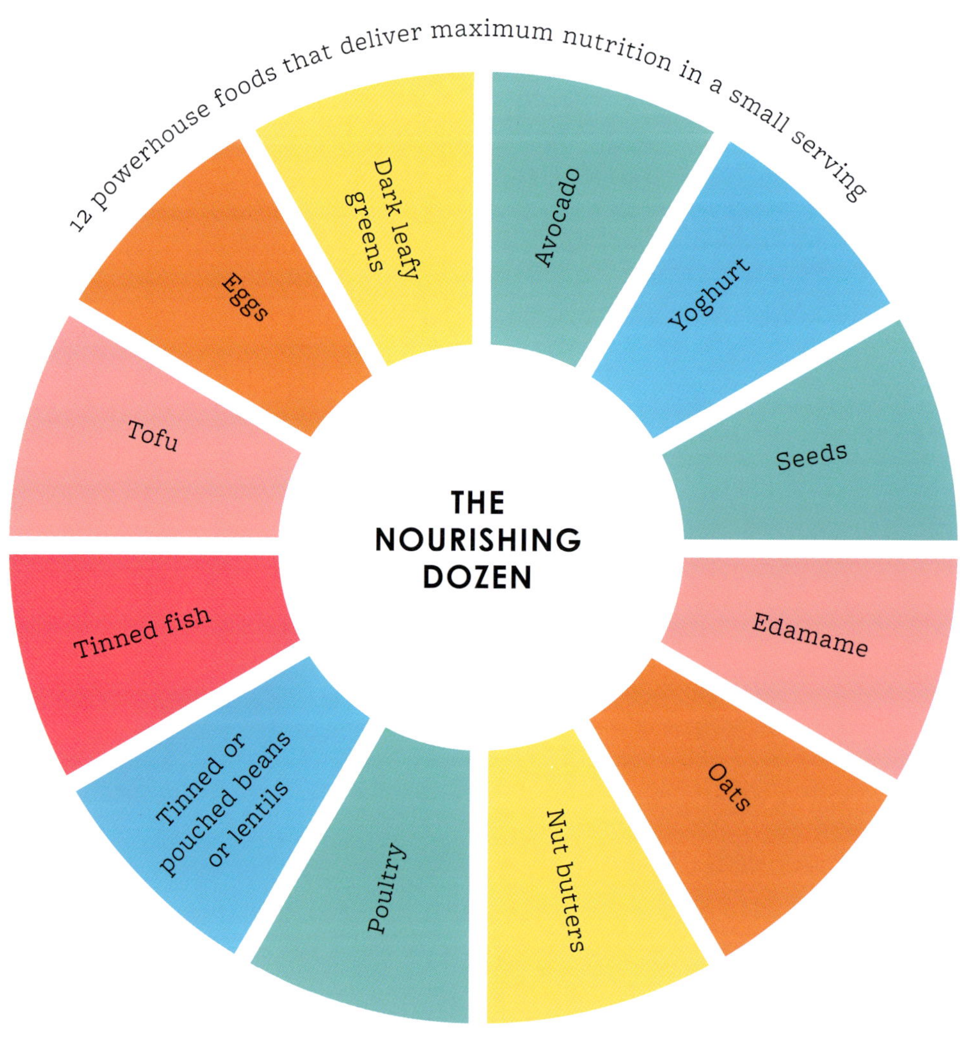

12 POWERHOUSE FOODS THAT DELIVER MAXIMUM NUTRITION IN A SMALL SERVING

Food	What it delivers
Eggs	Eggs are one of the best all-rounders. They are packed with high-quality protein, vitamin B12, choline (important for brain health) and iron. They are soft, easy to digest and versatile across meals.
Tinned fish	Tinned fish such as tuna, salmon, sardines or mackerel provide lean protein in a convenient format. Oily fish like salmon, sardines and mackerel are rich in omega-3 fats for heart and brain health; eating the bones can also provide a useful source of calcium.
Tofu	Tofu is a gentle source of complete plant protein, along with calcium and iron. Its soft texture and neutral flavour make it easy to digest and ideal when your appetite is low.
Oats	Oats provide beta-glucan fibre for heart and gut health and slow-release carbohydrates for energy; they also help regulate blood sugar. A small bowl can go a long way and works well in breakfasts and snacks.
Tinned or pouched beans and lentils	Tinned or pouched beans and lentils are full of fibre, plant protein and essential minerals such as iron, magnesium and folate. They are quick to use and easily added to soups, stews and salads when energy or appetite is limited.
Nut butters	Nut butters are energy-dense and provide healthy unsaturated fats, vitamin E and a small amount of protein in a serving. Just a spoonful can add nourishment and creaminess to porridge, toast or smoothies.
Avocado	Avocado is rich in monounsaturated fats, fibre and potassium. Its naturally soft texture and mild flavour make it a good option when your appetite or digestion is sensitive.
Yoghurt (Greek, fortified plant-based or skyr)	Yoghurt is high in protein and calcium and often contains live bacteria that support gut health. Fortified plant-based versions can also provide vitamins B12 and D, and soya is the highest in protein. Yoghurt works well as a snack, for breakfast or as a creamy base for other dishes. Skyr is a high-protein yoghurt that adds richness without excess fat.
Dark leafy greens	Dark leafy greens such as spinach, kale and chard are highly nutritious, offering folate, iron, magnesium and vitamin K. Just a small handful can significantly increase the nutritional quality of a meal.
Edamame	Edamame is an example of a complete plant protein, meaning that it contains significant amounts of all nine essential amino acids. It is also rich in fibre, folate and iron. It is convenient when bought frozen and can be added to stir-fries, bowls or soups without changing the flavour. These beans also have a vibrant colour that can make dishes more visually appealing.
Seeds	Seeds are rich in healthy fats, magnesium, zinc and plant-based protein. Chia seeds are especially high in fibre and protein. You can sprinkle seeds on yoghurt, porridge or salads, or make a ready-to-go topping using the toasted seed mix recipe on page 199.
Poultry	Poultry such as chicken and turkey provide lean protein, B vitamins, selenium and iron. Cooked slices are soft and easy to chew and can be added to sandwiches, soups or salads when your appetite is low.

PROTEIN AND MUSCLE MASS

Muscle mass isn't just about strength or appearance, it plays a vital role in your metabolism, supports immune function and helps maintain mobility, balance and resilience as you age.

While muscle doesn't 'store' protein in the traditional sense, it acts as the body's largest reservoir of amino acids. During periods of illness, stress or undernutrition, your body can break down muscle tissue to release these amino acids, which are then used to fuel immune responses, repair tissues and support essential bodily functions.

Muscle also functions as an active endocrine organ, meaning it releases hormone-like signalling molecules into the bloodstream. When you move, your muscles release compounds called myokines, which help regulate inflammation, support metabolic health and influence immune activity throughout the body.

If your intake of calories or protein is too low, especially over time, your body may begin breaking down muscle to meet its needs. This can lead to:

- Decreased muscle strength and stamina
- Reduced energy levels and slower recovery
- Impaired mobility or exercise tolerance
- Greater risk of falls, injury or overuse strain
- Harder recovery from illness, surgery or physical stress

A study published in *Diabetes, Obesity and Metabolism* in 2025 looked at how body composition changed during weight loss with the GLP-1 medication tirzepatide.[3, 4] Over 72 weeks, people taking the drug lost an average of 21 per cent of their body weight. About three-quarters of that weight loss came from body fat, and the rest came from lean tissue, measured using a body scan called DXA. This is similar to what's seen with weight loss from dieting or surgery.

Because people on tirzepatide lost more weight overall (and did so more quickly) the total amount of lean tissue lost was also higher, about 5.6kg on average, compared to just 1.2kg in the placebo group, who received lifestyle advice only. This has raised concerns about losing muscle, especially in people at risk of age-related muscle loss (sarcopenia).

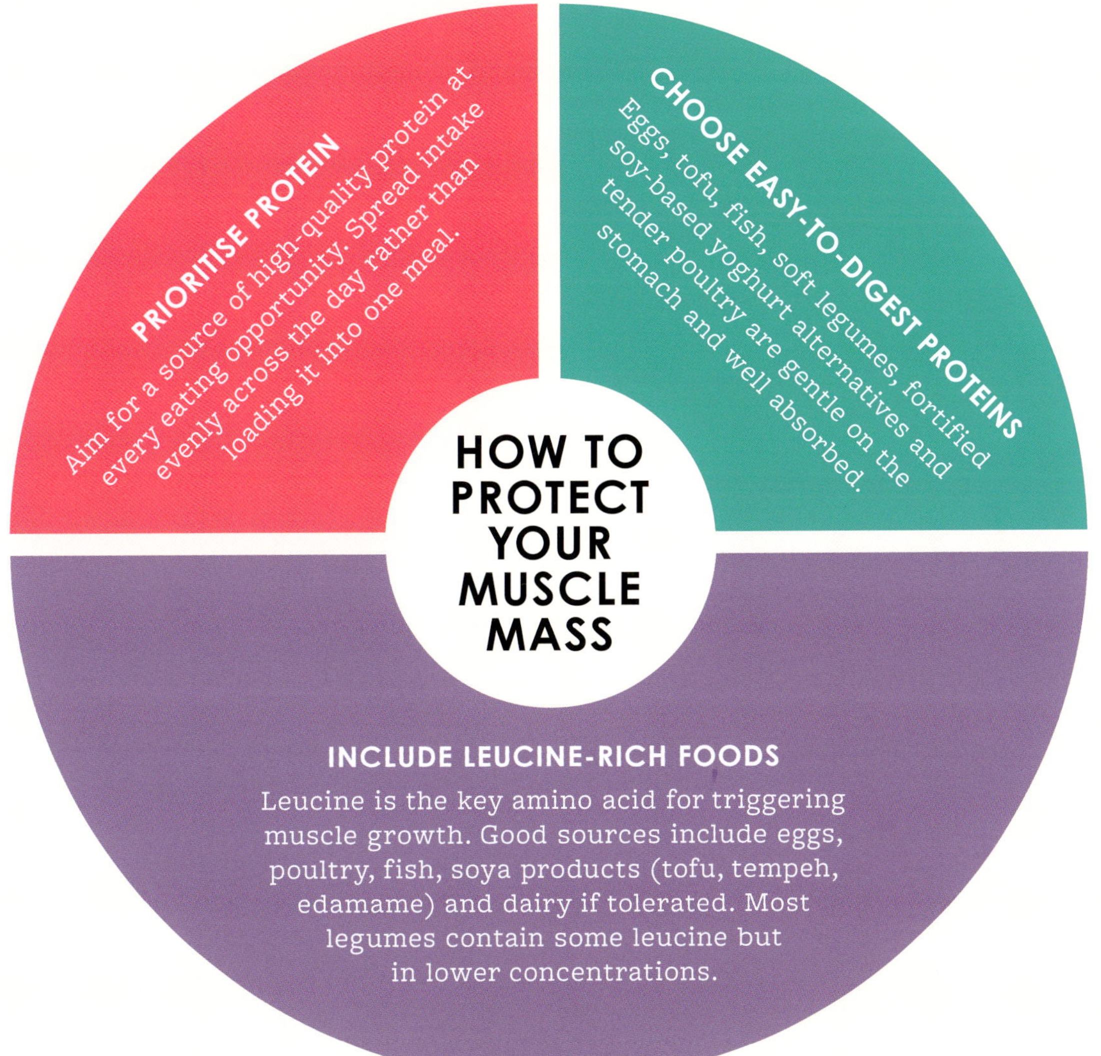

Although this study showed a typical fat-to-lean loss pattern, other research has found a wide range, with lean tissue making up anywhere from 15 to 60 per cent of total weight lost. It's also important to know that DXA scans don't just measure muscle, they include organs, fluid and other tissues, so not all lean tissue loss is muscle. Regardless, because these medications lead to such fast and effective weight loss, it's important to eat enough protein and include strength training to help protect muscle and support long-term health.

Protein targets

The Recommended Dietary Allowance (RDA) for protein is 0.8g per kilogram of body weight per day, but this is designed to prevent deficiency and not to support optimal health, especially during periods of low food intake or weight loss. In these situations, your body needs more protein to help preserve muscle mass and support recovery.

Research suggests that to preserve muscle during periods of low intake or weight loss, you may need around 1.2–1.6g of protein per kilogram of body weight per day. For someone weighing 70kg (about 11 stone), that's roughly 84–112g of protein per day, ideally spaced across small, manageable meals.

While the study I referenced on page 20 used an upper range of up to 2g of protein per kilogram of body weight per day, this was based on research in people following very low-calorie or aggressive weight-loss diets, where the risk of muscle loss is higher. This higher intake can also be relevant for GLP-1 medication users, since appetite and calorie intake are often significantly reduced. However, in practice, most people with a smaller appetite will find it more realistic to aim for 1.2–1.6g/kg/day, which is still a highly effective and evidence-based range for preserving lean mass during weight loss.

If that number sounds a little daunting, don't worry. You don't need to get there all at once. Think of protein as something you can build up gradually. Small increases across meals and snacks can make a big difference over time, especially if you're starting from a lower baseline.

WHAT DOES THAT LOOK LIKE?

The table on the next page shows the protein content of everyday foods in both standard portions and reduced portions designed for people with smaller appetites, including those using GLP-1 medications. While a few of these foods can provide close to 20g or more protein in a smaller serving, many will need to be combined with others to help you reach your protein target for the meal.

These are not rigid recommendations, but rather practical estimates to help you build high-protein meals. If you're able to eat closer to the standard portion size, that's one of the easiest ways to strengthen your protein intake. But if not, combining foods (like tuna and beans, lentils and chicken or edamame beans with seeds) can help you reach your goal in a more manageable way.

In this book, I've aimed to include a good amount of protein in every recipe, usually around 20g per serving or more, which is especially important when you're eating less overall. All recipes have been nutritionally analysed so you can see exactly how much protein they contain, helping you track your intake with ease. Breakfast and plant-based meal options can be tricky to ramp up the protein in small servings, but you can make up for it with high-protein snacks or a mini-meal later in the day. You'll see suggestions on the opposite page.

There are also dedicated 'protein-packed' recipes (25g+ per serving) for those with higher needs. And if a dish falls short of your target, you'll find quick tips after each recipe to help increase the protein, like adding extra meat, tofu, nuts, seeds, protein powder or a simple side.

PROTEIN FOODS (COOKED OR READY-TO-EAT WEIGHTS)

Food	Normal Portion	Normal Protein	Reduced Portion (70%)	Reduced Protein (70%)
Chicken breast	90g	27.0g	65g	19.5g
Salmon fillet	140g	35.3g	100g	25.2g
Cod fillet	140g	33.5g	100g	23.9g
Tinned fish (average)	110g	27.4g	77g	19.2g
Beef mince (lean)	90g	19.6g	65g	14.2g
Pork (lean)	90g	24.3g	65g	17.6g
Lamb (lean)	90g	23.9g	65g	17.3g
Eggs	2 medium (120g)	16.9g	2 small (100g)	14.1g
Prawns	100g	16.2g	70g	11.3g
Tofu (firm)	100g	12.0g	70g	8.4g
Whey protein powder	30g	24.0g	–	–
Plant-based protein powder	30g	22.0g	–	–
Greek yoghurt	150g	8.5g	105g	5.7g
Soya yoghurt (fortified)	150g	5.0g	105g	3.3g
Skyr	150g	15.9g	105g	11.6g
Dairy milk	200ml	6.8g	140ml	4.8g
Soya milk (fortified)	200ml	4.8g	140ml	3.4g
Cheese	30g	7.5g	20g	5g
Cottage cheese	100g	9.4g	70g	6.6g
Chickpeas	150g	12.6g	105g	8.8g
Lentils (average)	150g	11.7g	105g	8.2g
Beans (average)	150g	11.2g	105g	7.8g
Edamame beans	150g	18.0g	105g	12.6g
Peas	80g	4.2g	60g	3.2g
Nordic seeded loaf	45g	5.0g	–	–
Nuts	30g	7.1g	–	–
Seeds	30g	7.3g	–	–

Note: The Nordic Seeded Loaf, nuts and seeds are not shown with a 30 per cent reduction, as they are already used in smaller, practical amounts in recipes (e.g. 1–2 tbsp for nuts/seeds; portioned slices for the loaf).

HIGH-PROTEIN SNACKS AND MINI MEALS

Skyr or Greek yoghurt with seeds	Mini egg muffin (see page 86)	Cooked chicken slice with cherry tomatoes
Protein smoothie (homemade or ready-made)	Plain tofu cubes seasoned with tamari or chilli flakes	Mini lentil or bean salad pots dressed with olive oil and lemon
Boiled egg sprinkled with smoked paprika, chilli flakes or celery salt	Whipped cottage cheese (see page 202) with chopped fruit, berries or spooned onto a rye cracker, oatcake or toast	Slice of Nordic seed loaf (see page 194) topped with hummus or smoked salmon
Tinned mackerel mashed onto a wholegrain or seeded cracker	Small serving of chia pudding (see page 82) with chopped fruit	Cottage cheese with grated apple and a wholegrain or seeded cracker
Smoked salmon with a small slice of rye cracker	Cheese portion with sliced pear, apple, cucumber or cherry tomatoes	Edamame beans tossed with lime juice and flaked sea salt

Topping up with protein powders and clear protein drinks

If you're struggling to meet your protein target, protein powders and clear protein waters can be incredibly helpful. Nutritionally balanced meal replacement products can also offer a convenient option when your appetite is low, or time is short. Many are fortified with key vitamins, minerals and fibre, making them useful as a short-term tool or a fallback on difficult days.

Yes, they fall under the category of ultra-processed foods (UPFs), but in this context they can be a strategic and valuable addition. When used to complement a whole food diet (rather than replace it) they offer a practical way to bridge nutritional gaps without adding bulk to meals.

Clear whey or protein water is especially helpful if you feel too full for traditional shakes or food-based snacks. These lighter drinks are often easier to tolerate, particularly between meals or after exercise, and still deliver around 15–25g of protein per serving.

HOW TO USE THESE PRODUCTS WITH A SMALL APPETITE

Used mindfully, these products can take the pressure off your meals, giving you flexibility and confidence that you're hitting your targets, even on days when your appetite is particularly low or you have skipped meals.

- Start small – even half a scoop or half a bottle can contribute 10–12g protein
- Split a shake into two mini servings so have one mid-morning and another mid-afternoon
- Use clear whey or protein water between meals when you're not ready to eat
- Stir unflavoured protein powder into soups, oats or mashed veg

How to calculate your protein needs when you are overweight

If you're currently overweight, using your actual weight to calculate protein needs might overestimate how much you require. This is likely to be the case if you are taking GLP-1 medication. A more realistic and effective approach is to base your intake on your ideal or target weight, that is, the weight you're aiming to maintain for health or performance reasons. To do this you can use the body mass index or BMI.

While BMI is far from perfect as a diagnostic tool, especially because it doesn't account for muscle mass, bone structure or body composition, it's still useful for rough estimations. For the purpose of calculating protein needs, it provides a simple and practical starting point when more detailed assessments aren't available.

HERE'S HOW TO DO IT:

Step 1: Estimate your ideal weight. A practical way to do this is to use the midpoint of the healthy BMI range (22–23). For example, if you're 170cm tall (about 5ft 7), your ideal weight range is 63–67kg.

Step 2: Multiply your ideal weight by 1.2–1.6g of protein per kg to get your daily protein target. This gives you a personalised range based on your needs and goals.

Example: If your ideal weight is 65kg:
→ 65kg × 1.2g = 78g
→ 65kg × 1.6g = 104g
Your daily protein target would fall between 78g and 104g.

Protein per meal: what to aim for

To make your intake manageable, spread your protein across the day and aim for at least 20g of protein in a full meal. It's not as easy to get this amount of protein in a breakfast or snack but if you make them protein based then you can get close. Most people benefit from 3–5 eating opportunities per day that include protein.

This approach not only supports muscle maintenance, but also improves satiety, helps balance blood sugar and contributes to better recovery if you're physically active or unwell.

SAMPLE HIGH-PROTEIN MENU PLANS

PLAN 1: USING RECIPES FROM THE BOOK

Meal	Recipe	Protein
Breakfast	Miso scrambled eggs with 1 slice wholemeal toast	19g
Lunch	Herby salmon bowl with radish and pesto	30g
Dinner	Lentil, chicken and roast carrot protein bowl	31g
Optional Snack	1 x Mini egg muffin with spinach, sweetcorn and feta	11.2g
Optional Snack	Edamame and pomegranate seeded salad	14g
Optional Evening	150–200ml clear protein drink	8–12g

Protein from main meals: 80g

Protein including all optional extras: 113.2g–117.2g

PLAN 2: USING STORE CUPBOARD INGREDIENTS

Meal	What to Eat	Protein
Breakfast	30g oats cooked with 200ml milk + 1 tbsp peanut butter + 2 tsp seeds	16.4g
Lunch	80g tinned tuna + 100g tinned white beans mashed with lemon + 1 small wholemeal pitta bread	31.0g
Dinner	Lentil and chicken stew with 100g cooked lentils, 80g cooked chicken breast and 100g frozen veg	32.6g
Optional Snack	1 boiled egg	8.4g
Optional Snack	100g Greek yoghurt + 1 tbsp seeds + few berries	9.4g
Optional Evening	150–200ml clear protein drink	8–12g

Protein from main meals: 80g

Protein including all optional extras: 105.8–109.8g

DON'T FORGET YOUR BONES

Bone health is another hidden risk when your appetite is low, especially if you're not getting enough calcium and vitamin D. Bones are living tissue and, like muscle, they need regular stimulation through movement and a steady supply of nutrients to stay strong. If you're also moving less, then your bones don't get the usual mechanical pressure they need, which can accelerate bone loss.

KEY STRATEGIES TO SUPPORT BONE HEALTH

- Include calcium-rich foods at every opportunity. Think fortified plant-based milks, small fish with bones (like tinned salmon or sardines), tofu, almonds, tahini and dark leafy greens like kale or spring greens.
- Get enough vitamin D. This nutrient helps your body absorb calcium. It's hard to get from food alone (only oily fish, mushrooms grown under UV light, egg yolks and fortified foods), so a supplement is often necessary, especially during autumn and winter in the UK, or year-round if you're indoors often, have darker skin, are postmenopausal or at risk of osteoporosis.
- Add resistance exercise if possible. Light resistance bands, bodyweight squats or even gentle stair climbing can help stimulate bone maintenance by placing safe stress on the skeletal system.
- Don't overlook magnesium and vitamin K. Both support calcium regulation and bone mineralisation. Magnesium is found in nuts, seeds, wholegrains and leafy greens. Vitamin K2 is found in small amounts in fermented foods like aged cheese and natto, as well as in egg yolks. Vitamin K1, which also plays a role in bone health, is rich in green vegetables such as kale, spinach, broccoli, Brussels sprouts, cabbage and spring greens.

THE THING ABOUT FIBRE

Fibre might not be the first thing that comes to mind when you're eating less, but it's one of the most important nutrients to keep an eye on. It supports your gut health, helps regulate digestion and plays a key role in keeping you fuller for longer, which matters even more when you're working with smaller meals.

Fibre also feeds your friendly gut bacteria. These bacteria produce compounds that help regulate immunity, reduce inflammation and may even influence mood. When fibre is consistently lacking in your diet, your gut microbiome may become imbalanced, which in turn affects your overall health in ways you might not immediately link to your appetite.

Why fibre matters

The UK recommendation is 30g of fibre per day, but most adults fall far short of this. When your appetite is small, that target can feel even more out of reach. But fibre matters as it helps regulate blood sugar, supports bowel regularity and plays a central role in maintaining a healthy gut microbiome. It also contributes to heart health and helps protect against colorectal cancer – benefits supported by decades of research.

By feeding beneficial gut bacteria, fibre supports the production of anti-inflammatory compounds that protect your immune system and may have positive effects on mood and mental wellbeing. It's also one of the reasons why meals that include both fibre and protein feel more satisfying and help you stay full for longer even in modest portions.

One of the simplest ways to boost your fibre is to include more fruit and vegetables across the day. While they're not as fibre-dense as beans, pulses or wholegrains, they're often easier to eat in small amounts, especially if your appetite is low or you're using GLP-1 medications. Fruits and vegetables also come with added benefits of vitamins, minerals, antioxidants and plant compounds that act like nature's multivitamins.

Even small additions can make a meaningful difference – think a handful of berries, a few tablespoons of peas, frozen spinach stirred into a stew, or sliced tomato on toast. Go for colour and variety, and make the most of frozen, tinned or pre-prepped options to keep things simple and more convenient.

Fibre goals, not pressure

Hitting 30g of fibre a day might not be realistic every single day and that's okay. Think of it as a long-term goal to move towards, not something to hit perfectly. The fibre content of the recipes in this book varies and not all of them are high in fibre, but each recipe tells you the amount per serving to help you keep track without the guesswork. And many of the 'nutrient booster' suggestions will help to increase the fibre content of the dish.

You might also find it helpful to include a fibre-focused snack during the day like a small pot of chia pudding (see page 82), dried fruit and nuts, a seeded cracker with hummus or handful of edamame beans. These are low-effort options that can add 3–5g of fibre without requiring a big meal.

Fibre stacking

One of the most effective strategies to get enough fibre in your diet is fibre stacking, which means layering smaller amounts of fibre-rich foods together to improve your intake without adding bulk. For example, pair a slice of seeded bread (see page 194) with hummus and top it with a spoonful of cooked lentils or stir ground flaxseed into porridge made with oats and fortified milk. You'll also find toppers like the seed mix, the dukkha and the avocado nut and seed smash in the recipe section (see page 199, 198 and 201), which are an easy way to add fibre, texture and flavour to soups, dips, yoghurt bowls or vegetables – all in just a couple of teaspoons.

The challenge with fibre on a small appetite

Not everyone with a small appetite will find fibre difficult, but for some people, especially those on GLP-1 medications, who are recovering from illness, or with a sensitive gut, bulky or fermentable fibres can feel uncomfortable. If you're eating less than usual, and especially if your fibre intake has been low for a while, a sudden increase in high-fibre foods can lead to bloating, slowed digestion or a feeling of fullness that gets in the way of eating enough of the right foods.

Some nutritious foods can feel heavy or gassy when reintroduced too quickly or in large amounts. That's why it's helpful to build up fibre gradually, and start with gentler, easier-to-digest sources, especially if your digestion feels sensitive. Once your digestion has adjusted and your appetite improves, you can gradually reintroduce small amounts of more fibrous foods.

SOFTER FIBRES like oats, stewed fruits (apples and pears), cooked vegetables, peeled sweet potatoes, mashed lentils or beans, ground flaxseed, smooth dips, soft wholegrains, tinned fruit in juice (peaches and pears) or ripe fruits such as banana, mango, melon, peaches and plums

Introduce small amounts of well-cooked, more FIBROUS FOODS: beans, lentils, wholegrains, seeds and cruciferous vegetables (e.g. cabbage, broccoli, cauliflower) – try blending into soups, dhals and stews

PREBIOTIC AND PROBIOTIC FOODS

It's also worth thinking about how to support the beneficial bacteria in your gut with both prebiotic and probiotic foods. Prebiotics are types of fibre that feed your gut bacteria and help them thrive. You'll find them in foods like onions, garlic, leeks, asparagus, oats, bananas and legumes. Probiotics, on the other hand, are foods that contain live beneficial bacteria. You'll often find these in yoghurt with live cultures and kefir, which typically contain strains of Lactobacillus and Bifidobacterium. Traditionally fermented vegetables such as sauerkraut and kimchi can also provide live microbes if they're unpasteurised and kept in the fridge. While these may not always meet the strict scientific definition of a probiotic, they still offer a rich variety of live cultures that can support gut health.

Adding a spoonful of fermented veg can be a simple way to liven up a meal while supporting your gut health. They can be added to anything like salads, protein bowls, roasted veg, grilled meat and fish, or even soups and dhal. While not essential for everyone, these foods can be a flavourful and gut-friendly addition, especially if you enjoy tangy, savoury flavours, which is common for those on GLP-1 medication.

HOW MUCH SHOULD YOU EAT WHEN YOUR APPETITE IS LOW?

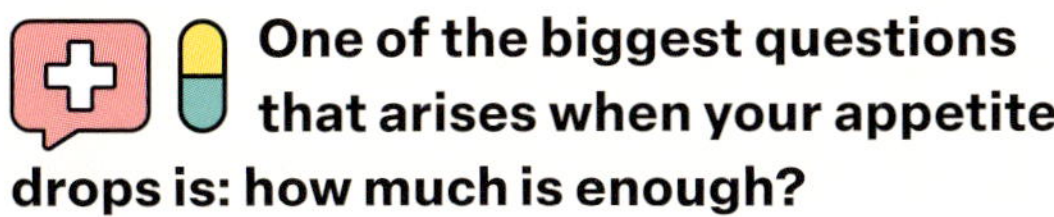

One of the biggest questions that arises when your appetite drops is: how much is enough?

When you're eating less, it's natural to wonder if you're getting what your body needs, but the answer is a lot more flexible than you might think.

Why there is no 'one size fits all'

When appetite is low, eating isn't about forcing down large meals or chasing calorie targets. It's about supporting your body's actual needs in a way that feels doable. And because everyone's situation is different, there's no single template for how much you should eat. Some people with a small appetite still have higher calorie or nutrient needs while others may need far less. That's why flexibility matters more than fixed rules.

Factors that affect how much you need might include:

- Your overall health and activity level
- Whether you're recovering from illness, injury or surgery
- Whether you're taking GLP-1 medications
- Age and life stage (older adults often need more protein)
- Your body size and composition as taller or heavier individuals, or those aiming to maintain or build lean muscle, typically need more protein

Understanding calorie needs when appetite is low

When your appetite drops, your total calorie intake naturally falls too. While average daily

DAILY CALORIE INTAKE RANGES FOR LOW APPETITE

Calorie Range	Who For	Typical Scenario
800–1,200 kcal	Very low appetite individuals	Starting GLP-1 meds, recovering from illness or surgery, older adults, high stress or fatigue
1,200–1,600 kcal	Moderate low appetite	Many women, older adults or moderately active people eating small, regular meals
1,600–2,000 kcal	Higher energy needs despite low appetite	Men, larger bodies or active individuals preserving muscle while managing smaller meals

needs are around 2,000–2,500 calories for most adults, people with a low appetite often fall somewhere between 800 and 1,600 calories per day.

These numbers are not strict targets as calorie needs depend on factors like age, sex, weight, activity level, medical history and how long appetite has been reduced. They're simply a guide to help you feel reassured that you're broadly on track, especially if your appetite is smaller than it used to be.

What matters most is the quality of the food you eat, the consistency of your eating pattern, and how you feel in yourself.

USING CALORIES AS A GENTLE GUIDE

While this book is primarily about eating in a way that supports your body when your appetite is low, it can still be helpful to use calories as a broad guide, especially if you're unsure whether you're getting enough energy across the day.

If you're regularly feeling low on energy or worried that your intake is too small, you can gently increase it by adding a few nourishing snacks. Some people find it easier to eat small amounts regularly rather than sitting down to full meals, and that's completely fine. What matters is that you're steadily fuelling your body in a way that feels manageable and sustainable for you.

HOW TO TELL IF YOU'RE EATING ENOUGH

Signs that you're broadly meeting your needs include:

- Stable or gently decreasing body weight (if weight loss is your goal)
- Steady energy levels during the day
- Maintaining or improving muscle strength (alongside strength exercise)
- Feeling mentally clear and emotionally stable
- Regular bowel movements without constipation

If you're frequently dizzy, losing strength quickly, catching infections easily or feeling deeply fatigued, these can be signs that you're not eating enough and may need more structured support.

THE LOW APPETITE SURVIVAL GUIDE

This chapter is your toolkit for making food work for you with less pressure, more flexibility and realistic strategies that fit into your day. If you need help structuring meals or managing emotional or physical barriers, everything here is designed to help you stay nourished, even when eating doesn't come easily.

Foundations for eating when you're not hungry

Use the following tips as a guide and to help build a routine around food.

FOCUS ON FREQUENCY, NOT VOLUME

If your appetite is small, large meals can feel overwhelming or unappealing. Instead, shift your focus to eating smaller amounts more frequently. Spreading food out across 4–6 smaller eating occasions makes nourishment feel more achievable and helps stabilise energy, blood sugar and mood. You're more likely to meet your nutritional needs when meals feel manageable.

For many people, a realistic portion might be one-third to half the size of what they used to eat but packed with foods that offer real value. Think quality over quantity. Here's what a well-balanced, smaller meal might look like:

- A mini wholemeal wrap filled with shredded chicken, hummus and spinach
- A small bowl of lentil soup with half a slice of wholemeal toast
- Half a salmon fillet with a few spoonfuls of roasted vegetables and brown rice
- A small yoghurt bowl with a spoonful of nuts and a few berries

EAT WITH INTENTION

When you're eating less, every bite needs to work harder for you. Focus on compact, high-value foods that deliver protein, fibre, healthy fats and essential micronutrients without the need for large portions. The Nourishing Dozen (see page 17) is your go-to list, so choose from these foods regularly to help maintain overall nutritional balance.

CHOOSE SMART SNACKS THAT ACTUALLY NOURISH

Snacks aren't just optional extras; they're essential opportunities to get nutrients in when main meals feel too much. The most effective snacks combine protein (for strength and satiety) with fibre (for digestion and fullness). These pairings help you feel energised and nourished between meals without overloading your appetite. Try these nourishing snack combinations:

- Greek-style or fortified soya yoghurt + berries + chia seeds
- Boiled egg + rye bread + tomato
- Hummus + seeded crackers + cucumber
- Nut butter + pear slices + cinnamon
- Smoked mackerel + mashed avocado + rye cracker
- Edamame + lime + flaked salt
- Chia pudding with milk + chopped fruit
- Cottage cheese + grated apple + seeds

ANCHOR EATING TO ACTIVITIES

When hunger is subtle or hardly felt at all, you can miss meals without realising. To stay on track, pair eating with something you already do every day, like having breakfast after a shower, a snack after answering emails, or lunch following a short walk. These routine cues help create structure and consistency without relying on physical hunger alone. Over time, they help retrain your body's appetite rhythms.

DON'T WAIT FOR STRONG HUNGER

Hunger isn't a prerequisite for nourishment – your body still needs fuel regardless of whether it's sending out hunger cues. Strong hunger won't always appear, especially if your appetite is low or you're using GLP-1 medications. Instead, take mild cues like a neutral sense of emptiness or a dip in energy as your green light to eat. You don't need to wait for a growling stomach. Gentle, consistent meals help maintain your strength, prevent crashes later and support your overall wellbeing.

Don't forget about fluids, as thirst can be just as muted as hunger. Drinking enough water or other hydrating fluids supports digestion, energy and concentration, and helps prevent further appetite suppression caused by dehydration. If you're struggling to eat enough, try sipping fluids between meals rather than right before or during, as drinking too much at mealtimes can make small meals feel even more filling.

STRUCTURING YOUR EATING DAY

A structured day of small, flexible meals takes the pressure off large portions and helps spread nutrients across the day. Here's an example of what a low appetite-friendly day might look like.

This structure is flexible, and designed for nourishment, not perfection. If you miss a snack or meal, it's okay. The aim is to keep things steady and sustainable. GLP-1 users may not eat this frequently so will adapt the timing and number of meals to suit their own rhythm.

Easing your way back into food

When your appetite has been low for a while, maybe due to illness, surgery or mental health, then getting back to regular eating takes time. It's not just about eating more; it's about easing back in, gradually increasing what you can manage and finding a rhythm that works for you.

Even if you're not eating three meals a day, what matters is creating a gentle routine that works for you. The focus here isn't on timing gaps between meals, it's on nourishing your body regularly in a way that feels manageable.

Progress might be uneven. Some days you'll manage more, others less, and that's okay. What matters is the general direction. Even a few consistent eating opportunities each day can start to build strength, energy and focus.

1. **START WITH SMALL, SPACED MEALS**
   Experiment with smaller portions at regular intervals, to help you stay comfortably nourished but without overwhelming your appetite.
2. **CHOOSE SOFT, EASY TEXTURES**
   Foods that are gentle to chew and digest tend to be better tolerated.
3. **ADD LIGHT FLAVOUR**
   If food tastes dull or unappealing, lift it gently with flavour: chopped herbs, vinegar, garlic or ginger.
4. **BUILD UP GRADUALLY**
   Increase portions slightly, add an extra snack or enrich meals without adding bulk.
5. **FOCUS ON HIGHLY NOURISHING FOODS**
   Make small portions work harder by choosing foods rich in protein, healthy fats and key nutrients (see the Nourishing Dozen on page 17).
6. **GET THE TEMPERATURE RIGHT**
   Some people find they tolerate warm or room-temperature meals better than cold ones, while others prefer cooler, lighter foods when appetite is low.
7. **ADD ROUTINE**
   Eating at regular times, even if it's just a few bites, can help reset your body's rhythm.

When eating feels like too much

Low appetite isn't just about not feeling hungry. It affects how you shop, cook and plan your days and how you relate to food emotionally. It can create frustration, guilt and isolation, especially when others expect you to eat normally. These are some common barriers you might face.

LOW MOTIVATION TO COOK OR EAT

When energy is low, even small tasks like opening the fridge, deciding what to eat or washing up can feel like too much. The idea of cooking a meal may be completely unrealistic, which often leads to skipped meals or reaching for nutritionally poor, ultra-processed snacks. Over time, this widens nutritional gaps and deepens fatigue.

Solution: Batch-prep on better days When your energy is higher, prepare basic components like cooked grains, boiled eggs, roasted vegetables or homemade sauces and dips. Freeze small portions so they're ready to use when needed; many of the recipes in this book can be batch-cooked. Prepare protein and grain salads that will keep in the fridge for a few days so you can dip in and out of them as your appetite dictates. Snacks like energy balls (see pages 212–217) are great to cook in bulk and store in the fridge or freezer.

Solution: Keep smart convenience foods on hand Stock your fridge and cupboards with nutritious, low-effort staples: tinned fish, grain pouches, frozen vegetables, ready-cooked lentils and beans (even flavoured varieties), pre-washed salad, yoghurts and even cook-in sauces. These become your building blocks for meals when energy is low, and you don't feel like cooking much.

Solution: Use no-cook meal ideas Having a short list of easy, balanced no-cook meals can reduce decision fatigue so you get something nourishing with minimal effort. Some ideas might include:

- Wrap with hummus, grated carrot and lettuce
- Stuffed avocado halves with tuna or chickpeas
- Tinned mackerel on oatcakes
- Flavoured lentil or bean salad pots
- Cottage cheese with soft fruit and crushed walnuts
- Shop-bought falafel with salad leaves + simple dressing

Solution: Designate a 'grab-and-go' shelf Use one shelf in your fridge or cupboard for instant-access foods: fruit-and-nut bars, boiled eggs, hummus pots, mini smoothies, oatcakes and cheese portions. These reduce friction when appetite or motivation is low.

EMOTIONAL DISCONNECTION FROM FOOD

Sometimes you're not avoiding food because you're full, but because you simply don't care. You may feel emotionally disengaged from eating due to grief or mental health struggle and even favourite meals have lost their appeal, while cooking may feel pointless or draining.

Solution: Make meals more sensory Use fresh herbs, lemon juice, spices or bright ingredients and combine crunchy foods with soft to stimulate the senses. Build in visual interest with layers and colour: sprinkle toasted seeds or crumbled cheese, add chopped herbs or a swirl of tahini, yoghurt, flavoured oil or pesto to a dish. Appealing colours, aromas and texture can reignite interest when hunger is absent.

Solution: Keep it small and well presented
When food feels unappealing, oversized portions or messy meals can be offputting. Serving small, nicely plated portions can make food feel more manageable and less like a chore. A small bowl of roasted carrots, wholegrains and spinach with a drizzle of lemon-tahini dressing; rice cakes with avocado, tomatoes, sesame and lime; a ramekin of hummus topped with olive oil and smoked paprika or za'atar, served with sliced veg and seeded crackers; or a soft tortilla with black beans, mango salsa and lettuce. Keep things tidy, colourful and well-composed to help you engage with eating.

Solution: Create an inviting eating space
Eat in a clean, uncluttered space. Lay the table rather than eat on your lap, light a candle or sit by a window with a view and plenty of natural light, drink from a glass and not your water bottle or put music on in the background. Even subtle environmental cues can make mealtimes more inviting.

Solution: Return to comfort foods Now may not be the time to try new recipes. Lean on the familiar, like simple toast with toppings, comforting soups, creamy porridge, mashed potatoes or nostalgic foods and meals from childhood that feel familiar and comforting.

Solution: Use rituals that reconnect Simple habits like making tea at the same time each day, switching on the radio in the morning for breakfast, putting on your favourite podcast while cooking, pouring your drink into a nice glass with ice and lemon and even putting your mobile on 'do not disturb' during lunch creates a sense of intention.

When your body pushes back

Some days, eating may feel more difficult, whether due to nausea, early fullness or a lack of interest in food. This is common with GLP-1 medications and other causes of low appetite. On these days, stick to small, light meals and snacks that feel manageable, and sip fluids between meals to stay hydrated without worsening fullness. Flexibility is better than forcing food.

PHYSICAL DISCOMFORT AFTER EATING

Some people avoid eating not because they lack appetite, but because food causes bloating, nausea, cramps or early fullness. These symptoms can follow surgery, digestive disorders or medication and can create a strong aversion to eating.

Solution: Eat slowly and chew thoroughly
Taking the time to chew your food properly eases the digestive process and reduces bloating and early fullness. Take your time, pause between bites and avoid distractions while eating so your body has time to signal fullness more accurately. (See page 47 for more on mindful eating.) If bloating is an issue, try the tummy tea on page 207.

Solution: Choose gentle textures Soft, smooth or well-cooked foods tend to be easier to digest and are less likely to trigger symptoms like bloating, nausea or early fullness. That's why many recipes in this book use softer grains like short-grain brown rice, which cooks into a stickier, more digestible texture. However, for some people, especially if you're experiencing nausea or fatigue, switching to white rice, mashed potato or other refined carbs may feel more comfortable. Other gentle options include blended soups, softly scrambled eggs, puréed beans, mashed root vegetables and stewed lentils. For people using GLP-1 medications, overly rich or creamy textures (like thick sauces) may worsen nausea. In this case, aim for foods that are soft and light, such as steamed veg, brothy soups or gently poached fish.

Solution: Avoid heavy meals Stick to small portions with just a few well-chosen ingredients. Overly complex meals can be harder for your digestive system to handle, especially if they are high in fat, which takes longer to digest. This is an issue for those on GLP-1 medications as food moves through your digestive system more slowly.

Solution: Separate fluids from meals
Drinking too much liquid while eating can increase gastric pressure and cause discomfort. Instead, sip water between meals and keep fluids minimal during eating.

Eating out with a small appetite

Much of this book focuses on eating at home, where portion sizes, prep and timing are easier to manage. But eating out – at restaurants, cafés, the office or at social events – comes with different challenges, especially if you have a small appetite. Large portions, unfamiliar menus and social expectations can make these situations harder to navigate. This section offers strategies to help you feel more in control and make food choices that work for you.

ADJUSTING YOUR APPROACH

Eating out doesn't have to look the same as eating at home. You don't need to finish everything on your plate, match others' eating habits or explain your choices. Instead, focus on what works for your appetite and energy levels. You can:

- Leave food if you've had enough
- Order starters or small plates as mains
- Eat at your own pace or not at all, if you prefer to focus on the social setting
- Take food home for later

Comfort and satisfaction aren't based on how much you eat; they're about making choices that support your needs.

CHOOSING SMALLER PORTIONS AND SMARTER OPTIONS

Look for menus that offer flexibility, small plates, half portions or build-your-own combinations. These options allow you to eat in a way that suits your appetite without feeling restricted or overwhelmed.

Many restaurant menus now include small plates, starters or mix-and-match dishes. These are perfect when you don't want a heavy meal. Use the following strategies:

- Order two starters instead of a main
- Choose a 'light bites' menu or soup with a side of vegetables

- Ask if the kitchen can serve a half portion or package half to go
- Share a dish if portions are large
- Choose soft, simple dishes (soup, grilled fish) that are easier to eat and digest

PRACTICAL TIPS FOR EATING ON THE GO

When you're out and unsure what food will be available or whether you'll feel like eating, portable snacks and pre-planning are your allies. Carry easy snacks like:

- Seed and nut mixes
- Dried fruit bars
- Seaweed thins
- Dates
- Plain mini rice cakes
- Banana
- Roasted chickpeas
- Olive pouches

Many shops and cafés now offer the following meals and snacks:

- Protein pots (eggs, prawns, hummus, falafel)
- Edamame beans
- Hummus with carrot sticks
- Boiled eggs
- Greek yoghurt and oat or chia pots
- Soup pots or broths
- Wholefood salad boxes with protein
- Sushi (sashimi and protein salads)

MAKING THE HIGH STREET WORK FOR YOU

Supermarket meal deals and food-to-go options can feel carb-heavy and protein-light. Here's how to build a more balanced, low-appetite-friendly meal:

START WITH PROTEIN
Look for lean meat, eggs, beans, tofu or fish. Avoid carb-only options like pasta pots with creamy sauces and no protein.

ADD COLOUR
Include at least one portion of vegetables or salad. Many high street shops offer protein salads or veg snack packs.

DON'T FORGET FIBRE
Choose wholegrain wraps, bread or crackers, but always build your meal around protein. Look out for small, easy, fibre-rich extras like a pouch of edamame beans, a small pack of roasted chickpeas, a mini fruit and nut snack pack, or a sprinkle of mixed seeds from a salad bar.

OPTIONAL EXTRAS
Add a boiled egg, hummus pot or some nuts/seeds to enhance the nutritional quality of your meal.

WHEN YOU'D RATHER NOT EAT

Sometimes, it's okay to skip the food and still join the social occasion. Having a plan helps. For example:

- Eat a small snack before going out
- Bring something in your bag just in case
- Order tea, water or a light drink to stay present at the table

If you're drinking alcohol, it can have a stronger effect when you haven't eaten much and may reduce your appetite even further. A small snack can help buffer the effects and protect your energy.

UNDERSTANDING GLP-1 MEDICATIONS

GLP-1 medications like Ozempic, Wegovy and Mounjaro have completely changed the way many people experience hunger. Originally developed to support blood sugar control in type 2 diabetes, these drugs are now widely used for weight management because of their ability to dramatically reduce appetite.

For many, this drop in appetite feels like a breakthrough; eating less, or even skipping meals, may seem like a positive thing, especially after years of struggling with cravings, overeating or weight gain. But while these medications can be powerful tools, they also introduce a new set of nutritional challenges. Eating less isn't automatically better, especially if it means missing out on the nutrients your body still needs to stay strong, energised and well.

It's also worth noting that GLP-1 medications can come with side effects like nausea, constipation and fatigue, and the long-term health impacts, especially for people using them for weight management rather than diabetes are still being studied. That's why good nutrition matters even more while you're on them.

This chapter explains what GLP-1 medications do, how they affect appetite and digestion and – most importantly – what you need to know about nourishing yourself properly if you're taking one.

What are GLP-1 medications?

GLP-1 stands for glucagon-like peptide-1, a hormone that your body naturally releases after eating. It plays several roles:

- Telling your brain you're full
- Slowing down the emptying of your stomach
- Helping to regulate blood sugar levels

GLP-1 medications mimic the effects of this hormone but in a more powerful and longer-lasting way. The result? You feel full much faster, often after just a few bites, and hunger signals become much less intense.

THE MOST COMMON GLP-1 DRUGS USED TODAY INCLUDE:

- **Semaglutide** – found in Ozempic (for type 2 diabetes), Wegovy (for weight loss), Rybelsus (oral tablet – less commonly used in the UK)

- **Tirzepatide** – found in Mounjaro (currently approved for type 2 diabetes and weight loss in the UK; approved for weight loss in the US under the name Zepbound)

These drugs can lead to substantial weight loss, but they also create a very different experience of eating, one that needs careful attention to nutrition.

How do GLP-1 medications affect appetite?

MOST PEOPLE ON GLP-1 MEDICATIONS EXPERIENCE:

- Earlier satiety (feeling full sooner)
- Reduced 'food noise', which is that constant background chatter about food that many people live with
- Less frequent hunger and sometimes forgetting to eat for long stretches
- Smaller portion tolerance, as larger meals can feel uncomfortable or even cause nausea

Studies suggest that people on GLP-1 medications eat, on average, a third fewer calories per meal compared to those not on the medication. Many users report that a full restaurant meal now feels daunting or unnecessary as they simply can't – and don't want to – eat as much as before. In fact, there has been a growing interest in the demand for smaller portion sizes in restaurants and food outlets to cater for people with a low appetite and this includes those on GLP-1s.

Portion sizes on GLP-1 vs 'normal' appetite

One of the most common questions people ask when using GLP-1 medications is: how much should I be eating now? The answer is less than you're used to, but what you do eat needs to work hard nutritionally.

These medications slow gastric emptying and reduce appetite, which can make normal portion sizes feel too much, too fast. The goal is to build smaller meals that give you everything you need nutritionally with less volume.

In this book, most portion sizes are reduced by around one-third to reflect the typical changes seen in people taking GLP-1 medications. A well-conducted clinical study found that adults on 2.4mg of semaglutide ate approximately 35 per cent less energy than those not on the medication, due to earlier fullness and reduced appetite signals.[5] You'll find the full portion tables in Appendix 1, which offer a practical, evidence-based starting point, not a strict rule. Appetite can vary day to day and person to person, so listen to your body and adjust your portions as needed.

The recipes in this book have been nutritionally analysed to make sure you are getting what you need; on the whole the portion sizes reflect those in the tables on pages 229–231. However, when you are putting a meal together from individual components, understanding what to put on your plate can be useful and help avoid unnecessary food waste or preparing meals that aren't nourishing or satisfying.

Is everyone affected in the same way?

Not exactly. How strongly GLP-1 medications affect your appetite can depend on:

- Dose of the medication (higher doses tend to suppress appetite more)
- Length of time taking the drug (some people adapt slightly over time)
- Individual metabolism and physiology
- Pre-existing eating behaviours and relationships with food

Some people feel a near-complete absence of hunger ('silent stomach'), while others describe a gentle softening of cravings. A few still experience occasional strong appetite, especially if their dose is low or if the effect starts to wear off before the next injection.

What happens to food preferences?

GLP-1 medications don't just change how much you want to eat; they can change what you want to eat, too. Common changes include:

- Preference for lighter, fresher foods like salads, lean proteins and soups
- Decreased interest in greasy, heavy meals like fried foods, creamy dishes or rich takeaways as well as indulgent snacks such as crisps, pastries and chocolate, which may feel too rich or trigger nausea
- Increased sensitivity to rich or sweet foods as they may taste too strong or feel unappealing
- Craving for simple, easy-to-digest foods

Some people even report subtle changes in how food tastes. Fatty foods, in particular, can feel unpleasant, possibly because GLP-1 affects digestion and the brain's reward centres related to high-calorie foods.

A PRACTICAL LOOK: A TYPICAL DAY BEFORE AND AFTER STARTING GLP-1 MEDICATION

Time	Before GLP-1	After GLP-1
Breakfast	Large bowl of cereal + toast	Half a yoghurt pot with berries and seeds
Mid-morning	Biscuit snack	Small handful of nuts
Lunch	Sandwich + crisps + drink	Mini wrap with chicken and spinach
Mid-afternoon	Chocolate bar or coffee	Protein smoothie
Dinner	Full plate of pasta and sauce	Small portion of salmon with roasted vegetables
Evening	Dessert	Rarely hungry

Key nutritional priorities on GLP-1s

If you're using GLP-1 medication, you've already seen how appetite can shrink dramatically. That's why nutrient quality becomes more important than quantity. This is a quick recap of the core focus areas to help guide your food choices day to day:

- **Protein** – protects muscle mass and supports metabolism
- **Calcium + vitamin D** – essential for bone health, especially if dairy or fortified foods are limited
- **Iron + B vitamins** – help maintain energy and cognitive function
- **Healthy fats** – support hormone balance and absorption of key vitamins
- **Fibre** – encourages regular digestion and supports your gut health
- **Magnesium** – supports muscle function, sleep and energy, and can help maintain regular digestion, which may be affected by GLP-1 medications

Think of these as your foundation. You'll see them woven throughout the book.

Managing digestive side effects

It's completely normal to experience some digestive side effects, especially in the first few weeks or after a dose increase of GLP-1 medications. These work by slowing down digestion and promoting fullness, which can be helpful for appetite control, but also means your gut may take some time to adjust. Common side effects include:

- Nausea
- Bloating
- Constipation
- Early fullness (feeling full after just a few bites)
- Reflux or heartburn

For most people, these symptoms improve as your body adapts. But in the meantime, there's a lot you can do through food and meal structure to reduce discomfort and support digestion.

EAT LITTLE AND OFTEN

Smaller, more frequent meals are much easier to manage than three large ones. This approach reduces pressure on your digestive system and helps prevent nausea or bloating, giving you more opportunities to take in the nutrients your body needs.

FOCUS ON SOFT, EASY-TO-DIGEST TEXTURES

When your stomach feels sensitive or you're only managing a few bites at a time, softer foods may be easier to handle. Think creamy, blended or gently cooked – nothing that takes much effort to chew or feels too heavy.

Try things like mashed root veg, soft scrambled eggs, blended soups, lentil dhal, silken tofu or a spoonful of porridge with mashed banana. Even a soft frittata or a baked apple with yoghurt can go down more easily than crunchy or dry foods. That said, everyone responds differently, and some people may find soft or creamy foods worsen their nausea, while cooler or more textured options (like crisp veg or plain crackers) feel more palatable. Pay attention to what feels manageable for you.

AVOID RICH, FATTY MEALS

Foods that are high in fat (especially greasy or fried meals) can slow digestion further and often make nausea worse. Stick to lighter cooking methods like steaming, poaching, baking or slow roasting.

DRINK BETWEEN MEALS, NOT DURING

Sipping water or herbal teas throughout the day supports hydration and can help ease constipation – both common concerns when appetite is low or you're using GLP-1 medications. A few sips before eating may gently support digestion, but try to avoid drinking large volumes of fluid right before or during meals. This can lead to early fullness and make it harder to eat enough, especially if you're already working with small portions.

CHOOSE GUT-FRIENDLY FIBRE

Constipation is common with GLP-1 medications, so aim to include gentle fibre sources like oats, berries, ground flaxseed, cooked vegetables and pulses in small amounts. Raw salads and tough cruciferous veg may be harder to tolerate early on, so cooked is usually better.

How to navigate the silence

One of the most striking effects of GLP-1 medications is the silencing of what's often called food noise, which is that constant mental hum about what to eat next, how much, when and whether you've earned it.

For many people, this quiet is profoundly freeing. You're no longer consumed by cravings or compelled to raid the kitchen every few hours – often out of boredom as much as hunger. But that silence comes with a flip side, which is that it's easy to forget to eat, skip meals or drift through the day under-nourished simply because hunger doesn't knock loudly any more. This is particularly important to recognise if you're using GLP-1s for weight loss or metabolic health. Eating less isn't the only goal, as eating enough of the right things still matters for energy, immunity, mood and muscle mass.

EAT BY THE CLOCK, NOT BY CUES

Relying on hunger signals won't cut it any more. Set reminders on your phone, anchor meals to other habits (like your morning coffee or post-walk snack), or create a loose eating structure that includes three small meals and 1–2 snacks across the day.

FOLLOW A LOOSE FOOD PLAN

Planning ahead makes eating feel more automatic and less like a negotiation. It doesn't need to be strict. A rough outline of what and when to eat helps you stay consistent, even when you're not feeling driven to eat. This book's recipes are portioned to help you build those meals without guesswork.

Fridge / Chilled	Cupboard / Shelf-stable
Ready-to-drink protein shakes or clear protein waters	Nut butter sachets (great with fruit or rice cakes)
Mini pots of Greek-style yoghurt or dairy-free alternatives	Seed or fruit bars
Boiled eggs or pre-cooked beetroot	Tinned mackerel or sardines (pair with rye crispbread)
Mini Babybel or sliced Cheddar	Cooked lentil or grain pouches
Sliced avocado, cottage cheese or soft cheese (for crackers)	Mini rice cakes or oat crackers
Hummus or other nourishing dips	Chopped fresh fruit and veg (or ready-cut snack packs)
Olives or gherkins	

PRIORITISE 'EASY WINS'

These kinds of 'easy wins' are even easier when you've stocked up on quick, ready-to-eat-staples. These are highly nutritious foods that need no prep and can be grabbed when motivation is low. Above are some ideas for ready-to-go foods to keep in your fridge or cupboard.

Building balanced meals on GLP-1: the small plate framework

When you're eating less, whether due to GLP-1 medication or simply having a smaller appetite, it's not always easy to know how to build a meal that feels satisfying but doesn't overwhelm. That's where a small plate framework comes in.

This approach is widely used in nutrition care for people with low appetites, and it's designed to help you hit your nutritional needs even when your meals are modest. It focuses on what matters most: protein first, followed by fibre-rich vegetables, complex carbohydrates and healthy fats.

While the recipes in this book are already built to do that, you won't always be cooking from scratch. Some days you'll be grazing, grabbing leftovers or building a quick meal from whatever's in the fridge. This simple plate structure is something you can fall back on when energy or appetite is low.

Choose a smaller plate (around 18–20cm – roughly the size of a standard side plate) and build it roughly as follows:

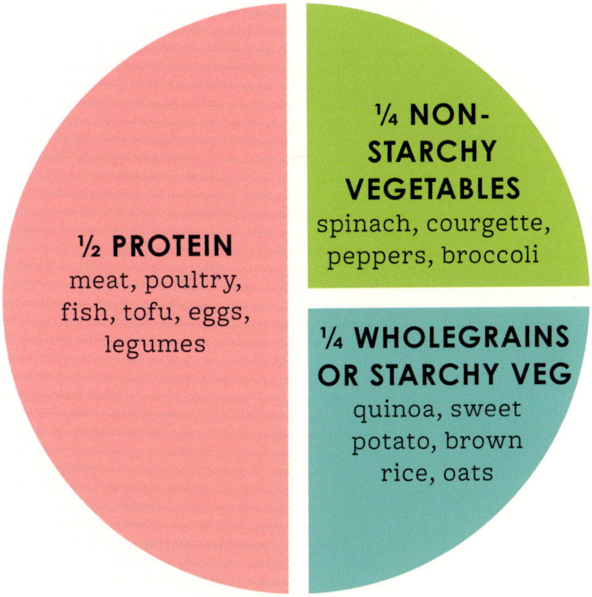

This layout helps you prioritise protein, support fibre intake and get enough energy without overfilling your stomach. It's a visual shortcut for building meals that are nourishing, not random. However, this isn't a rigid rule – it's a flexible guide to help you plate up when your appetite is unpredictable. It's especially useful if you're eating intuitively or assembling quick meals rather than following recipes.

YOU CAN NOW ADD SOME OPTIONAL EXTRAS:

- A drizzle or spoonful of healthy fat (olive oil, avocado, nuts/seeds)
- A calcium-rich food (yoghurt, fortified plant milk, cheese, tofu)

HERE'S WHAT THAT MIGHT LOOK LIKE ON THE PLATE:

- A small bowl of quinoa topped with roasted chickpeas, spinach, grilled courgette and tahini
- Two eggs with mashed sweet potato and sautéed kale
- Tofu stir-fry with peppers, broccoli and a scoop of brown rice
- Tuna and bean salad with cherry tomatoes, green beans and olive oil
- A seeded sandwich with chicken, salad and avocado, served with veggie sticks or soup

Being mindful of starchy carbs when you're on GLP-1s for weight loss

If you're using a GLP-1 medication for weight loss, it's still important to be mindful of how much starchy carbohydrate you're eating. These include foods like bread, pasta, rice, potatoes and other grain-based products. While these foods aren't off limits, eating large amounts of them can spike your blood sugar, which can compete with the appetite-regulating effect of your medication.

Starchy carbs also take up valuable space in your stomach, and since GLP-1s slow down digestion, you'll feel fuller quicker. That makes it even more important to prioritise protein, fibre-rich veg and healthy fats, which are more satiating and richer in nutrients.

Focus on smaller portions of wholegrain versions or starchy vegetables like sweet potato or squash, and pair them with protein and non-starchy vegetables to help keep your blood sugar stable and support sustained weight loss.

How you eat matters as well

When you're dealing with a low appetite, especially if you're using GLP-1 medications, how you eat can be just as important as what you eat. With appetite signals dialled down and fullness arriving quickly, slowing down and becoming more intentional with mealtimes can make all the difference.

Eating too quickly when you have a small appetite can lead to discomfort, nausea, bloating and a missed opportunity to meet your nutritional needs. GLP-1 medications slow down how quickly food moves through your stomach (known as gastric emptying), so rushing through meals can leave you feeling overly full and reluctant to eat again later.

This doesn't mean mealtimes have to be overly formal or time-consuming. It's about small shifts in how you approach food that can improve comfort, digestion and appetite over time.

Try these strategies:

1.

Eat slowly and chew thoroughly

Give your stomach time to register fullness. Chewing properly also helps break food down for easier digestion and better nutrient absorption.

2.

Take smaller bites

Use a small spoon or fork to slow the pace. It may sound basic, but it can really help if fullness comes on quickly.

3.

Pause between bites

Put your cutlery down for a few seconds between mouthfuls to give your body time to respond.

4.

Sit down to eat

Wherever possible, sit at a table and avoid eating on the move. This helps reduce mindless eating and makes the food feel more intentional.

5.

Minimise distractions

Try to avoid phones, TV or working through meals. Focusing on your food, even just for 10 minutes, makes it easier to tune into your hunger and fullness signals.

6.

Choose visually appealing, aromatic foods

Appetite is multisensory. Colourful, well-presented meals with a nice aroma can help you engage more with food and stimulate a desire to eat.

7.

Reheat food gently

Warm food tends to be more aromatic and easier to digest than cold leftovers, which can feel unappealing when appetite is low.

What happens when you stop taking GLP-1s?

At some point, many people stop taking GLP-1 medications, whether it's because they've reached their health or weight goal, experienced side effects, or simply decided it's time. And when that happens, two of the biggest concerns are, 'will my appetite come back?' and 'can I maintain the progress I've made?'

The short answer to the first question is yes – you can continue to eat well without medication, but it helps to understand what's going on in your body, and how to support yourself through the transition.

GLP-1 medications don't permanently change your appetite. Once you stop taking them, your body gradually returns to its usual hormone rhythms. This means:

- Hunger may return within days or up to a week after stopping the medication, especially with shorter-acting GLP-1s. This is completely normal, though it can feel intense or unfamiliar at first
- Food noise (the mental chatter about what to eat) may increase
- Fullness might take longer to register or feel less satisfying
- You may crave foods you haven't wanted in months and that can feel confusing

None of this means you've failed. It's your biology recalibrating. What matters now is acknowledging this shift and having the tools to respond and not react to this change.

WHY THIS BOOK STILL WORKS AFTER GLP-1S

If you've been using this book while taking GLP-1s, you've already been building the habits that will help you most now:

- You're eating smaller, high-protein, high-fibre meals
- You're spacing your meals and snacks to avoid big energy dips
- You've simplified your kitchen so eating feels doable even on low-energy days

This structure supports your appetite, whether it's low or rising again. It's not about restriction. It's about consistency.

Supporting natural GLP-1 through food

In response to the question on maintaining progress, while you can't replicate the drug's effects with food alone, you can support your body's GLP-1 hormone release through what and how you eat. Building meals that support fullness naturally without relying on extreme restriction is the long-term strategy.

1. Eat more protein at each meal

Protein-rich foods stimulate GLP-1 release and help you feel full. Aim for at least 20g of protein per main meal (these recipes are designed with that in mind). If you find your appetite increasing, scale the portion size up, especially the protein component. Add some of the protein-rich 'nutrient boosters' from the recipe section, like nut and seed mixes, high-protein breads, cashew nut cream and whipped cottage cheese to dishes.

2. Increase fibre gradually

Fibre, especially soluble fibre from oats, beans, lentils, ground flaxseed and cooked vegetables, supports slower digestion and steadier appetite signals. Try increasing the veg portions, adding a spoonful of lentils or beans, or serving with a small portion of a wholegrain like brown rice or quinoa. The homemade bread recipes are naturally high in fibre, and there's a simple seed mix and dukkha you can sprinkle over many meals to improve texture and fibre content.

3.

Chew your food well and eat slowly

This isn't just good manners; slower eating leads to a more robust GLP-1 response. Taking time to eat helps you better notice when you've had enough, especially now your natural appetite cues are returning.

4.

Include healthy fats

Small amounts of healthy fat (like extra virgin olive oil, tahini, avocado or seeds) help prolong satiety and support the release of fullness hormones, including GLP-1. Many of the recipes in this book already include these fats in small, balanced amounts.

5.

Drink mint tea or ginger tea after meals

Herbal teas like mint or ginger can support digestion, help manage cravings and provide a gentle sense of closure after eating. Avoid mint tea if you have heartburn, as it encourages stomach acid to enter the oesophagus and worsen things.

You don't need to chase fullness

One of the challenges after stopping medication is the expectation that fullness should feel the same. It won't. Your goal now isn't to suppress hunger, it's to meet it calmly, with meals that are balanced, satisfying and grounded in your needs.

This is where the book's flexible approach helps. You don't need to overhaul your meals, just keep building small, protein- and fibre-rich meals that suit your appetite. The structure stays but the portions shift slightly.

RECONNECTING WITH YOUR NATURAL HUNGER CUES

GLP-1s can mute hunger and when it returns, it can feel unfamiliar or even unsettling, especially if you associated hunger with overeating or feeling out of control. But hunger is your body's way of communicating its needs. After stopping medication, this is your opportunity to build a healthy relationship with hunger, learning to respond, not restrict. So take note of your appetite signals when you start to feel peckish, when meals satisfy you and when you're genuinely full. These cues may feel blunt at first, but they sharpen with time and consistency.

A GENTLE APPROACH: REVERSE DIETING

Reverse dieting, a term borrowed from sports nutrition, means gradually increasing food intake after a period of restriction or appetite suppression. This gentle approach may help prevent rebound eating, support your metabolism, and ease the pressure of 'going back to normal'. Rather than jumping into large meals or old habits, it's about slowly building on what already works: protein-first meals, balanced plates, and regular eating patterns.

Coming off medication is not back to square one; it's the next phase of your journey. If you eat to support satiety, blood sugar balance and nourishment you give your body and brain the best chance to stay steady.

FIVE FIXES TO MAKE EVERY BITE COUNT

You're probably very familiar with the central idea of the book at this point: when your appetite is small, nutrition matters more. But what happens on the days when even small meals feel like too much? When you're hitting that familiar wall of early fullness, bloating, low energy or just general disinterest in eating?

Fix 1: Use nutrient boosters liberally

If you can't eat more food, you can make the food you do eat work harder. Nutrient boosters are small additions that drastically increase the nutrient value of your meals, without increasing the portion size. These boosters are especially important when:

- You're eating soft or blended meals that may be lower in calories
- You want to hit key micronutrient targets (iron, omega-3, calcium)
- You need to start gaining weight after a period of low appetite and weight loss

EFFORTLESS PROTEIN BOOSTERS

Use these to instantly increase the protein in your meals with no cooking required. Stir them into porridge, soups, dips or spreads, or sprinkle them over toast, salads and grain bowls.

Protein Booster	Portion	Protein
Chia seeds	1 tbsp	2.5g
Ground flaxseed	1 tbsp	3.5g
Hemp seeds	1 tbsp	4.7g
Nut butter (e.g. peanut)	1 tbsp	3.8g
Tahini	1 tbsp	4g
Whey protein powder	1 scoop	24g
Plant-based protein powder	1 scoop	22g
Nutritional yeast	1 tbsp	7g
Greek yoghurt	2 tbsp	3.4g
Cottage cheese	2 tbsp	4.7g
Edamame	40g	4.8g
Skyr	2 tbsp	6.4g
Silken tofu (blended)	75g (¼ block)	5.2g

EFFORTLESS FIBRE BOOSTERS

These small additions can make a big difference to your fibre intake without increasing the size or effort of your meals. They're ideal for stirring into porridge, yoghurt, soups or dips, or sprinkling over toast, roasted veg or grain bowls.

Fibre Booster	Portion	Fibre
Chia seeds	1 tbsp	5.1g
Ground flaxseed	1 tbsp	3.1g
Mixed seeds (hemp, pumpkin, sunflower)	1 tbsp	1.5g
Chopped nuts (almonds, walnuts)	1 tbsp	0.9g
Nut butter (e.g. peanut)	1 tbsp	1.1g
Oats	1 tbsp	1.1g
Psyllium husk	1 tsp	2g
Cooked lentils	2 heaped tbsp	1.9g
Cooked chickpeas	2 heaped tbsp	2.4g
Cooked beans	2 heaped tbsp	3g

DON'T FORGET TO ADD SOME COLOUR TO YOUR PLATE

Fruit and vegetables really are nature's multivitamins and one of the easiest ways to lift the nutritional value of a meal with minimal effort. Keep a stash of frozen spinach, peas, mixed veg or berries in the freezer so you can throw them into soups, stews, curries or yoghurt and smoothies without any prep. Even small handfuls make a difference, and using a mix of colours helps cover more nutritional bases across the day.

Fix 2: The Rule of Four: protein + colour + healthy fat + wholefood

This is your go-to formula for building quick meals and it ensures every bite works hard for you, supporting strength, energy and long-term health. Unlike the Small Plate Framework (see page 45), which is designed for plated meals and helps with visual portioning (especially useful for GLP-1 users) the Rule of Four is more adaptable and a formula I used to help me build the recipes in this book. It's your go-to for quick meals that don't follow a traditional plate layout, like a wrap, grain bowl or fridge-raid combo. It offers structure without needing to measure or divide a plate, making it ideal for when you want to eat well, fast.

Think of the Rule of Four as the core structure of your meal. You can always build on it with extra elements that suit your tastes or needs, like fresh herbs, spices, nuts, seeds, fermented foods, more grains and legumes or a dressing. These additional elements add interest, texture and even more nutritional benefits.

- **Protein:** The anchor of every meal. It supports muscle, metabolism and blood sugar balance. Aim for at least 20g per serving.
- **Colour:** A fruit or vegetable adds fibre, antioxidants and visual appeal.
- **Healthy fat:** Adds flavour and mouthfeel, calories and omega-3; helps you absorb vitamins A, D, E and K.
- **Wholefood:** A grain or legume provides fibre and nutrients like iron and magnesium as well as slow-burning energy. Often the smallest part of the meal in this instance, but still important.

RULE OF FOUR INGREDIENTS

Protein	Colour	Healthy Fat	Wholefood
Poultry (chicken, turkey)	Fresh green herbs (coriander, chives)	Extra virgin olive oil	Oats
Oily fish (salmon, mackerel)	Dark green leafy vegetables (kale, spring greens)	Avocado	Wholemeal breads (pitta, wraps)
Tinned fish (tuna, salmon, mackerel)	Root vegetables (carrots, beetroot)	Tahini	Wholegrains (quinoa, barley, brown rice)
Tofu, tempeh, edamame beans	Salad vegetables (red pepper, lettuce)	Hummus	Pasta (wholewheat, legume-based)
Eggs	Frozen fruits and vegetables (berries, spinach, peas)	Nut butter (almond, peanut)	Rice (brown, wild, red)
Legumes (beans/lentils)*	Orchard fruits (apples, pears, citrus fruits)	Nuts (almonds, walnuts)	Starchy vegetables (sweet potato, parsnips, potatoes)
Hard cheese (halloumi, feta)	Berries (strawberries, raspberries, blueberries)	Seeds (chia, pumpkin)	Legumes (beans/lentils)*
Cottage cheese, paneer	Jarred vegetables (red peppers, artichoke, asparagus)	Cashew cream	Puffed grains (wholemeal rice cakes, quinoa, brown rice)
Seafood (prawns, crab)	Tropical fruits (mango, pineapple)	Olives	Crackers (rye, oat, seed)
Yoghurt, skyr, fortified soya yoghurt	Processed tomatoes (tinned, purée, sun-dried)	Dukkah (nut, seed and spice mix)	Breakfast cereals (fortified, low sugar)

** Legumes count as both a protein and a wholefood because they provide plant-based protein **and** are rich in fibre and slow-releasing carbohydrates.*

GOOD EXAMPLES OF RULE OF FOUR MEALS

Poached egg + Sautéed spinach + Avocado + Seeded bread

Lentil dhal + Roasted squash + Coconut milk (swirl) + Lentil dhal

Chicken slices + Roasted carrots + Tahini dressing + Cooked lentils

Grilled halloumi + Mixed salad + Hummus + Wholemeal wrap

Tofu + Stir-fry vegetables + Peanut sauce + Brown rice

Fix 3: The Rule of Three: base + protein + flavour

For those moments when you're short on time, energy or appetite, an even simpler approach might be what's needed. That's where the Rule of Three comes in. This is your fast-track formula for snacks. It's not meant to be perfectly balanced; it's meant to be doable.

Base: A neutral carrier like wholegrain toast, oatcakes, seeded crackers (see page 200) rice cakes, rye crackers or veggie slices.

Protein: The star of the show again. Even a little can help support muscle and energy.

Flavour: Adds appeal through spice, acidity, crunch or sweetness, which is essential when appetite is low.

GOOD EXAMPLES OF THE RULE OF THREE SNACKS OR MINI MEALS

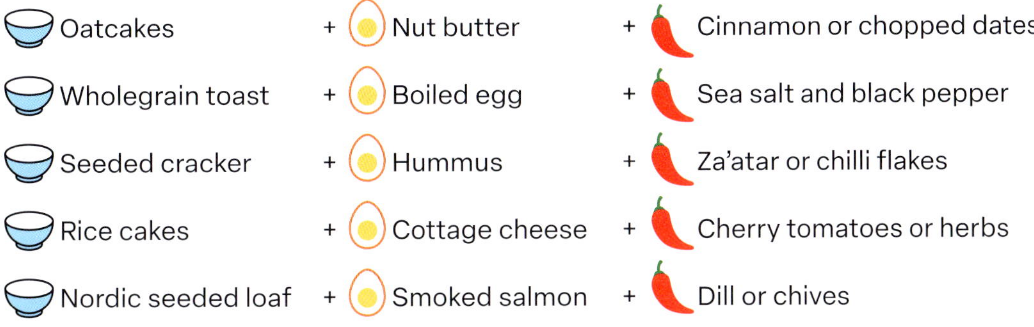

Base		Protein		Flavour
Oatcakes	+	Nut butter	+	Cinnamon or chopped dates
Wholegrain toast	+	Boiled egg	+	Sea salt and black pepper
Seeded cracker	+	Hummus	+	Za'atar or chilli flakes
Rice cakes	+	Cottage cheese	+	Cherry tomatoes or herbs
Nordic seeded loaf	+	Smoked salmon	+	Dill or chives

The Rule of Three is about removing pressure. You don't have to tick every nutritional box, just create something nourishing enough to get you through. If you have more appetite later, you can always build on it.

WHY SIDE PLATES AND SMALL BOWLS WORK

Smaller crockery does more than reduce portion sizes, it helps create a visual and psychological shift that's especially useful when appetite is low. Here's why it matters:

- Smaller portions feel more doable, which reduces meal-time stress
- A full side plate feels 'abundant', even if the meal is modest
- You avoid wasting food or feeling like you need to finish a plate that's too full

Using a side plate isn't about tricking yourself, it's about making meals feel more approachable. Try keeping mini bowls and ramekins for small snacks and mini meals.

YOU DON'T HAVE TO AIM FOR PERFECTION ON EVERY PLATE

When meals are smaller and more frequent, it helps to let go of the idea that each one needs to tick every nutrition box. Instead, aim for balance across the day or even over two days if your appetite is particularly low.

If lunch is light on veg then add fruit, mixed green vegetables or a salad at dinner.

If there is very little protein in your evening snack, then include a boiled egg or yoghurt the next morning. This flexible mindset gives you more freedom and makes it easier to keep eating without pressure.

Fix 4: Adding Calories Without Bulk

If you need more energy but find it hard to eat larger meals, the solution is to fortify what you're already eating. Here are some simple, nutrient-dense additions that add calories without increasing volume too much:

- Drizzle extra virgin olive oil over cooked veg, soups or grains
- Stir coconut milk or tahini into porridge or smoothies
- Add a splash of soy cream, blended silken tofu or cashew nut cream (see page 203) to plant-based soups, stews, curries and other one-pot meals
- Sprinkle lightly crushed seeds or chopped nuts onto bowls, salads or soups

These additions are small but powerful. For example, 1 tablespoon of extra virgin olive oil adds around 120 calories and supports the absorption of fat-soluble vitamins.

This isn't about better or worse, it's about what's appropriate for you. Right-sized meals still nourish; they just do it without overwhelming your system.

Fix 5: Smart Supplementation

When your appetite is small, it can be hard to meet all your nutritional needs through food alone, even with the best intentions. Whole foods are always the priority and offer benefits a pill can't replicate, but strategic supplementation and fortified foods can help fill the gaps when needed.

These options are also incredibly convenient. Even a splash of fortified milk in tea, a few spoonfuls of fortified cereal, or a daily multivitamin can offer useful nutritional insurance when your food intake is low. They're low-effort ways to top up key nutrients, especially on days when cooking or eating much just isn't realistic.

Think of these additions as tools, not crutches. If your diet is limited, you've lost weight quickly, or fatigue makes cooking and eating difficult, these small extras can help keep your body supported. Supplements aren't always necessary, but you might benefit from them if:

- You're eating much less than usual for more than a few weeks
- You've lost weight quickly or unintentionally
- You're relying heavily on the same few foods
- You follow a restrictive or plant-based diet
- You feel tired, weak or notice changes like pale skin, hair thinning or poor wound healing
- You avoid food groups like dairy
- You've been advised by a GP or dietitian

SUPPLEMENTS TO CONSIDER

- Multivitamin – choose one that suits your age and diet (e.g. vegan-friendly)
- Protein powder – handy when you're eating less. Look for versions with added vitamins and minerals
- Calcium + vitamin D – especially important if you avoid dairy or fortified foods. The UK Government recommends 10mcg vitamin D daily from October to April for everyone, but postmenopausal women and those at higher risk of deficiency may benefit from taking it year-round to support bone health.
- Iron – only take if you're low and advised by your GP
- Vitamin B12 – important for those on plant-based diets
- Omega-3 – if you don't eat oily fish, try an algae-based EPA + DHA supplement

FORTIFIED FOODS: EASY WINS WHEN EATING LESS

- Breakfast cereals (check for added iron, B vitamins, folate)
- Plant milks (many have calcium, iodine, vitamins D and B12)
- Dairy-free yoghurts (look for calcium + B12)
- High-protein yoghurt and milk (extra protein)
- Nutritional yeast (B12 + folate)
- Spreads with vitamin D

HOW TO FUEL EXERCISE WITH LOW APPETITE

Exercise plays a crucial role in maintaining health, supporting mood, enhancing overall vitality and – importantly – helping to preserve muscle mass, especially when you're eating less.

But when your appetite is low, fuelling your body for movement can feel like a balancing act. You want to support your workouts, but eating before (or after) may feel challenging due to early fullness, digestive discomfort or simply a lack of interest in food.

You might be coming back to exercise after a break, perhaps because your appetite and energy were low for a while. Or maybe you've started losing weight on GLP-1 medication and now feel more inspired to move your body again. Either way, nutrition plays a key role in getting the most out of your workouts and protecting your health as you become more active.

The good news is you don't need large meals or traditional 'athlete-style' fuelling plans to benefit from being active. You can use small, strategic eating moments around exercise to nourish your body, support recovery and avoid fatigue, all while working with your appetite, not against it.

Why exercise still matters

When you're eating less overall, your body actually needs more careful support to stay strong and energised. Exercise helps maintain lean mass, protects your bones, supports mood and keeps your metabolism

ADAPTING YOUR EXERCISE TYPE FOR LOW APPETITE

More Manageable	Use Caution
Strength or resistance training Helps protect muscle mass, even with lower calorie intake	**Long cardio sessions without food** Can lead to fatigue and low energy
Walking, cycling, swimming Low intensity but effective for health and mood	**Intense HIIT workouts on an empty stomach** May feel draining and hard to recover from
Yoga or Pilates Support flexibility, core strength and stress management	**Hot yoga or strong core-focused classes** Can be dehydrating or uncomfortable if energy or digestion is low

steady, but those benefits rely on getting enough protein, energy and hydration throughout the day.

WITHOUT FUELLING PROPERLY, EXERCISE CAN LEAD TO:

- Muscle loss instead of gain or maintenance
- Poor recovery and ongoing soreness
- Increased risk of injury
- Low mood, fatigue or burnout

Even light or moderate activity needs nutritional support. It doesn't take much food, just the right food at the right time.

TIP: Creatine can be a helpful addition if you're doing resistance training. When paired with a protein-rich diet, it supports muscle strength, performance and recovery, which is all especially important when you're eating less. Choose the monohydrate form, ideally as a powder rather than pills. There's

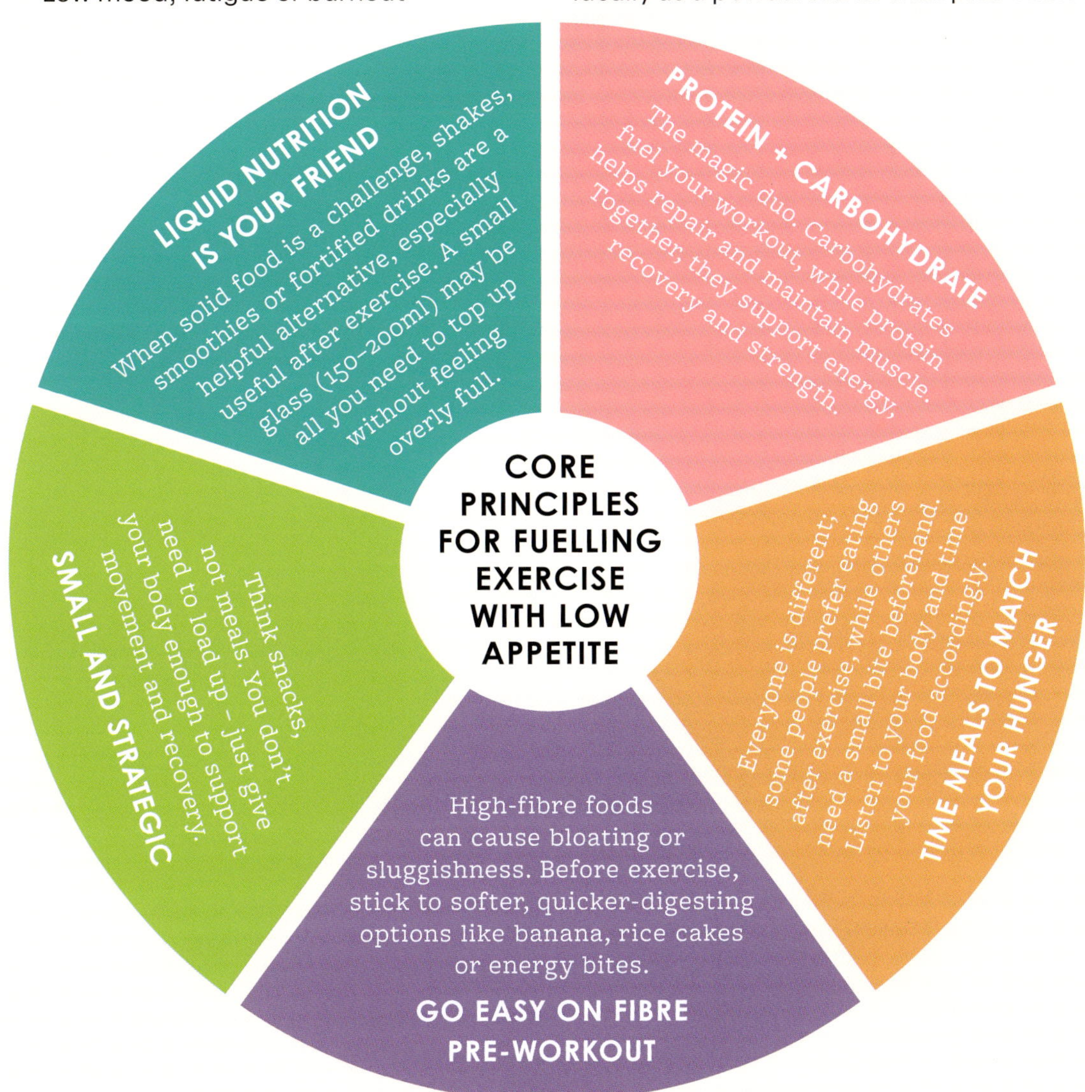

also growing interest in its benefits for brain health, including memory and cognition in older adults.

Pre-exercise nutrition

What you eat before exercise can make a real difference to how you feel and perform, helping to top up your energy, stabilise blood sugar and reduce the risk of dizziness, fatigue or underperforming. When your appetite is low, you might not feel like eating much, and that's absolutely fine. Even a few bites of the right kind of food can go a long way.

In Pre-workout Snacks (pages 212–217), I've included a range of simple, quick-to-digest snacks designed to give you a small hit of carbohydrate before training. Think dried fruit energy balls, oats, rice cakes and soft wraps – all easy to manage and designed to fuel your session without weighing you down. Aim to eat them around 30 to 60 minutes before you start exercising, depending on your tolerance and how heavy the snack feels for you.

That said, you don't always have to eat before you exercise, especially if it's a short or low-intensity session, or if you feel better training on an empty stomach. Everyone's tolerance is different, and some people find they have more energy eating afterwards instead. The key is to listen to your body, find what works for you and fuel up at a time that supports your recovery and energy levels.

IDEAL PRE-EXERCISE OPTIONS

If you're not making homemade pre-workout snacks, you can still grab something simple from your store cupboard to get you through your session. For morning workouts, appetite may be even lower than usual, and that's totally normal as not all of us are morning people. You don't need a full snack, sometimes just a few bites of banana or a sip of smoothie is enough to take the edge off and help you move comfortably.

The goal here isn't to load up, it's to give your body just enough fuel to feel steady and energised, without feeling weighed down.

- Half a banana
- Rice cakes with nut butter
- A few sips of smoothie
- A handful of dried fruit
- 1–2 Medjool dates (plain or stuffed with a walnut half)
- 1 slice of soft toast with honey
- Mini low-fibre wrap with mashed banana
- Fruit purée pouch
- Soft dried apricots or mango slices

Post-exercise nutrition

Eating after exercise is one of the most effective times to refuel. Your muscles are primed to absorb nutrients, and what you eat during this window can support recovery, replenish energy stores and help you maintain lean muscle mass, even when your overall appetite is low.

That said, it's not just about what you eat right after training. It's the protein that you eat across the whole day that matters most, so don't worry if you feel you can only manage a small amount straight after exercise. The key is to include a little protein and carbohydrate within about an hour of finishing, then continue fuelling as your appetite allows.

You don't need to track grams unless you want to. As a guide:

- 15–30g of protein = a portion of tofu, small serving of chicken, a protein shake, 2 boiled eggs, a small bowl of yoghurt or skyr topped with nuts and seeds
- 20–50g of carbohydrate = a banana, 3 dates, a mini wrap, small bowl of porridge or slice of toast

EASY POST-WORKOUT OPTIONS

In Post-workout Snacks (pages 218–221) you'll find a handful of recipes that are ideal for post-workout recovery. Use what works for you and your schedule and remember: consistency over the day is what really supports your body, not perfection after every session. Here are some other options that require little preparation and use store cupboard ingredients:

- Protein rich smoothie (try the gut-loving breakfast shake on page 85)
- Scrambled egg or tofu on wholemeal toast or egg muffins (see page 80)
- A couple of rice cakes with cottage cheese and tomato
- Yoghurt or skyr with berries and hemp seeds
- Small wholemeal wrap with turkey and avocado
- Small slice of wholemeal toast with hummus and sliced boiled egg
- 2 Medjool dates and a small protein drink

KEEP PROTEIN-RICH LEFTOVERS IN THE FRIDGE

Cooked quinoa, lentils, tofu, roasted chicken or veggie chilli can be quickly turned into a post-workout meal when paired with something like brown rice, oatcakes, seeded or rye crackers, mini wholemeal pitta breads or a small wholemeal wrap. This is also a smart way to use up proteins like chicken or fish when you've bought more than you need for one small meal.

IF SOLID FOOD FEELS DIFFICULT

- Try a ready-to-drink protein or homemade protein drink (see page 207)
- Sip a smoothie slowly over 30–60 minutes
- Break your recovery into two stages: something liquid now, something soft or savoury later

TIME MEALS AROUND YOUR WORKOUT

If you're already eating at set times to help manage a low appetite, planning your workout around those meals can save time and reduce the pressure of figuring out what to eat before and after. For example, training just before a planned snack or meal means you can eat straight after without needing to add anything extra. It's a simple way to stay nourished without overthinking it.

A workout day with low appetite

PRE-WORKOUT
A few bites of banana + a sip or two of protein shake
(A light start to take the edge off hunger before movement)

SHORT STRENGTH WORKOUT
(30 minutes)

POST-WORKOUT RECOVERY
Small smoothie (150–200ml) with milk or a fortified alternative, protein powder, frozen berries and almond butter
(Liquid nutrition to support muscle recovery without overwhelming your appetite)

LIGHT LUNCH
Small soft wholemeal wrap with chicken (or black beans), hummus and sliced vegetables
(A protein-rich leftover used smartly that is easy to chew and digest)

SNACK
Yoghurt or fortified alternative with cinnamon, grated apple and hemp seeds
(A light, wholesome snack to top up protein, calcium and omega-3s)

EVENING MEAL
Grilled tofu or salmon with brown rice + wilted greens drizzled with a spoonful of tahini
(Small, warm and comforting; easy to portion and adapt to appetite)

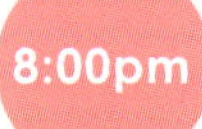

EVENING WIND-DOWN
Herbal tea + 1–2 Medjool dates
(A little end-of-day nourishment without feeling heavy)

Staying hydrated

Hydration is just as important as food, especially with reduced appetite. Dehydration can worsen fatigue and make you less likely to want to eat.

- Drink water or diluted juice in small sips throughout the day
- Use electrolyte tablets or powders if you're sweating heavily
- Try warm fluids like broth or herbal teas for hydration without bloat
- Avoid gulping large amounts at once so space your drinks out

HEALTH HACKS FOR MEALTIMES

When your appetite is low, eating well isn't just about food choices, it's about reducing friction. Health hacks are a core strategy in this book because they take the pressure off and help you eat more consistently, with less effort and more ease.

Whether it's a five-minute fix or a smart set-up in your kitchen, these little nudges add up. Think of this chapter as your go-to list of small, actionable tweaks that can make a real difference. Many of these have been mentioned throughout the previous chapters, so see this as your quick reference list.

Prep hacks

1. Build a power-up box

Keep a tray or small box in your fridge or cupboard filled with nutrient-rich add-ins that require zero prep. Think toasted seeds, a jar of tahini, a bottle of extra virgin olive oil, lemon wedges, a tub of hummus, nutritional yeast or a scoop-ready protein powder. These are compact ingredients that pack a nutritional punch and can be stirred into soup, spooned over porridge or sprinkled on toast. Having a power-up box takes the thinking out of upgrading your meals.

2. Create a go-to meal list

Think about a handful of meals or snacks you enjoy and that feel good after eating, even on low-energy days. Write them on a note on the fridge or save them in your phone for easy access. These meals should be low effort, feel achievable and bring some satisfaction. Having this personal shortlist means you won't find yourself standing in front of the fridge wondering what to eat when you're already feeling depleted.

3. Cook once, eat often

Instead of cooking from scratch every time, prepare a few core ingredients at the start of the week that can be used in multiple ways. A tray of roasted vegetables can become part of a grain bowl, a wrap, or even be blended into a soup. Cooked lentils can be added to a salad one day and stirred into soup or mash the next, while hard-boiled eggs are a valuable high-protein snack. These flexible foundations allow you to eat well without constant decision-making.

4. Keep three 'no-brainer plates' in the fridge

Choose three simple, balanced plate ideas that you can keep components for in the fridge. Think pouched puy lentils, cherry tomatoes and feta; hard-boiled egg, avocado and rye crispbread or Nordic seeded loaf (see page 194), smoked salmon and cucumber. Having these familiar combos on hand removes barriers to eating and gives you an easy default on days when energy is low.

5. Layer 'smart stack' meals

Stack three or four nourishing elements together to create a satisfying plate without needing a big main dish. This approach works well when your appetite is low, but you still want variety and nutrition. Try a small slice of seeded toast topped with smoked salmon and fresh dill, or for a more substantial stack, combine roast chicken slices with puy lentils (from a pouch), cherry tomatoes and a drizzle of tahini, which gives you a gentle but balanced meal with protein, fibre and healthy fats. These 'stacks' offer variety, texture and flavour without overwhelming your appetite with one large meal. (See also pages 51 and 53 for Rule of Three and Rule of Four.)

Presentation hacks

1. Use smaller bowls and plates

Smaller crockery can help visually reframe your portion. A modest serving can look more generous in a small bowl or plate, making you more likely to feel satisfied rather than underwhelmed. Use side plates, ramekins, tapas bowls or even espresso cups for soup – anything that makes the food feel manageable and inviting.

2. Make it look as good as it tastes

We eat with our eyes first. Keep a few colourful toppers like chopped herbs, sliced radishes, pomegranate seeds or flaked almonds handy. A sprinkle of something vibrant can turn a dull dish into something you feel more inclined to eat. Visual stimulation can make a big difference when appetite is low.

3. Create a 'comfort bowl' set-up

Keep one favourite bowl or plate for meals that need to feel familiar and soothing. Build your meal around soft, easy-to-digest foods like mash, roasted veg, lentils or eggs, with a simple drizzle or topping. Changing the ingredients but keeping the format consistent creates a mental shortcut that lowers resistance to eating.

Appetite hacks

1.

Eat to a gentle schedule

Instead of waiting to feel hungry, which may not happen, use time cues to remind you to eat. Try eating something every 3–4 hours, even if it's just a few bites. Setting gentle reminders on your phone or pairing meals with regular parts of your day (like post-shower or after a walk) can help create a rhythm that retrains your appetite over time.

2.

Move first, eat after

Even a little movement before eating – a walk around the block, five minutes of light stretching or tidying the kitchen – can stimulate digestion and bring on a hint of hunger. Movement increases circulation and can kick-start your appetite by gently prompting your body to prepare for food.

3.

Warm it up

Warm food gives off more aroma, which can subtly stimulate your appetite. Even if you're grabbing leftovers or a pre-made meal, a quick reheat can improve flavour and make eating more appealing. This also applies to soft fruits or stewed dishes: warm apples, pears or compotes can feel more comforting than cold alternatives.

4.

Use light and fresh air

Your environment matters. Sitting near a window, eating outside or just opening a window can help stimulate your senses and appetite. Natural light and airflow can lift your mood and subtly tell your body that it's time to eat. Even playing gentle background sounds or nature noise can make a meal feel more enjoyable.

5.

Limit large drinks pre-meal

Big drinks just before meals can take up space in your stomach and reduce your desire to eat. Try sipping water or herbal teas between meals instead. If you do want a drink during your meal, go for something small and gentle like diluted juice or warm tea in a small cup, rather than a full glass.

Mindset hacks

1.

Pair eating with something enjoyable

Not every meal needs to be eaten in silence at the table. If you find it hard to eat, try pairing meals with a relaxing or low-pressure activity like listening to music or a podcast, or even chatting with someone on the phone if you're eating alone. Gentle distraction can lower the emotional barrier to eating.

2.

Celebrate the wins

Focus on what you did eat, not what you didn't. Maybe it was just half a bowl or a spoonful more than yesterday, but that still counts. Small wins build momentum, so keep a mental or physical note if it helps remind you that you're making progress, even if it's slow.

3.

Create a 'low bar' eating cue

Place a sticky note in your kitchen or on your fridge that says something like: 'Have you had three bites today?' or 'Something is better than nothing'. These non-judgemental nudges can gently prompt you to eat without pressure or guilt, especially when motivation is low.

4.

Notice what works

After you eat, take 30 seconds to ask yourself: Did I enjoy that? Did it sit well? Was it satisfying? These quick reflections help you learn, which meals feel good not just physically, but emotionally too. Over time, this self-awareness makes food choices feel less random and more intuitive.

MANAGING LEFTOVERS AND GETTING ORGANISED IN THE KITCHEN

One of the realities of low appetite eating, and smaller portion recipes, is that you often end up with leftover ingredients.

This can be because it's harder to buy 'single serving' quantities of foods like beans, grains or vegetables, or because appetite fluctuations mean you may not finish planned meals. A few spoonfuls of cooked grains, half a tin of beans, half an avocado, a handful of wilted spinach – if you're not prepared, these leftovers can quickly turn into food waste or feel like a source of stress rather than a helpful resource.

Instead of fighting it, the key is to build a system that embraces and uses leftovers.

The basics: get organised

INVEST IN A GOOD SET OF CONTAINERS

Small, stackable containers are essential. Look for a variety of sizes, especially smaller ones (100–500ml). Top choices:

- Glass containers (better for visibility and reheating)
- Small jars for sauces, dressings, dips
- Freezer-safe bags for batch-cooked foods like grains or lentils

LABEL EVERYTHING

Use masking tape and a marker or purpose-made freezer labels. Label the contents and the date it was cooked or opened so you know when to use it by.

CREATE A 'LEFTOVER SHELF'

Designate a small section of your fridge and kitchen cupboards for leftover items. It keeps them visible and reminds you to use them up.

Clever ways to use up common leftovers

HALF-USED AVOCADOS

- Mash onto toast with lemon juice
- Blitz down into a dressing with extra virgin olive oil, lemon juice and herbs
- Blend into smoothies
- Make a quick guacamole
- Fill with an egg and bake
- Mix with unsweetened cocoa powder, honey and coconut oil for a healthy mousse
- Freeze in small portions to use later

COOKED GRAINS

- Add to soups, stews and other one-pot dishes
- Toss into salads with a lemon and olive oil dressing
- Stir-fry with leftover vegetables and a protein source
- Blend into veggie burger mixes
- Make simple grain bowls with leftover vegetables and protein

TINNED LEGUMES

- Mash with herbs and olive oil for a quick dip or spread for mini wraps
- Blend into sauces or use to thicken dishes
- Use as a base for veggie burgers or falafel
- Add to scrambled eggs or tofu
- Mix into soups, stews, curries and salads as a good fibre and protein booster
- Stir into cooked grains for extra nutrition

LEFTOVER VEGETABLES

- Add to any dish or serve as a side
- Roast into mixed vegetable trays
- Blitz into soups or smoothies
- Chop or grate into frittatas, egg muffins (see page 86) or scrambled egg
- Blend into dips like beetroot hummus or red pepper and walnut

STORING LEFTOVER HERBS

I love using lots of fresh herbs as they add flavour and brightness, but when you're cooking small servings of food you don't need much of them and they can often wilt before you get a chance to use them all. Here's how to keep them fresher for longer and reduce waste:

- **Fridge:** Wrap soft herbs (parsley, mint, coriander) in damp kitchen paper and store in a zip-lock bag or container. Keeps them fresh and reduces wilting.
- **Freeze (dry):** Wash, dry and freeze chopped or whole herbs on a tray, then transfer to a bag. Best for cooking, as the texture changes when defrosted.
- **Freeze (in cubes):** Chop herbs and freeze in ice-cube trays with water or olive oil. Drop straight into soups, stews or sauces.

What to do with leftover meat and fish

Leftover portions of cooked meat, tinned tuna or minced beef and lamb are common in small-portion cooking, and they can be easily repurposed into nourishing meals with very little effort. These additions help raise the protein content of meals without extra prep, and they're great options for people who may not feel up to cooking from scratch.

To avoid leftovers in the first place, consider buying your meat or fish at the supermarket counter rather than picking up pre-packed trays; this way you can ask for exactly the amount you need. It's a useful strategy if you're cooking for one or two, or planning a few smaller meals in advance.

Also remember to batch-cook recipes in this book that use just half packets of minced meats, so you're never left with awkward portions or waste.

TINNED TUNA

- Mix with a little olive oil, lemon juice and chopped herbs and serve on toast or crackers
- Stir into cooked pasta with leftover vegetables and a spoonful of pesto
- Add to a baked sweet potato with chopped tomato or red pepper for a quick meal
- Combine with mashed chickpeas and a little avocado and lemon to make a tuna spread

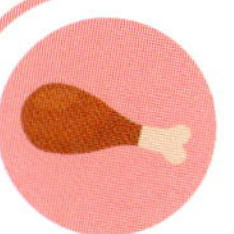

COOKED CHICKEN OR TURKEY

- Shred and toss into soups, stews or broths to increase protein
- Add to a simple grain bowl with vegetables and tasty dressings
- Mix with yoghurt and curry powder for a quick coronation-style salad or topping for rye crackers

LEFTOVER LAMB OR BEEF MINCE

- Add to a vegetable soup or tomato-based sauce for added richness and depth
- Use in a one-pan hash with potatoes, onions and leftover greens
- Combine with cooked lentils and spices to fill peppers or courgettes and bake

FLEXIBLE MEALS YOU CAN MAKE FROM LEFTOVERS

These easy recipes help you make the most of what's already open or cooked without needing to batch cook. They're gently flavoured, versatile and quick to prepare, and ideal for turning bits and pieces into nourishing little meals.

SAVOURY VEG AND CHICKPEA MASH

Mash soft, cooked veg (sweet potato, carrot, parsnip, courgette) with 2–3 tbsp tinned chickpeas or cannellini beans. Add olive oil, lemon juice and a pinch of smoked paprika or cumin. Warm in a pan or microwave. Serve with toast, oatcakes or over grains.

VEGETABLE FRITTERS OR PATTIES

Grate or finely chop leftover veg (courgette, carrot, sweetcorn, broccoli). Mix with 2–3 tbsp mashed beans/lentils, 1 tbsp oats or flour and 1 egg (or flaxseed egg). Season, shape into patties and pan-fry in olive oil for 2–3 minutes each side.

LEFTOVER VEG SOUP SHOT

Sauté chopped leftover veg in olive oil. Add a splash of stock and 1 tbsp tinned beans, lentils or grains. Simmer for 5–10 minutes, then blend until smooth. Season to taste and serve warm in a mug or bowl.

MINI TRAYBAKE WITH LEFTOVERS

In a small oven dish, mix cooked veg with 2–3 tbsp cooked grains (quinoa, wholemeal couscous). Add herbs, crumble in feta and drizzle with olive oil. Bake at 180°C/160°C fan/Gas 4 for 15–20 minutes.

SMALL-BATCH HUMMUS OR BEAN DIP

Blend ½ tin chickpeas, butter beans or cannellini beans with 1 tbsp olive oil, juice of ½ lemon, 1 small garlic clove and a pinch of salt. Add leftover roasted veg if using. Blend until smooth. Serve as a dip or spread.

CRISPY TOP BUBBLE AND SQUEAK

Mash 1 cup cooked potato/sweet potato/ root veg with cooked greens (spinach, kale) and 2–3 tbsp mashed beans or tofu. Press into a small baking dish, top with breadcrumbs and olive oil. Bake at 200°C/180°C fan/Gas 6 for 15–20 minutes.

ONE-POT NOURISH BOWL

Warm leftover grains, chopped veg and pulses in a pan with a splash of stock, water or a spoon of tahini or pesto. Stir until hot. Top with seeds or a soft-boiled egg.

QUICK STUFFED VEG

Halve and core a pepper, courgette or large mushroom. Fill with cooked grains, chopped veg, mashed beans and herbs. Top with cheese or seeds and bake at 180°C/160°C fan/Gas 4 for 20 minutes.

EGG OR TOFU SCRAMBLE WITH VEG

Sauté chopped cooked veg in olive oil. Add 1–2 beaten eggs and stir gently until just set OR crumble in tofu with turmeric and a splash of plant milk.

Your low effort kitchen toolkit

When appetite is low, the last thing you want is complicated cooking. Having the right kitchen tools can make a big difference and a few smart basics can make it easier to cook, store and eat well when you're working with less appetite and energy.

- Makes cooking quicker and simpler when energy is low
- Helps store leftovers safely and conveniently
- Encourages small-batch prep
- Keeps portion sizes realistic to avoid waste

MUST-HAVE TOOLS FOR LOW APPETITE EATING

These are my essentials to help you prepare and store the recipes in throughout this book, many of which you will probably already have in your kitchen cupboards.

- **Small storage containers (100–500ml sizes):** to store leftovers, prepped ingredients and small batch meals. Reusable, ideally glass and freezer-safe.
- **Small non-stick frying pan (20cm):** perfect for mini meals like scrambled egg or tofu, quick sautéed vegetables, mini frittatas or patties and small portions of meat and fish.
- **Stick blender:** useful for blitzing soups, smoothies, dressings and blending dips like guacamole.
- **Mini chopping board and sharp knife:** a small board and a good-quality chef's knife will do 90 per cent of the work.
- **Small and medium non-stick saucepans:** useful for reheating leftovers, cooking grains or warming up soups and broths. Essential for cooking one-pot dishes in smaller serving sizes.
- **Measuring spoons:** helpful when following recipes to help portion realistically and avoid waste.
- **Small non-stick baking trays:** these are ideal for roasting a small number of vegetables, baking single portions of meat and fish or reheating leftovers.
- **Non-stick 6-cup muffin tin:** these are great for making breakfast muffins. You can also use them to freeze cooked grains like quinoa, couscous or brown rice into handy single portions. Once frozen, pop them out and store in a freezer bag – ideal for days when you only want a small amount without cooking a full batch.
- **Ice cube trays:** good for freezing sauces, stocks and chopped herbs.
- **Digital kitchen scales:** accurate, no-waste measuring and useful when preparing small servings of food.
- **Attractive small bowls and side plates:** when your appetite is low, presentation really matters. Smaller bowls (12cm diameter) help food look inviting rather than overwhelming or lost on a large plate. Choosing dishes you actually like to use can make mealtimes feel more enjoyable too.

Set your kitchen up for success

I can't cook unless my kitchen is really organised. If I don't know where things are or the space feels messy, it ruins the whole experience and makes me far less inclined to cook at all. A tidy, well-arranged kitchen isn't just about efficiency, it sets the tone for how enjoyable and doable cooking feels, especially when you're starting from scratch.

- **Keep your tools visible and accessible:** if your blender lives in a cupboard behind the ironing board, it won't get used.
- **Group your 'leftover kit' together:** keep all your storage containers in one place and get plenty of them as they are also great for storing leftover ingredients, which you will encounter when cooking small servings of food. Store oatcakes, tinned fish, nut butter, grain pouches and other minimal-prep staples somewhere visible and easy to reach.
- **Create a 'quick meal shelf':** keep store cupboard foods like tinned fish, grain pouches, tinned lentils and beans, oats, nut butter, crackers, tinned tomatoes and a few go-to spices in a visible, easy-to-reach spot. When your appetite is low or energy is lacking, these familiar basics make it easier to pull together something nourishing without overthinking or cooking a full meal from scratch.

You don't need a big kitchen or a cupboard full of gadgets to eat well when your appetite is small. A few smart tools that are easy to use, easy to clean and built for small portions can turn low appetite eating from a chore into something simple and manageable.

BUILDING A LOW APPETITE STORE CUPBOARD

When your appetite is low, the way you shop and stock your kitchen may need to shift. Even if you're cooking for others, it helps to build a personalised toolkit of small, easy, flexible foods just for you and options that support your nourishment with minimal effort and waste.

Why a thoughtful store cupboard matters

A well-stocked store cupboard can make low appetite eating feel less like a chore. When the right ingredients are on hand, it becomes easier to build quick, nourishing meals, even on low-energy days. Here's why it matters:

- **Removes friction:** you can respond quickly when you feel like eating, without starting from scratch.
- **Reduces waste:** shelf-stable and small-batch items mean you use what you have, not what goes off.
- **Supports consistency:** helps you build small, regular meals with less stress.
- **Suits your needs:** you can meet taste preferences (salty, savoury, sweet) with less overwhelm.
- **Connects to the Nourishing Dozen:** a well-stocked store cupboard makes it easier to consistently include foods from the Nourishing Dozen (see page 17). From tinned beans and grains to nut butters and leafy greens, these everyday building blocks help you tick off important nutrients without needing big meals.

Store cupboard must-haves for low appetite eating

SHELF-STABLE STAPLES

These items form the backbone of quick meals.

- Tinned legumes (chickpeas, cannellini, black beans, lentils) – look for smaller 215g tins
- Tinned oily fish (sardines, mackerel, salmon)
- Tinned tomatoes and tomato purée (for fast sauces and soups) – look for smaller 227g tins
- Nut butters and tahini
- Wholegrain oatcakes, crispbreads, crackers
- Seeds (especially chia seeds and ground flaxseeds for fibre and for adding to smoothies, puddings) and nuts
- Protein powders (plant or whey-based)

- Long-life plant milks (fortified with calcium and vitamin D)
- Grains: brown rice, quinoa, wholemeal pasta, quick-cook spelt (dry and ready cooked pouches), oats. (I tend to use short-grain brown rice as it is softer and less husky)
- Cartons of vegetable and chicken stock – decant into smaller containers and freeze
- Herbs, spices, flavour pastes (pesto, tahini, soy sauce, miso, harissa)

FRIDGE BASICS

- Eggs (versatile for quick and easy nourishing meals)
- Greek or fortified soya yoghurt
- Avocados
- Dips like hummus or guacamole
- Leafy greens (spinach, rocket, chard, pak choi, cabbage)
- Raw and pre-cooked chicken
- Firm tofu
- Fresh herbs or citrus (lemon, lime, grapefruit)
- Cottage cheese, feta

FREEZER STAPLES

- Frozen vegetables (spinach, peas, mixed)
- Frozen edamame (shelled)
- Frozen berries (for smoothies, breakfasts)
- Leftovers or batched meals (soups, dahls, one-pot dishes)
- Cooked grains (freeze in small bags)

HOW TO USE YOUR STORE CUPBOARD

- Assemble no-cook meals and nourishing snacks on low-energy days
- Respond quickly to appetite when it appears
- Batch-prep breakfasts when energy is higher (chia puddings, overnight oats, quinoa porridge)
- Build around cravings for creamy, savoury, salty, sweet
- Make the Nourishing Dozen easier to hit with less effort

Smart store cupboard hacks

Your store cupboard doesn't need to be perfect, but you can organise it in a way that makes things easier and saves a bit of time and effort when you're cooking.

ORGANISE BY SPEED: put fast-grab foods (crackers, tinned fish, nut butter) in front.

CREATE A RESCUE SHELF: stock this with no-effort go-to options: pre-cooked grains, tinned soup, oatcakes

GROUP BY USE: keep ingredients you often use together on the same shelf or in a basket

STORE SMALL: use jars or containers for grains/seeds and take only what you need.

Tailor your store cupboard to your taste

The best store cupboard is one you want to eat from, so start with the basics, then personalise it to your tastes.

- **Savoury over sweet breakfast:** eggs, avocado, sweet potato, spinach, tinned mackerel, smoked salmon
- **Love Mediterranean flavours:** olives, sun-dried tomatoes, passata, pesto sauce, jarred roasted red peppers, tahini, wholemeal couscous
- **Prefer Asian-inspired flavours:** tamari, sesame oil, frozen edamame beans, miso, ginger, coriander, curry pastes, noodles
- **More plant-based:** Extra tinned or pouched legumes and grains, tofu, seeds, dips, nutritional yeast

Your store cupboard is a safety net, not a storage unit, and it should reduce pressure, not add to it. You don't need dozens of ingredients, just the right ones. With a small, flexible stock of nutrient-dense, low-prep foods, you can build simple meals in minutes, even when appetite and energy are both running low.

NO-COOK RECIPE IDEAS

Breakfasts

- Protein smoothie (include powder) with oats, banana and nut butter
- Mashed avocado on wholegrain toast topped with poached egg and chilli flakes
- Porridge made with unflavoured protein powder, milk and stewed or fresh fruit
- Skyr with granola (low sugar), berries and seed sprinkle
- Greek yoghurt or fortified soya yoghurt with nut butter, tinned peach slices and toasted oats or flaked almonds
- Mashed banana and Greek yoghurt or fortified soya yoghurt topped with chopped dates, tahini and cinnamon
- Greek yoghurt, fortified soya yoghurt or skyr with unsweetened cocoa powder and honey (optional) topped with cherries or berries and sunflower seeds

Snacks

- Banana wrapped in an almond butter-spread wholemeal tortilla wrap
- Rice cakes with almond butter and banana
- Oatcakes with cottage cheese and cucumber slices
- Hard-boiled egg with cherry tomato and olives
- Hummus sprinkled with seed mix and carrot sticks
- Guacamole sprinkled with pumpkin seeds and red pepper slices
- Mini falafel with yoghurt dip and sliced baby spinach
- Edamame and cucumber with lime juice and sea salt
- Turkey slices rolled with hummus and spinach leaves or cream cheese and chopped walnuts
- Roasted almonds, halved cherry tomatoes and feta cubes
- Greek yoghurt or fortified soya yoghurt with chopped pear and flaxseeds
- Peanut butter on apple slices with sunflower seeds
- Date stuffed with nut butter and sprinkle of sesame seeds
- Tinned or fresh peach slices with cottage cheese and mixed seeds
- Ricotta on wholegrain toast with lemon zest and black pepper
- Boiled egg mashed with avocado on rye crispbread
- Tinned tuna with chopped celery and Greek yoghurt
- Mashed beans (cannelloni or butterbean) on rye cracker with extra virgin olive oil
- Mackerel pate with oatcakes and cucumber

- Halved boiled egg with pinch of smoked paprika and hummus
- Mini cheese cubes with pickles and wholegrain crackers
- Cottage cheese with tinned or fresh pineapple chunks and chia seeds
- Skyr or fortified soya yoghurt with chopped apple and peanut butter
- Skyr or fortified soya yoghurt with grated carrot, sultanas, pumpkin seeds
- Cold roast chicken strips with shredded lettuce and pesto
- Chickpeas mashed with tahini on rye crackers with sliced spring onion
- Roasted chickpeas
- Ricotta with olive tapenade on wholegrain toast

Lunches & light meals

- Slice of homemade vegetable frittata and avocado slices
- Soft-boiled egg with hummus and grated carrot on wholegrain crackers
- Boiled egg with black beans, avocado, spinach, olive oil, smoked paprika
- Small mackerel fillet with cooked beetroot, cooked quinoa, rocket, extra virgin olive oil and lemon juice
- Chickpeas and avocado mashed with lemon juice and cumin spread on wholegrain toast
- Leftover roasted sweet potato or butternut squash, black beans, yoghurt, lime juice and coriander
- Mashed avocado and edamame with lemon juice and chilli flakes on wholegrain toast
- Shredded cooked chicken, apple, celery and walnut with Greek-style yoghurt and rye crackers
- Shredded cooked chicken, curry powder, peas, yoghurt, coriander, brown rice
- Tinned tuna, cherry tomatoes, cucumber, chickpeas, lemon juice, extra virgin olive oil and oregano
- Tinned tuna, tinned lentils, red onion, sliced olives, parsley, lemon juice, extra virgin olive oil
- Cottage cheese, chickpeas, avocado, cherry tomatoes, spring onions and toasted seeds
- Falafel and hummus with cooked wholewheat couscous, grated carrot, sultanas, cumin, parsley and lemon juice
- Boiled egg, cooked lentils, chopped spinach and cucumber with tahini, yoghurt and lemon juice dressing
- Tinned or fresh cooked salmon with lentils, cherry tomatoes and tzatziki
- Falafel with hummus, shredded cabbage and carrot and cooked mixed wholegrains grains from a pouch

Dinners

- Wholemeal couscous with roasted red pepper, chickpeas, feta and a drizzle of extra virgin olive oil and lemon juice
- Cooked cold chicken breast with mixed wholegrains from pouch, roasted courgette, with pesto and yoghurt
- Tinned salmon mixed with mashed potato and peas, shaped into small patties and pan-fried in extra virgin olive oil, served with green veggies
- Salmon flakes with cooked lentils with spinach, dill, lemon juice and olive oil
- Cooked salmon, boiled new potatoes, green beans, dill and olive oil and mustard dressing

BREAKFAST

Roasted Sweet Potato and Egg Stack with Tahini

This colourful sweet potato and egg stack is a satisfying small meal that's rich in flavour and packed with nourishing ingredients. Sweet potato provides a natural source of vitamin A and fibre, and tahini and seeds add healthy fats and magnesium. This dish is a smart choice for supporting energy and immune health. It's best served warm and fresh, and it's quick enough to enjoy any day of the week.

1 medium sweet potato (200g)
2 tsp extra virgin olive oil
2 medium eggs
4 tsp tahini
4 tsp mixed seeds, toasted
Pinch of smoked paprika or za'atar
Sea salt

1. Preheat the oven to 200°C/180°C fan/Gas 6.
2. Slice the sweet potato into 1cm rounds then toss them in the olive oil. Lay them out on a non-stick baking sheet and roast for 20–25 minutes, flipping halfway, until golden and tender.
3. Once the sweet potato is cooked, poach the eggs in simmering water for about 4 minutes for a soft yolk, or longer if preferred.
4. Arrange the sweet potato rounds on 2 plates, drizzle over the tahini and top with the seeds.
5. Place the eggs on top, sprinkle over the spices and season with salt.

➔ NUTRIENTS MORE THAN 15% RDA
Folate, iron, magnesium, zinc, vitamins B1, B2, B6, C, E.

➔ NUTRIENTS MORE THAN 30% RDA
Phosphorus, vitamins A, B12.

➔ PROTEIN BOOSTER
Serve with a dollop of yoghurt or skyr or add an extra egg.

➔ NUTRIENT BOOSTER
Stir the tahini through a small handful of wilted spinach, then use to top the sweet potato slices.

➔ TAKE TO WORK
Not suitable.

➔ NOTE
This dish also makes a great small meal during the day.

Miso Scrambled Eggs with Chives and Pumpkin Seeds

A twist on a classic, this recipe gives breakfast a subtle umami upgrade. It works just as well for lunch or a light supper, especially when your appetite's low but you still want something nourishing. Eggs are naturally packed with protein and a wide range of essential nutrients, including B vitamins, selenium and zinc. The sprinkle of pumpkin seeds on top adds crunch and extra minerals like magnesium.

- 4 medium eggs
- 1 tsp white miso paste
- 2 tbsp milk or unsweetened fortified soya milk
- 1 tsp extra virgin olive oil
- 1 tsp sesame oil
- 1 tbsp chopped chives
- 2 tsp pumpkin seeds
- Sea salt and black pepper
- 2 small slices of toasted wholegrain bread, to serve

1. Crack the eggs into a bowl and whisk together with the miso paste and milk until smooth and slightly frothy.
2. Heat the olive oil and sesame oil in a non-stick pan over a medium heat.
3. Pour in the egg mixture and gently stir with a spatula, slowly folding until softly scrambled and creamy, about 3–5 minutes.
4. Remove from the heat while the eggs are still slightly runny (they will finish cooking off the heat), then stir in the chives and a pinch of salt and pepper.
5. Sprinkle with pumpkin seeds and serve warm over toast.

➔ NUTRIENTS MORE THAN 15% RDA
Calcium, chromium, iodine, iron, magnesium, selenium, zinc, vitamins B1, B3, B6, D, E, K.

➔ NUTRIENTS MORE THAN 30% RDA
Folate, phosphorus, vitamins A, B2, B12.

➔ PROTEIN BOOSTER
Increase the egg or add egg white from a carton. Spread the toast with mashed soft white (cannellini) beans.

➔ NUTRIENT BOOSTER
Add some chopped cherry tomatoes or sliced spinach – gently sauté in the oil before adding the egg.

➔ TAKE TO WORK
Not suitable.

➔ NOTES
Soya milk has more protein than other plant milks – look for one that is fortified.

Raspberry Almond Quinoa Porridge

Quinoa porridge is a lighter alternative to oats – ideal if you don't have a good appetite first thing. It's naturally sweet, gently creamy and packed with fibre and key nutrients like calcium and magnesium, making it a great choice for supporting bone health. You can enjoy it warm or serve it cold; if you have any left over, it also makes a nourishing snack straight from the fridge.

60g dry quinoa
400ml milk or unsweetened fortified soya milk
1 tbsp ground flaxseed
100g raspberries (fresh or frozen and defrosted)
1 tsp maple syrup or honey
1 tbsp toasted flaked almonds

1. Tip the quinoa into a sieve and rinse thoroughly under cold water.
2. Add it to a non-stick saucepan with the milk and flaxseed then give it a good stir. Place over a medium heat and bring to a simmer, then reduce the heat and cook gently for about 20 minutes, stirring occasionally, until the quinoa is soft and porridge-like. Add a splash more milk if needed.
3. Stir in most of the raspberries (saving a few for the top) and the maple syrup or honey, then cook for 1–2 minutes more.
4. Spoon into small bowls and top with flaked almonds and remaining raspberries. Serve warm.

➔ NUTRIENTS MORE THAN 15% RDA
Chromium, iron, zinc, vitamins B1, B2, B6, E.

➔ NUTRIENTS MORE THAN 30% RDA
Calcium, folate, magnesium, phosphorus, vitamins B12, C.

➔ PROTEIN BOOSTER
Serve with a dollop of yoghurt or skyr or stir in a scoop of plant-based protein powder when cooking.

➔ STORAGE
This will keep in the fridge for up to 3 days.

➔ NUTRIENT BOOSTER
Add extra almonds, mixed seeds or a small handful of blueberries or sliced banana.

➔ TAKE TO WORK
Yes – cold.

➔ NOTES
Try making with tricolour quinoa. If you are serving it cold you may need to add more milk or water to loosen the mixture.

Coconut Chia Pudding with Mango and Toasted Almonds

This tropical-inspired chia pudding is a refreshing, make-ahead option that works just as well for breakfast or a nourishing snack. It's rich in fibre and plant-based protein, with chia seeds and almonds offering plenty of nutritional value in just a few mouthfuls.

- 4 tbsp chia seeds
- 125ml fortified coconut milk drink (not tinned)
- 125ml milk or unsweetened fortified soya milk
- 1 tsp maple syrup or honey (optional)
- 100g mango, diced into little pieces
- 30g toasted flaked almonds

1. In a bowl or container, mix the chia seeds, coconut milk, milk, soya milk and maple syrup or honey (if using), then stir well.
2. Refrigerate for at least 4 hours or overnight, stirring once or twice early on to prevent clumping.
3. When ready to serve, give the pudding another stir. Serve in a small bowl or ramekin and top with the diced mango and toasted almonds.

➔ NUTRIENTS MORE THAN 15% RDA
Chromium, folate, iodine, iron, zinc, vitamins B1, B2, E.

➔ NUTRIENTS MORE THAN 30% RDA
Calcium, magnesium, phosphorus, vitamins B12, C.

➔ PROTEIN BOOSTER
Add protein powder to the pudding mixture. Spread 1–2 tablespoons of skyr or natural yoghurt on top of the chia pudding to create a layered effect.

➔ STORAGE
This can kept in the fridge without toppings for up to 5 days in a sealed container.

➔ NUTRIENT BOOSTER
Sprinkle over hemp seeds or halved blueberries.

➔ TAKE TO WORK
Yes.

➔ NOTES
If your appetite is particularly low in the morning and you find this portion size too much then it will keep in the fridge for breakfast another day; a smaller serving also makes a great snack during the day. It can also be scaled up and eaten over several days.

Nutty Banana Power Pancakes

MAKES 6

267 KCAL

13.3G PROTEIN

3.4G FIBRE

These soft, nutty pancakes are a great way to start the day or enjoy as a snack. Packed with protein and natural sweetness from banana, they're easy to prep and even easier to eat. Even better, any leftovers keep well for another day.

1 ripe banana (120g)
2 medium eggs
30g oat flour (see Note)
1 tbsp almond or peanut butter
½ tsp ground cinnamon
½ tsp baking powder
1 tsp extra virgin olive oil, for cooking

1. Mash the banana in a bowl until smooth, then whisk in the eggs.
2. Stir in the oat flour, nut butter, cinnamon and baking powder. Let the batter sit for 5–10 minutes to thicken. It should be thick but pourable, like yoghurt.
3. Place a non-stick frying pan over a medium heat and add a little olive oil. Swirl to coat the base.
4. Spoon in small amounts of batter (about 2 tablespoons per pancake). Cook for 2–3 minutes until you see small bubbles form on the surface and the edges start to set. This is when you know they're ready to flip.
5. Flip gently with a spatula and cook for another 2 minutes until golden and just firm.
6. Serve warm with a few berries or a dollop of yoghurt, if you like.

➔ NUTRIENTS MORE THAN 15% RDA
Chromium, folate, iron, magnesium, vitamins A, B1, B2, B3, B6, C.

➔ NUTRIENTS MORE THAN 30% RDA
Phosphorus, vitamin B12.

➔ PROTEIN BOOSTER
Serve with a dollop of yoghurt or skyr.

➔ STORAGE
Store in an airtight container in the fridge for up to 3 days. They're great cold or gently reheated.

➔ NUTRIENT BOOSTER
Add a spoonful of flaxseed or chia seeds into the batter for more fibre and healthy fats.

➔ TAKE TO WORK
Yes – but if you're taking them out for the day, keep them cool and eat within a few hours.

➔ NOTE
You can make your own oat flour by blitzing rolled oats in the food processor.

Gut-loving Kefir Breakfast Shake

This nourishing kefir shake is ideal if you don't feel like eating breakfast in the morning. It's packed with gut-friendly bacteria from kefir to help support a healthy microbiome, alongside fibre, protein and natural sweetness from fruit and oats. With skyr, flaxseed and nut butter, it's satisfying enough to stand in as a protein-rich snack or mini meal later in the day. Experiment with different types of fruit and anything you might have left over in the fridge.

300ml natural dairy kefir
2 tbsp skyr or Greek yoghurt
1 small banana
2 tbsp rolled oats
1 tbsp nut butter or tahini
1 tbsp ground flaxseed
80g mixed frozen berries
¼ tsp ground cinnamon
1 tsp maple syrup or honey

1. Add all the ingredients to a blender or food processor and blend until smooth and creamy.
2. Pour into glasses and serve chilled.

➔ NUTRIENTS MORE THAN 15% RDA
Chromium, folate, iodine, iron, magnesium, vitamins B1, B6, C, E.

➔ NUTRIENTS MORE THAN 30% RDA
Calcium, phosphorus, vitamins B2, B12.

➔ PROTEIN BOOSTER
Add 1 scoop of protein powder. Serve with a handful of walnuts.

➔ NUTRIENT BOOSTER
Add 1 teaspoon of unsweetened cocoa powder or a small handful of spinach.

➔ TAKE TO WORK
Yes.

➔ NOTES
You can use 50g silken tofu instead of skyr.

Mini Egg Muffins with Spinach, Sweetcorn and Feta

These small savoury muffins are ideal if you prefer lighter, more frequent meals. Eggs are an excellent source of high-quality protein and essential nutrients like B12, iodine and selenium, while sweetcorn and spinach bring fibre, colour and extra flavour. These muffins are easy to prep ahead and great for breakfast on the go or a protein-rich snack during the day. Delicious served with sriracha or tomato ketchup.

- 1 tsp extra virgin olive oil
- 4 medium eggs
- 40g feta cheese, crumbled
- 100g sweetcorn (tinned or frozen and defrosted)
- 30g spinach, finely chopped
- 1 tsp chopped dill or chives (optional)
- 2 tsp pumpkin seeds
- Sea salt and black pepper

1. Preheat the oven to 180°C/160°C fan/Gas 4. Lightly oil 4 holes of a muffin tin.
2. Whisk the eggs in a bowl, then stir in the feta, sweetcorn, spinach and herbs (if using), then season with salt and black pepper.
3. Divide the mixture between the muffin moulds and sprinkle the pumpkin seeds on the top.
4. Bake for 18–20 minutes, or until just set. Leave to cool in the oven with the door open – this will help prevent them from sinking. Serve warm or cold.

➔ NUTRIENTS MORE THAN 15% RDA
Folate, iodine, magnesium, vitamins B2, K.

➔ NUTRIENTS MORE THAN 30% RDA
Phosphorus, vitamins A, B12.

➔ PROTEIN BOOSTER
Crumble in some firm tofu.

➔ STORAGE
Store in an airtight container in the fridge for up to 3 days and the freezer for 2 months.

➔ NUTRIENT BOOSTER
Stir finely chopped red pepper or grated courgette through the egg mixture.

➔ TAKE TO WORK
Yes – warmed up or served cold.

➔ NOTE
You can also use dried herbs in this recipe: ¼ teaspoon dried oregano or mixed herbs works well.

Spiced Apple and Hazelnut Chia Skyr Pot

This thick and creamy pot is made with skyr, a high-protein yoghurt that adds richness without excess fat. Paired with fibre-rich chia seeds, crunchy hazelnuts and naturally sweet apple, it's a satisfying way to start the day or fuel up with a protein-packed mini meal or snack. It keeps well in the fridge, making it a great option for those mornings when you need something to grab and go.

250g skyr or Greek yoghurt or fortified soya yoghurt
1 small apple, grated
2 tbsp chia seeds
½ tsp ground cinnamon
1 tsp maple syrup or honey (optional)
2 tbsp roasted chopped hazelnuts or 2 tsp nut butter

1. Place the skyr in a bowl and add 2 tablespoons of water to thin the texture. Stir in the grated apple, chia seeds, cinnamon and maple syrup or honey (if using).
2. Divide into 2 small bowls or ramekins and chill for 20 minutes (or overnight) until thickened. It may become quite thick overnight in a very cold fridge so just add a splash of milk or water to loosen the mixture.
3. Top with hazelnuts or nut butter.

➔ NUTRIENTS MORE THAN 15% RDA
Folate, iodine, iron, magnesium, vitamins B2, E.

➔ NUTRIENTS MORE THAN 30% RDA
Calcium, phosphorus, vitamin B12.

➔ PROTEIN BOOSTER
Add a scoop of plant-based protein powder (with a few tablespoons of water). Sprinkle over hemp seeds.

➔ STORAGE
This recipe can be kept in the fridge without toppings in a sealed container for up to 5 days.

➔ NUTRIENT BOOSTER
Top with chopped dried figs or sultanas.

➔ TAKE TO WORK
Yes.

➔ NOTES
This is a great chia pot alternative if you're not a fan of the texture of traditional chia seed pudding. It's easy to scale up too.

Baked Oats with Blueberries and Honey

Soft, gently sweet and full of comfort, this warm baked oat bowl is ideal for breakfast or a mid-afternoon snack. It bakes into a spongy yet spoonable texture, almost like a soft, set porridge. You can use regular milk or switch to fortified soya milk, which offers a similar amount of protein and makes this completely plant-based. This is a generous portion so you might prefer to eat half and save the rest.

60g rolled oats
½ tsp baking powder
½ tsp ground cinnamon
1 tbsp chia seeds
Pinch of sea salt
160ml milk or unsweetened fortified soya milk
1 medium egg
1–2 tsp maple syrup or honey
100g fresh or frozen and defrosted blueberries

1. Preheat the oven to 180°C/160°C fan/Gas 4. Grease or line a 900g loaf tin with parchment paper.
2. Combine the oats, baking powder, cinnamon, chia seeds and salt in a bowl.
3. In a separate bowl, whisk together the milk, egg and maple syrup or honey until well combined, then pour these wet ingredients into the dry ingredients and stir until fully incorporated.
4. Gently fold in the blueberries, then pour the mixture into the prepared tin.
5. Bake for 25 minutes, or until the oats are set and golden brown on top.
6. Let it cool slightly before serving – it's great with a dollop of coconut yoghurt.

➔ NUTRIENTS MORE THAN 15% RDA
Calcium, chromium, folate, iron, magnesium, vitamins B1, B2.

➔ NUTRIENTS MORE THAN 30% RDA
Phosphorus, vitamin B12.

➔ PROTEIN BOOSTER
Serve with skyr, coconut yoghurt, Greek yoghurt or whipped cottage cheese (see page 202). Top with chopped nuts.

➔ STORAGE
This will keep in the fridge for up to 3 days. Once chilled, it firms up and can be eaten cold or gently reheated with a splash of milk or yoghurt.

➔ NUTRIENT BOOSTER
Swap the blueberries for blackberries to increase the vitamin C. Add sunflower seeds to the oat mixture.

➔ TAKE TO WORK
Yes – can be warmed or eaten cold.

➔ NOTES
For a firmer, sliceable texture when serving cold, add another tablespoon of chia seeds to the mix before baking. Once chilled, remove from the tin and cut into bars. You could also bake this in a 20 x 20cm brownie tin (check after 20 minutes in the oven).

LUNCH

LIGHT & ENERGISING 92

PROTEIN PACKED 109

EASY TO DIGEST 116

COMFORTING & WARMING 125

Herby Lentils with Whipped Feta, Cumin, Carrots and Toasted Almonds

This dish is a great example of simple ingredients coming together to create something nourishing and full of flavour. The lentils and whipped feta offer a good source of protein, while toasted almonds and spices add interest and texture. It's light, satisfying and ideal if you're after a lighter meal that still delivers on nutrition.

- 100g feta cheese
- 100g skyr or Greek yoghurt
- 1 large carrot, peeled and halved lengthways
- 1 tsp cumin seeds
- 1 small garlic clove, finely chopped or grated
- 2 tsp extra virgin olive oil, plus extra for drizzling
- Zest and juice of ¼ lemon
- 1 tbsp roughly chopped flat-leaf parsley
- 90g cooked puy lentils
- 1 heaped tbsp toasted flaked almonds
- Sea salt

1. Bring a medium saucepan of water to the boil.
2. Blend the feta and skyr using a stick blender until smooth or beat in a large bowl with a spatula. Season with a little salt then set aside.
3. Simmer the carrot for 3 minutes in the pan of boiling water. Drain and leave to steam-dry before cutting into diagonal slices.
4. Toast the cumin seeds in a dry pan for 30 seconds.
5. In a bowl, combine the garlic, olive oil, lemon zest and juice, toasted cumin seeds, parsley and carrots with a pinch of salt. Toss gently to coat.
6. Spread the whipped feta between 2 small plates then top with the lentils and the carrot salad. Finish with almonds and a small drizzle of olive oil.

➔ NUTRIENTS MORE THAN 15% RDA
Iodine, iron, magnesium, zinc, vitamins B1, B2, B6, E.

➔ NUTRIENTS MORE THAN 30% RDA
Calcium, phosphorus, folate, vitamins A, B12.

➔ PROTEIN BOOSTER
Increase the lentils or combine with leftover cooked quinoa.

➔ NUTRIENT BOOSTER
Mix finely shredded spinach or rocket into the lentils. Top with a small handful of pomegranate seeds.

➔ TAKE TO WORK
Yes – try layering it in a small Kilner jar or container.

➔ NOTES
Try swapping carrots for roasted beetroot. Use cooked puy lentils from a pouch or tin, or cook 30g dry lentils to get 90g cooked.

SERVES 2

350 KCAL

20G PROTEIN

5G FIBRE

Tofu Noodles with Peanut and Sesame Dressing

This noodle dish is fresh, vibrant and full of flavour without feeling too heavy – perfect for those with smaller appetites. Tofu brings a boost of plant-based protein, along with iron and calcium, and pairs beautifully with the creamy, nutty dressing. The mix of peanut butter, tahini, lime and soy gives you that savoury-sweet balance with a zingy lift. It's easy to adapt, too.

70g fine egg noodles (dry weight)
150g firm tofu, pressed and cut into 1cm cubes
2 tsp cornflour
1 tsp extra virgin olive oil
½ small red pepper, thinly sliced
1 small carrot, julienned or grated
1 spring onion, thinly sliced
1 tbsp chopped coriander and mint

For the dressing
½ tbsp peanut butter
½ tbsp tahini
½ tbsp light soy sauce
½ tbsp lime juice
1 tbsp natural yoghurt
½ tsp maple syrup or honey
1–2 tbsp warm water, to loosen

1. Bring a saucepan of water to the boil and cook the noodles for 3–4 minutes. Drain and rinse under cold water to prevent sticking. Set aside.
2. Toss the tofu in the cornflour. Heat the olive oil in a frying pan over a medium heat and lightly fry the tofu cubes until golden on all sides. Set aside to cool.
3. In a small bowl, whisk together the dressing ingredients, adding just enough warm water to make a pourable dressing.
4. In a large bowl, toss the cooked noodles with the tofu, red pepper, carrot, spring onion and herbs, then pour over the dressing and mix gently until everything is coated. Serve.

➔ NUTRIENTS MORE THAN 15% RDA
Folate, potassium, zinc, vitamins A, B1, B2, B3, C, E.

➔ NUTRIENTS MORE THAN 30% RDA
Calcium, iron, magnesium, phosphorus, vitamin B6.

➔ PROTEIN BOOSTER
Add extra tofu or edamame beans. Swap egg noodles for soba noodles. Blend silken tofu into the dressing.

➔ STORAGE
Keep the salad and dressing separately in the fridge for 2–3 days.

➔ NUTRIENT BOOSTER
Add shredded baby spinach, avocado or mixed seeds.

➔ TAKE TO WORK
Yes – pack the dressing separately.

➔ NOTE
If you find the dressing too rich, just drizzle it over the salad rather than tossing through it.

SERVES 2

390 KCAL

23G PROTEIN

6G FIBRE

Zesty Tuna and Brown Rice Nourish Bowl

This bowl brings together bold flavours and satisfying textures in a simple, energising meal. The citrus, herbs and gentle chilli kick help wake up the taste buds, which can be especially helpful if your appetite is low. It will give you a good hit of protein and fibre, and it's quick to pull together using mostly store cupboard ingredients and vegetables.

---

1 x 145g tin tuna in olive oil, drained
Juice of 1 lime
2 tsp extra virgin olive oil
¼ small red chilli, finely chopped (optional)
180g cooked short-grain brown rice
1 small avocado, diced
½ small red pepper, finely diced
6cm piece of cucumber, halved, deseeded and diced
1 spring onion, thinly sliced
Small handful of baby spinach, shredded
1 tbsp chopped coriander
1 tbsp pumpkin seeds
Drizzle of sriracha
Sea salt

1. Flake the tuna into a bowl and mix with the lime juice, olive oil, chopped chilli (if using) and a pinch of salt.
2. Divide the cooked rice between 2 small bowls.
3. Top with tuna mixture, diced avocado, red pepper, cucumber, spring onion and spinach.
4. Finish with chopped coriander, pumpkin seeds and a drizzle of sriracha. Serve chilled or at room temperature.

➔ NUTRIENTS MORE THAN 15% RDA
Chromium, iron, magnesium, potassium, zinc, vitamins A, B1, B2, B6, E.

➔ NUTRIENTS MORE THAN 30% RDA
Folate, phosphorus, selenium, vitamins B3, B12, C, K.

➔ PROTEIN BOOSTER
Add more tuna. Swap the cucumber for edamame beans. Add extra seeds.

➔ NUTRIENT BOOSTER
Mix tinned black beans or leftover cooked quinoa with the rice.

➔ TAKE TO WORK
Yes.

➔ NOTES
This dish is best made fresh, but you can prep the rice and tuna mix ahead of time and store them separately in the fridge. Use cooked rice from a pouch, or cook 60g dry brown rice to get 180g cooked.

Crunchy Tofu Wraps with Peanut Drizzle

These flavour-packed wraps are perfect when you want something satisfying yet light. Tofu is a brilliant source of plant-based protein, and roasting it gives a lovely texture that pairs perfectly with the rich peanut drizzle. Using lettuce leaves as wraps keeps the meal light and gives it a refreshing crunch. Paired with a simple slaw and toasted sesame seeds, this hits all the right notes for taste and texture.

200g firm tofu, cut into 2cm cubes
2½ tbsp smooth peanut butter
1 tbsp light soy sauce
1 tbsp lime juice
1 tsp maple syrup or honey
2 tsp sesame oil
50g grated carrot
50g shredded red cabbage
1 spring onion, thinly sliced
4 large lettuce leaves (such as romaine or little gem)
2 tsp sesame seeds
Coriander leaves (optional)

1. Preheat the oven to 200°C/180°C fan/Gas 6. Spread the tofu cubes out on a lined baking tray and roast for 20 minutes, turning halfway until crisp and golden.
2. Meanwhile, whisk together the peanut butter, soy sauce, lime juice, maple syrup or honey and sesame oil to create a smooth, pourable dressing. Add a splash of warm water if needed.
3. In a bowl, mix the grated carrot, shredded red cabbage and spring onion to make a crunchy slaw.
4. Toss the roasted tofu in the peanut dressing while still warm so it's well coated.
5. Lay out the lettuce leaves and fill with the slaw, followed by the saucy tofu.
6. Sprinkle with sesame seeds and coriander leaves (if using) and enjoy.

➔ NUTRIENTS MORE THAN 15% RDA
Chromium, potassium, zinc, vitamins B1, B2, B3, B6.

➔ NUTRIENTS MORE THAN 30% RDA
Calcium, folate, iron, magnesium, phosphorus, vitamins A, C, K.

➔ PROTEIN BOOSTER
Increase the tofu or add edamame beans and pumpkin seeds to the slaw.

➔ NUTRIENT BOOSTER
Serve with a small portion of brown rice or quinoa in the lettuce wrap.

➔ TAKE TO WORK
Not suitable.

➔ NOTE
This also works well with cooked shredded chicken instead of roasted tofu.

SERVES 2

392 KCAL

15.1G PROTEIN

6G FIBRE

Dukkah-topped Avocado and Cottage Cheese

This is one of those throw-together meals that still feels a bit special. The cottage cheese mix adds flavour and protein, while avocado brings healthy fats and a soft, satisfying texture. A sprinkle of dukkah finishes it all off with crunch and spice. It's simple and nourishing and you can serve both halves for lunch, or just one for a quick, balanced snack.

- 200g cottage cheese
- 1 roasted red pepper (from a jar), finely chopped
- 1 spring onion, thinly sliced
- 1 tsp lemon juice
- 1 tsp extra virgin olive oil
- 1 tbsp chopped chives or parsley
- 2 medium ripe avocados, halved and pitted
- 4 tsp dukkah (see page 198)
- Pinch of chilli flakes (optional)
- Sea salt and black pepper

1. In a small bowl, mix the cottage cheese with chopped roasted red pepper, spring onion, lemon juice, olive oil and herbs. Season with salt and black pepper.
2. Spoon the mixture evenly into the avocado halves and sprinkle each half with the dukkah and a small pinch of chilli flakes (if using).
3. Serve immediately or chill for later.

➔ NUTRIENTS MORE THAN 15% RDA
Calcium, iodine, iron, magnesium, potassium, vitamins A, B1, B2, B6, E.

➔ NUTRIENTS MORE THAN 30% RDA
Folate, phosphorus, vitamins B12, C, K.

➔ PROTEIN BOOSTER
Mix the cottage cheese with skyr or Greek yoghurt. Switch to high-protein cottage cheese.

➔ STORAGE
This will keep in the fridge for 1 day in an airtight container. The cottage cheese mix will last 2–3 days in the fridge.

➔ NUTRIENT BOOSTER
Serve with seeded crackers (see page 200).

➔ TAKE TO WORK
Yes.

➔ NOTE
This also works as a nourishing snack with rye or seeded crackers (see page 200).

Smoked Mackerel and Avocado Mash On Rye

This is another great dip-style recipe that works perfectly as a nourishing light meal served on rye bread or with rye crackers. Avocado adds a creamy texture along with heart-healthy fats, fibre and a whole mix of vitamins and minerals. Smoked mackerel is not only rich in protein and omega-3 fats but also one of the few natural food sources of vitamin D, which helps your body absorb calcium to keep your bones strong.

½ small ripe avocado
1 tbsp Greek-style yoghurt or skyr
Squeeze of lemon juice
120g smoked mackerel fillet, skin removed
2 small slices of rye bread
Sea salt and black pepper

1. In a bowl, mash the avocado with the yoghurt and lemon juice until smooth.
2. Flake the mackerel into small pieces and fold gently through the avocado mash. Season with salt and a pinch of black pepper.
3. Toast the rye bread, then spread the mackerel and avocado mash evenly over the slices.
4. Cut into halves or quarters and serve.

➔ NUTRIENTS MORE THAN 15% RDA
Chromium, folate, iodine, magnesium, vitamins A, K.

➔ NUTRIENTS MORE THAN 30% RDA
Phosphorus, selenium, vitamins B3, B6, B12, D. Contains omega-3.

➔ PROTEIN BOOSTER
Add extra smoked mackerel or top with sliced boiled egg or pumpkin seeds.

➔ STORAGE
It will last 1–2 days in the fridge.

➔ NUTRIENT BOOSTER
Top with watercress or rocket, halved cherry tomatoes or cucumber slices.

➔ TAKE TO WORK
Yes – pack separately with rye bread or crackers and sliced vegetables like carrot, red pepper and cucumber.

➔ NOTES
If you're sensitive to oily fish or rich foods, try a smaller serving and keep leftovers in the fridge for later meals and snacks. Don't toast the bread if you find it hard to digest.

Crab, Mango and Noodle Salad with Sesame-Lime Dressing

This light, refreshing salad is full of bright flavours and soft textures, making it ideal if you're after something nourishing but easy to eat. It's high in protein thanks to white crab meat, with a punchy sesame-lime dressing and the natural sweetness of mango to lift the dish. A good source of selenium and vitamins A and C for immunity, it's a simple, energising meal.

80g ribbon rice noodles
120g fresh or tinned white crab meat
½ small ripe mango, thinly sliced
6cm piece of cucumber, halved, deseeded and thinly sliced diagonally
2 tbsp chopped coriander
2 tbsp chopped Thai basil (or regular basil)
1 heaped tbsp raw peanuts, chopped

For the dressing
2 tsp fish sauce
2 tsp rice vinegar
½ tsp sugar
Juice of ½ lime
1 tsp sesame oil

1. Cook the rice noodles according to the packet instructions, then drain and rinse under warm water.
2. In a small bowl, whisk together the fish sauce, rice vinegar, sugar, lime juice and sesame oil.
3. Toss the noodles into a bowl with the crab meat, mango, cucumber, chopped herbs and dressing.
4. Divide between 2 small bowls and top with the chopped peanuts.

➔ NUTRIENTS MORE THAN 15% RDA
Folate, iodine, iron, magnesium, zinc, vitamins B1, B2, B3, B6, E.

➔ NUTRIENTS MORE THAN 30% RDA
Phosphorus, selenium, vitamins A, B12, C.

➔ PROTEIN BOOSTER
Add extra crab, edamame beans or pumpkin seeds.

➔ NUTRIENT BOOSTER
Add julienned carrot, thinly sliced spinach leaves or diced avocado.

➔ TAKE TO WORK
Yes.

➔ NOTES
Leftover crab works well in an omelette using the same herbs and a teaspoon of fish sauce. Cook fresh rice noodles rather than buying ready-cooked, as they taste much better.

Sardine and White Bean Mash with Lemon and Capers

Tinned fish is one of the most underrated healthy foods, which is why it's earned a spot on my Nourishing Dozen list (see page 17). Sardines, in particular, are a great source of high-quality protein, omega-3 fats, calcium and vitamin D, all in one affordable tin. Here, they're folded through a creamy, lemony white bean mash and served with rye bread for a balanced plate, but crackers work just as well.

150g jarred white beans, rinsed
Zest and juice of ¼ lemon
1 tsp extra virgin olive oil
1 tbsp Greek yoghurt or skyr
1 x 120g tin sardines in olive oil, drained well
2 tsp small capers from a jar
1 tbsp chopped parsley
2 small slices of wholegrain bread or rye crackers
Sea salt and black pepper

1. In a bowl, mash the drained beans with lemon zest and juice, olive oil and yoghurt until creamy but still textured.
2. Flake the sardines and fold gently through the mash along with capers and parsley. Season with salt and pepper.
3. Spread the mash over the bread or rye crackers and serve.

➔ NUTRIENTS MORE THAN 15% RDA
Folate, potassium, zinc, vitamins B1, B2, B3, B6, E.

➔ NUTRIENTS MORE THAN 30% RDA
Calcium, iron, magnesium, phosphorus, selenium, vitamin B12. Contains omega-3.

➔ PROTEIN BOOSTER
Serve with high-protein crackers (normally seeded or made with legume flours like lentil) or top with a sliced boiled egg.

➔ STORAGE
The topping will keep in the fridge for up to 3 days.

➔ NUTRIENT BOOSTER
Stir in chopped baby spinach, chopped olives or grated celery or fennel.

➔ TAKE TO WORK
Yes – take with rye bread or crispbreads and vegetables like red peppers and carrots cut into batons.

➔ NOTE
If you find sardines in oil too rich then swap for tinned mackerel in brine.

Thai Prawn, Grapefruit, Cashew and Toasted Coconut Bites

These light, punchy lettuce cups are full of citrusy freshness and natural umami, making them a great high-protein choice when you don't want anything too heavy. The prawns deliver lean, complete protein, while the grapefruit, herbs and toasted coconut keep the dish bright and interesting.

- 2 tbsp desiccated coconut
- 2 tbsp cashew nuts, finely chopped
- 150g cooked peeled prawns, chopped
- ½ small pink grapefruit, peeled, segmented (flesh only) and finely chopped
- 1 spring onion, thinly sliced
- 2cm piece of fresh ginger, peeled and grated
- 1 tsp fish sauce
- ½ tsp light soy sauce
- Zest and juice of ½ lime
- ½ red chilli, deseeded and finely chopped (optional)
- Few coriander and torn mint leaves
- 4–6 baby gem lettuce leaves

1. Toast the desiccated coconut in a dry pan over a medium heat for 2–3 minutes until golden and fragrant. Set aside to cool. Add the chopped cashew nuts to the pan and toast for about 2 minutes until golden – watch them carefully as they burn easily.
2. Add the chopped prawns, grapefruit, spring onion, ginger, fish sauce, soy sauce, lime zest and juice, red chilli (if using), herbs and half the toasted cashew nuts to a medium bowl. Fold in the cooled coconut.
3. Spoon the mixture into baby gem lettuce leaves. Scatter over the remaining toasted cashews before serving on small plates.

➔ NUTRIENTS MORE THAN 15% RDA
Folate, iodine, zinc, vitamins B1, B2, B6.

➔ NUTRIENTS MORE THAN 30% RDA
Phosphorus, selenium, vitamins B12, C, E.

➔ PROTEIN BOOSTER
Add extra prawns, chopped edamame or black beans to the mixture.

➔ STORAGE
This will keep in the fridge for 1 day in an airtight container.

➔ NUTRIENT BOOSTER
Add 2 tablespoons coconut milk to the mixture or some chopped chives.

➔ TAKE TO WORK
Yes – take the prawn mixture and lettuce leaves separately.

➔ NOTE
The prawn mixture is also great as a salad, as a filling for a small wholemeal tortilla or folded into a small omelette.

Crunchy Chicken Salad with Lime and Sesame Dressing

Bright, crunchy veg, soft avocado and tender chicken come together with a punchy lime and sesame dressing that really lifts it. It's quick to make, full of texture and works well for lunch or a light dinner – especially good if you've got leftover roast chicken and other veg and herbs to use up.

150g cooked chicken breast, shredded
1 small carrot, peeled, grated or julienned
6cm piece of cucumber (80g), halved, deseeded and thinly sliced diagonally
50g red cabbage, finely shredded
½ small avocado (80g), diced
2 spring onions, thinly sliced
1 tbsp chopped coriander
1 tbsp chopped mint
1 tbsp toasted sesame seeds

For the dressing

1 tbsp light soy sauce
1 tsp runny honey
1 tsp sesame oil
Juice of ½ lime
2cm piece of fresh ginger, peeled and grated

1. In a small bowl, whisk together the soy sauce, honey, sesame oil, lime juice and ginger to make a dressing.
2. Combine the chicken, carrot, cucumber, cabbage, avocado, spring onions, coriander and mint in a bowl. Pour over the dressing and toss gently to coat.
3. Sprinkle with the toasted sesame seeds and serve immediately.

➔ NUTRIENTS MORE THAN 15% RDA
Calcium, magnesium, potassium, zinc, vitamins B1, B2, B12, E.

➔ NUTRIENTS MORE THAN 30% RDA
Folate, phosphorus, vitamins A, B3, B6, C, K.

➔ PROTEIN BOOSTER
Add extra chicken, edamame beans or chickpeas.

➔ NUTRIENT BOOSTER
Add thinly sliced red pepper. Add leftover cooked quinoa or puy lentils.

➔ TAKE TO WORK
Yes.

➔ NOTE
You can buy ready-cooked chicken to save time in the kitchen, or roast or poach 200g raw chicken to get 150g cooked.

Smoked Salmon and Quinoa Bowl with Dill Dressing

This colourful bowl has a Scandinavian vibe and is packed with nourishing ingredients. Smoked salmon is not only a great source of protein but also one of the best ways to get omega-3s, the healthy fats that support heart and brain health. The quinoa base gives this bowl some bite and, being a seed rather than a grain, it also delivers useful nutrients like magnesium and iron.

1 medium egg
150g cooked tri-coloured quinoa
60g smoked salmon, sliced or flaked
1 small avocado, cubed
6cm piece of cucumber, diced
2 radishes, thinly sliced
1 tbsp pumpkin seeds
Juice of ¼ lemon

For the dill dressing
2 tbsp natural yoghurt
1 tbsp chopped dill (or ½ tsp dried)
½ tsp Dijon mustard
Sea salt and black pepper

1. Bring a small saucepan of water to the boil, lower in the egg and cook to your liking (about 7 minutes for a jammy centre). Cool under running water, then peel and halve.
2. In a small bowl, whisk together all the dressing ingredients until smooth. Season with salt and pepper.
3. In 2 serving bowls, layer the quinoa, smoked salmon, avocado, cucumber, radishes, boiled egg and pumpkin seeds. Squeeze over the lemon juice. Finally, drizzle over the dressing before serving.

➔ NUTRIENTS MORE THAN 15% RDA
Folate, iodine, iron, magnesium, zinc, vitamins B1, C, E, K.

➔ NUTRIENTS MORE THAN 30% RDA
Phosphorus, selenium, vitamins B3, B12, D.

➔ PROTEIN BOOSTER
Add extra salmon, pumpkin seeds or an extra egg.

➔ NUTRIENT BOOSTER
Add shredded baby spinach or chopped skinless segments of orange or grapefruit.

➔ TAKE TO WORK
Yes.

➔ NOTES
Use a pouch of ready-cooked quinoa to save time, or cook 50g dried quinoa to get 150g cooked. You can use brown rice or wholemeal couscous if you don't have quinoa.

Cottage Cheese and Lentil Stuffed Peppers with Harissa

Stuffing vegetables is a great way to create a low-bulk meal that still delivers on nutrition. In this recipe, sweet roasted peppers are filled with a creamy mix of high-protein cottage cheese and lentils, making it ideal when you don't feel super-hungry but still want to eat well. The harissa brings warmth, while mint and lemon keep things fresh. It's light, satisfying and easy to prep in advance

- 1 red pepper, cut in half and deseeded
- 2 tsp extra virgin olive oil
- 2 tsp harissa paste
- 180g cooked green lentils (tinned is fine)
- 120g cottage cheese
- Zest and juice of ¼ lemon
- 1 tbsp chopped mint
- 1 tbsp sunflower seeds, toasted
- Sea salt and black pepper

1. Preheat the oven to 200°C/180°C fan/Gas 6. Place the pepper halves cut side up on a lined baking tray.
2. Mix the olive oil and harissa paste in a small bowl. Brush this mixture generously over the cut sides of the peppers.
3. Roast the peppers in the oven for 20–25 minutes until soft and slightly charred.
4. In a bowl, mix the cooked lentils with the cottage cheese, lemon zest and juice, mint and a good pinch of salt and pepper. Pop it back in the fridge until needed.
5. Once the peppers are cooked, spoon the mixture evenly into the roasted halves.
6. Sprinkle with toasted sunflower seeds and serve.

➔ NUTRIENTS MORE THAN 15% RDA
Calcium, iodine, iron, magnesium, potassium, selenium, zinc, vitamins B1, B2, B3, B6, E.

➔ NUTRIENTS MORE THAN 30% RDA
Folate, phosphorus, vitamins A, B12, C, K.

➔ PROTEIN BOOSTER
Add more cottage cheese (or use a high-protein cottage cheese).

➔ STORAGE
The lentil mixture will keep for up to 3 days in the fridge.

➔ NUTRIENT BOOSTER
Add sliced baby spinach, red pepper (fresh or roasted from a jar) or diced cucumber.

➔ TAKE TO WORK
Yes – it can be warmed up or served cold.

➔ NOTES
Serve with rye crackers or sliced vegetables like peppers and carrots. Use cooked lentils from a tin or pouch to save time or cook 60g dried lentils to get 180g cooked.

Herby Salmon Bowl with Radish and Pesto

This herby salmon bowl is fresh, high in protein and full of texture from the crisp radishes and creamy pesto dressing. It's satisfying without being heavy and works well warm or cold. Cooking quinoa from scratch is always going to taste better than using a pouch as the grains stay light and fluffy with just the right bite.

---

1 tsp extra virgin olive oil
200g skinless salmon fillet
1 tsp fresh basil pesto
1 tbsp Greek-style yoghurt
1 tsp lemon juice
150g cooked quinoa
50g frozen edamame beans, defrosted
4 radishes, thinly sliced
1 tbsp chopped parsley
1 tbsp chopped mint
Sea salt and black pepper

1. Heat the olive oil in a non-stick frying pan over a medium heat. Season the salmon fillets with salt and pepper, then add to the pan and cook for 4–5 minutes on each side until cooked through. Remove from the pan and drain on kitchen paper for a few minutes before flaking into bite-sized pieces.
2. In a small bowl, mix the pesto with the Greek yoghurt and lemon juice to create a creamy dressing. Add a pinch of salt.
3. In a large bowl, combine the cooked quinoa, edamame beans, radishes, parsley and mint. Gently toss with half of the creamy pesto dressing.
4. Divide the quinoa salad between 2 plates, top with the flaked salmon, and drizzle with the remaining pesto dressing. Serve warm or at room temperature.

➔ NUTRIENTS MORE THAN 15% RDA
Iodine, iron, potassium, zinc, vitamins C, E.

➔ NUTRIENTS MORE THAN 30% RDA
Chromium, folate, magnesium, phosphorus, selenium, vitamins B6, B12, D, K.

➔ PROTEIN BOOSTER
Add extra salmon. Stir leftover lentils through the quinoa.

➔ STORAGE
You can keep leftovers in the fridge for 2 days.

➔ NUTRIENT BOOSTER
Add shredded baby spinach and grated carrot.

➔ TAKE TO WORK
Yes.

➔ NOTE
I always recommend cooking a big portion of quinoa and keeping it in the fridge for a few days so it's ready to use in dishes like this; 50g dry quinoa will give you 150g cooked.

Sticky Soy Salmon with Edamame Rice

This dish delivers maximum flavour from minimal effort, with salmon caramelised in a sticky soy glaze and served over edamame rice. It's a great way to get in a good dose of protein and omega-3 fats, and the punchy glaze makes it feel a bit special even on low-effort days. If you're short on time, you can prep the glaze and rice ahead to make this even faster to finish.

- 150g cooked short-grain brown rice
- 40g frozen edamame beans, defrosted
- 1 tsp mirin
- 2 tbsp soy sauce
- 2 tsp honey
- 1 tsp sesame oil
- 2 tsp grated fresh ginger
- 1 garlic clove, minced
- 200g skinless and boneless salmon fillet, halved
- 1 tsp sesame seeds
- 2 spring onions, thinly sliced

1. Heat the rice then stir in the edamame and mirin, cover with foil or a lid, and set aside to keep warm.
2. In a small bowl, whisk together the soy sauce, honey, sesame oil, ginger and garlic.
3. Add a small drop of oil to a non-stick frying pan set over a medium heat. Place the salmon in the pan then brush with the glaze and cook for 3–4 minutes on each side, spooning over more glaze as it reduces and becomes sticky.
4. Serve the salmon over the edamame rice. Top with sesame seeds and sliced spring onions.

➔ NUTRIENTS MORE THAN 15% RDA
Folate, iodine, magnesium, potassium, vitamins B1, B2, K.

➔ NUTRIENTS MORE THAN 30% RDA
Phosphorus, selenium, vitamins B3, B6, B12, D. Contains omega-3.

➔ PROTEIN BOOSTER
Add extra salmon or edamame beans.

➔ NUTRIENT BOOSTER
Increase the amount of rice and serve with a side of Tenderstem broccoli or pak choi.

➔ TAKE TO WORK
Yes.

➔ NOTES
You can flake the salmon and roll it into nori sheets with the rice for a sushi-style version that's easy to eat with your hands. Use a pouch of ready-cooked brown rice if short on time, or cook 50g dried brown rice to get 150g cooked.

SERVES 2

320 KCAL

25G PROTEIN

6G FIBRE

Tuna and White Bean Mash On Seedy Crackers

This mash is a smart twist on a classic combo, bringing together tuna, avocado and yoghurt for a creamy, protein-rich topping. It's quick to prepare, satisfying without being heavy, and pairs brilliantly with crunchy seeded crackers for contrast. White beans from a jar are much softer than from a tin and work great in this recipe.

---

1 x 145g tin tuna in water, drained
100g jarred white beans, rinsed and drained
½ small avocado
2 tbsp skyr or Greek yoghurt
2 tsp extra virgin olive oil
1 tbsp lemon juice
1 tbsp chopped chives
4–6 small crackers (rye, oat or wholegrain rice)
2 tsp toasted seed mix (see page 199)
Sea salt and black pepper

1. In a bowl, mash the tuna, beans, avocado, yoghurt, olive oil and lemon juice until well combined but still slightly chunky.
2. Stir in the chopped chives and season with salt and pepper to taste.
3. Spoon the mixture generously over the crackers, then sprinkle with mixed seeds and serve immediately.

➔ NUTRIENTS MORE THAN 15% RDA
Calcium, iodine, magnesium, potassium, zinc, vitamins A, B1, B2, B6, E, K.

➔ NUTRIENTS MORE THAN 30% RDA
Folate, phosphorus, selenium, vitamins B3, B12.

➔ PROTEIN BOOSTER
Add extra tuna or top with a sliced hard-boiled egg.

➔ NUTRIENT BOOSTER
Add chopped capers and olives.

➔ TAKE TO WORK
Yes – the mash will last for up to 2 days in the fridge.

➔ NOTE
You can serve the mash in lettuce cups or spoon onto cucumber slices for a lighter version.

Rice Noodle and Chicken Broth with Lemongrass and Thai Basil

This gently spiced broth, with its mix of lean chicken, miso, fresh herbs and citrus, is full of Thai-inspired flavour but still feels clean and light. The veg and rice noodles make it more substantial so it's a good option when you want something warming that still feels energising. It's also quick to prepare, making it perfect for busy days or when your appetite is smaller.

- 80g dry rice noodles
- 1 tsp extra virgin olive oil
- 1 tsp sesame oil
- 1 garlic clove, sliced
- 2cm piece of fresh ginger, peeled and grated
- 500ml fresh chicken stock
- 1 lemongrass stalk, bruised
- 1 tsp white miso paste
- 1 tsp light soy sauce
- Juice of ½ lime
- 120g cooked chicken breast, shredded
- 1 small head of pak choi, shredded
- 1 small carrot, ribboned
- 2 tbsp frozen edamame beans, defrosted
- 1 spring onion, thinly sliced
- Handful of Thai basil or coriander

1. Cook the rice noodles in boiling water, according to the packet instructions. Drain, rinse and set aside.
2. Heat the oils in a non-stick saucepan set over a medium heat. Add the garlic and ginger and cook for 1 minute until fragrant.
3. Add the chicken stock and lemongrass, then simmer gently for 10 minutes to infuse, before removing the lemongrass.
4. Stir in the miso paste, soy sauce, lime juice and chicken and simmer for 2–3 minutes until warmed through, then add the pak choi, carrot and edamame beans and simmer for 1–2 minutes until the pak choi is just wilted.
5. Divide the noodles between 2 small bowls, ladle over the broth and vegetables and top with spring onion and Thai basil or coriander.

➔ NUTRIENTS MORE THAN 15% RDA
Magnesium, potassium, selenium, zinc, vitamins B1, B2, B6, C, K.

➔ NUTRIENTS MORE THAN 30% RDA
Folate, phosphorus, vitamins A, B3.

➔ PROTEIN BOOSTER
Add extra chicken or edamame beans.

➔ NUTRIENT BOOSTER
Sprinkle with pumpkin seeds.

➔ TAKE TO WORK
Yes.

➔ NOTES
You can buy ready-cooked chicken to save time in the kitchen, or roast or poach 200g raw chicken to get 150g cooked. You can also swap the chicken for silken tofu cubes.

Ginger Carrot Soup with Silken Tofu, Brown Rice and Turmeric Oil

This ginger carrot soup has a lively kick from fresh ginger that wakes up the senses without overwhelming. It's a great example of how simple ingredients like silken tofu can naturally boost protein and creaminess without heaviness. The turmeric oil drizzle adds a warm, comforting touch and brings extra anti-inflammatory benefits to this gentle, nourishing soup.

1 tbsp extra virgin olive oil
1 small onion, diced
1 garlic clove, finely chopped
4cm piece of fresh ginger, grated
200g carrots, peeled and chopped
½ medium potato (about 75g), peeled and diced
350ml vegetable stock
100g silken tofu
75g cooked short-grain brown rice (very soft)
Sea salt and black pepper

For the turmeric oil

1 tbsp extra virgin olive oil
½ tsp ground turmeric

1. Heat 1 teaspoon of the olive oil in a saucepan set over a medium heat. Add the onion and cook for 3–5 minutes until softened.
2. Stir in the garlic, ginger, carrots and potato. Cook for 3 minutes, then add the stock. Bring to a boil, then simmer for 20 minutes until the vegetables are very soft.
3. Add the silken tofu to the pan and use a stick blender to blend everything until completely smooth.
4. Stir in the cooked rice and gently reheat until warmed through. Season with salt and pepper.
5. To make the turmeric oil, warm the olive oil in a small pan with the turmeric for 30 seconds until fragrant. Drizzle the turmeric oil over the soup to serve.

➔ NUTRIENTS MORE THAN 15% RDA
Calcium, magnesium, potassium, vitamins B1, B6, E, K.

➔ NUTRIENTS MORE THAN 30% RDA
Folate, phosphorus, vitamins A, C.

➔ PROTEIN BOOSTER
Sprinkle with toasted pumpkin seeds or swirl with Greek-style yoghurt or fortified soya yoghurt.

➔ STORAGE
This soup freezes well, but loosen with water or stock when reheating. It will freeze for up to 3 months.

➔ NUTRIENT BOOSTER
Stir in finely chopped spinach, sprinkle with nutritional yeast, increase the amount of rice or use tofu.

➔ TAKE TO WORK
Yes.

➔ NOTES
It's best to cook the rice yourself as you want a really soft texture; 25g dried brown rice will give you 75g cooked. Alternatively, use a pouch of ready-cooked rice. If your digestion is sensitive, swap the brown rice for well-cooked white basmati rice.

Smoked Mackerel and Beetroot Toast

This brightly coloured toast is a great way to tempt the appetite as the beetroot gives it a bright pink colour and the horseradish adds a gentle kick that can help stimulate digestion. Smoked mackerel brings protein, omega-3 and vitamin B12, while the rye bread adds fibre to keep you feeling nourished. It's a punchy little dish that's quick to make and ideal when you fancy something light but sustaining.

75g smoked mackerel fillet, skin removed

1 small, cooked beetroot (60g), diced

3 tbsp natural Greek yoghurt or skyr

1 tsp horseradish

Juice of ¼ lemon

2 slices of seeded rye bread

Chopped dill, to garnish

Black pepper

1. In a food processor or using a stick blender pulse the mackerel, diced beetroot, yoghurt, horseradish and lemon juice with some black pepper. The texture should be smooth but with a little bite.
2. Lightly toast the bread and spread the mackerel mixture generously over each slice.
3. Cut into halves or quarters, garnish with dill and serve immediately.

➔ NUTRIENTS MORE THAN 15% RDA
Folate, iodine, vitamins B1, B2, B3, B6.

➔ NUTRIENTS MORE THAN 30% RDA
Phosphorus, selenium, vitamins B12, D. Contains omega-3.

➔ PROTEIN BOOSTER
Add some extra mackerel or top with sliced boiled egg.

➔ STORAGE
This will keep for up to 3 days in the fridge, but it's better to make this as needed.

➔ NUTRIENT BOOSTER
Top with watercress, rocket, cucumber slices or pumpkin seeds.

➔ TAKE TO WORK
Yes – take with rye bread or crispbreads with sliced vegetables like red pepper, carrot and cucumber.

➔ NOTE
Choose vacuum-packed beetroot cooked in water, which you can buy in a resealable bag.

SERVES 2

350 KCAL

16.5G PROTEIN

6.5G FIBRE

Silken Tofu and Brown Rice Bowl with Sesame, Lime and Avocado

Tofu can be a bit of a blank canvas, but that's not a bad thing as it soaks up flavour brilliantly if you get the dressing right. This bowl layers soft silken tofu over warm brown rice with creamy avocado, zingy lime and a savoury sesame-ginger dressing that brings it all together. It's light but satisfying, high in plant protein, and packed with folate, magnesium and calcium.

- 2 tsp light soy sauce
- Juice of ½ lime
- 2 tsp sesame oil
- 1cm piece of fresh ginger, peeled and grated
- 200g silken tofu
- 180g cooked short-grain brown rice
- 80g frozen edamame beans, defrosted
- ½ small avocado, diced
- 2 tsp toasted sesame seeds
- 1 tbsp chopped coriander

1. In a small bowl, whisk together the soy sauce, lime juice, sesame oil and grated ginger to make the dressing.
2. Gently warm the silken tofu until heated through, keeping it as intact as possible. You can do this in a steamer or by placing the tofu in a heatproof bowl inside a colander set over a saucepan of simmering water. Cover with a lid and steam for about 6 minutes.
3. Reheat the rice (pour boiling water over it in a bowl, then drain), then spoon into bowls and top with the edamame beans and diced avocado. Place the tofu on top of this and break it up slightly.
4. Drizzle over the dressing and finish with the toasted sesame seeds and chopped coriander. Serve warm.

➔ NUTRIENTS MORE THAN 15% RDA
Calcium, potassium, zinc, vitamins B1, B3, B6, C, E.

➔ NUTRIENTS MORE THAN 30% RDA
Folate, iron, magnesium, phosphorus, vitamin K.

➔ PROTEIN BOOSTER
Add extra tofu or swap the rice for quinoa.

➔ NUTRIENT BOOSTER
Add more avocado or finely diced cucumber. You can also add a tablespoon of leftover cooked puy lentils.

➔ TAKE TO WORK
Not suitable.

➔ NOTES
If you don't like the texture of silken tofu then use cubes of firm tofu tossed in cornflour and salt then cooked in the pan with a little extra virgin olive oil. If you are short on time use a pouch of ready-cooked brown rice, or cook from scratch: 60g dried rice will give you 180g cooked.

Mini Baby Spinach, Pea and Parmesan Omelette

This quick omelette is a great way to pack in protein and greens with very little effort. The peas and spinach add natural sweetness and fibre, while Parmesan gives a rich flavour without feeling heavy. Perfect for when you need something nourishing but light, it works as a speedy lunch or a protein-boosting snack.

3 medium eggs
30g grated Parmesan cheese
Handful of baby spinach, chopped
2 tbsp frozen peas
1 tbsp chives, chopped
1 tsp extra virgin olive oil
Sea salt and black pepper

1. Crack the eggs into a bowl and whisk well. Stir in the Parmesan, baby spinach, peas and chives and season with a good pinch of salt and black pepper.
2. Heat the olive oil in a non-stick frying pan over a medium heat.
3. Pour the egg mixture into the pan and cook gently until the edges begin to set, about 1–2 minutes. Push the edges to the centre of the pan, then place the lid on the pan and cook for another 2–3 minutes undisturbed until cooked through.
4. Fold and slice in half to serve.

➔ NUTRIENTS MORE THAN 15% RDA
Vitamins C, D.

➔ NUTRIENTS MORE THAN 30% RDA
Calcium, folate, iron, magnesium, phosphorus selenium, vitamins A, B1, B12, K.

➔ PROTEIN BOOSTER
Add another egg or some more peas or stir some leftover cooked puy lentils into the egg before cooking.

➔ NUTRIENT BOOSTER
Serve with a fresh tomato salsa on the side or simply chopped cherry tomatoes.

➔ TAKE TO WORK
Yes – enjoy cold. It will keep for up to 24 hours in an airtight container in the fridge.

➔ NOTE
You can turn this into a more substantial meal by serving with a small slice of seeded rye bread.

Tofu Scramble with Baby Spinach and Sun-dried Tomatoes

This is a great introduction to tofu if you haven't tried it before. The scramble is creamy, savoury and full of flavour, with richness from tahini and sharpness from sun-dried tomatoes. It's a high-protein, plant-based meal that's easy to digest and quick to make. Nutritional yeast is added here for a mild, cheesy flavour and a boost of protein. It's also rich in B vitamins, making it a useful ingredient to keep on hand.

200g firm tofu, crumbled
2 tsp extra virgin olive oil
½ tsp ground turmeric
1 tbsp nutritional yeast
1 tsp light soy sauce
1 spring onion, thinly sliced
Small handful of baby spinach, shredded
4 sun-dried tomato halves in oil, drained, patted dry and finely chopped
2 tsp tahini
Juice of ¼ lemon
Pinch of chilli flakes (optional)
Sea salt and black pepper

1. Drain and pat the tofu dry, then squeeze gently between sheets of kitchen paper to remove any excess moisture. Crumble it into small chunks using your hands or a fork, but don't make it too fine.
2. Heat the olive oil in a non-stick pan over a medium heat. Add the tofu, turmeric, nutritional yeast, soy sauce and spring onion. Cook for 5–6 minutes, stirring occasionally, until heated through and lightly golden.
3. Add the baby spinach and sun-dried tomatoes and cook for another 1–2 minutes until the spinach has wilted. Add a splash of water if needed to help it along.
4. Take the pan off the heat. Stir in the tahini along with the lemon juice to loosen it and bring everything together. Season well with salt and pepper.
5. Serve warm, topped with chilli flakes (if using).

➔ NUTRIENTS MORE THAN 15% RDA
Zinc, vitamins B2, B3, B6, C.

➔ NUTRIENTS MORE THAN 30% RDA
Calcium, folate, iron, magnesium, vitamins B1, K.

➔ PROTEIN BOOSTER
Add extra tofu or stir in defrosted frozen peas.

➔ NUTRIENT BOOSTER
Serve with toasted wholegrain bread or a side of chopped cherry tomatoes.

➔ TAKE TO WORK
Not suitable.

➔ NOTE
You can find nutritional yeast in health food shops or online, but don't worry if you don't have it as the dish still works well without it.

Carrot and Lentil Soup with Coconut And Lime

This vibrant soup is more than just comforting; it's packed with nourishing ingredients that work together to support your health. Red lentils are a great source of plant-based protein and fibre, helping to keep you full while supporting gut health. The addition of lime juice provides vitamin C, which helps your body absorb the iron from the lentils more effectively. A nutrient-rich meal you can batch-cook and freeze.

---

1 tsp extra virgin olive oil
½ onion, finely chopped
1 garlic clove, finely chopped
1 tsp grated fresh ginger
2 medium carrots (about 120g), peeled and diced
100g red lentils
400ml vegetable stock
150ml coconut milk
Juice of ½ lime, plus a little zest
2 tsp coconut yoghurt
1 tbsp chopped coriander
Sea salt and black pepper

1. Heat the oil in a saucepan. Add the onion, garlic and ginger and cook gently for 3–4 minutes until softened.
2. Stir in the carrots, lentils, stock and coconut milk. Bring to the boil, then reduce the heat and simmer for 15–20 minutes until everything is soft.
3. Add the lime juice and season to taste. Blend until smooth (or leave slightly textured if preferred).
4. Serve in bowls and top each portion with 1 teaspoon of coconut yoghurt, some chopped fresh coriander and a little lime zest.

➔ NUTRIENTS MORE THAN 15% RDA
Iron, magnesium, potassium, zinc, vitamins B1, B6, K.

➔ NUTRIENTS MORE THAN 30% RDA
Folate, phosphorus, vitamins A, C.

➔ PROTEIN BOOSTER
Add silken tofu or plant-based protein powder before blending or stir in some cooked quinoa after blending.

➔ STORAGE
This will keep in an airtight container in the fridge for up to 4 days or the freezer for up to 3 months.

➔ NUTRIENT BOOSTER
Sprinkle with toasted mixed seeds (see page 199). Add ½ red pepper with the onion and ginger. Add leftover brown rice, lentils or quinoa.

➔ TAKE TO WORK
Yes.

➔ NOTE
You can switch to reduced-fat coconut milk for a lighter version.

Soft Egg and Spinach Dhal with Coconut Yoghurt

Soft, comforting dhal combines creamy red lentils with tender spinach and gently spiced aromatics. Topped with soft-boiled eggs and a cooling dollop of coconut yoghurt, it's a simple, protein-rich meal that's easy on smaller appetites but still satisfying. Lentils are a great way to add both protein and fibre to your diet.

1 tsp extra virgin olive oil
½ onion, finely chopped
½ tsp ground turmeric
½ tsp ground cumin
¼ tsp ground coriander
1 small garlic clove, finely chopped
2cm piece of fresh ginger, peeled and grated
100g dried red lentils, rinsed
350ml vegetable stock
Big handful of spinach, chopped
2 medium eggs
2 tbsp coconut yoghurt
1 tbsp chopped coriander
Sea salt

1. Heat the olive oil in a saucepan over a medium heat. Add the onion and cook for 3–5 minutes until soft. Add the spices, garlic and ginger and stir gently for 1 minute until fragrant.
2. Stir in the rinsed lentils and pour in the stock. Bring to the boil, then reduce to a simmer and cook for 15–20 minutes, stirring occasionally, until the lentils are soft and thickened. Add a splash more water if needed – it should be thick, creamy and pourable.
3. Stir in the spinach and cook for 2 more minutes until just wilted. Season with salt to taste.
4. Meanwhile, soft-boil the eggs for 6–7 minutes, then cool slightly, peel and cut in half.
5. Spoon the dhal into bowls and top each with a halved egg and a spoonful of coconut yoghurt. Sprinkle with chopped coriander.

➔ NUTRIENTS MORE THAN 15% RDA
Calcium, iron, magnesium, potassium, selenium, zinc, vitamins B1, B2, B3, B6, C.

➔ NUTRIENTS MORE THAN 30% RDA
Folate, phosphorus, vitamins A, B12, K.

➔ PROTEIN BOOSTER
Add an extra egg, stir in some chickpeas or sprinkle with toasted pumpkin seeds.

➔ STORAGE
This will keep in the fridge for 3–4 days and freeze for up to 3 months (minus the egg) in an airtight container.

➔ NUTRIENT BOOSTER
Serve with a spoonful of fermented vegetables like sauerkraut or top with roasted beetroot. You can also serve with a small wholemeal flatbread.

➔ TAKE TO WORK
Yes.

➔ NOTES
You can use coconut oil instead of olive oil for a subtle flavour change. You can also dry-fry the egg in a non-stick frying pan rather than boiling if that's easier.

SERVES 2

310 KCAL

17G PROTEIN

2G FIBRE

Sticky Miso Tofu Bites with Tahini and Lime Dip

These crispy tofu bites are coated in a sticky-sweet miso glaze and served with a tangy tahini-lime dip that pulls everything together. It's the kind of dish that feels indulgent but delivers serious nutrition, thanks to tofu's protein, tahini's healthy fats, and the umami depth of fermented miso. As light meals go, it's bold, balanced and satisfying.

200g firm tofu
1 tbsp cornflour
1 tsp extra virgin olive oil
1 spring onion, thinly sliced
Sesame seeds, to garnish
Salt and black pepper

For the glaze
1 tbsp white miso paste
1 tbsp rice vinegar
2 tsp maple syrup or honey
2 tsp soy sauce
1 tsp grated fresh ginger

For the dip
1 tbsp tahini
Juice of ½ lime
1 tsp soy sauce
1 tsp maple syrup or honey
1 tbsp natural yoghurt
1 tbsp warm water (to loosen)

1. Press the tofu between a couple of sheets of kitchen paper to remove excess water, then cut into bite-sized cubes. Tip the cornflour into a bowl, season with salt and pepper and add the tofu. Toss until evenly coated.
2. Heat the olive oil in a non-stick pan over a medium-high heat. Fry the tofu until golden and crisp on all sides, turning regularly, about 6–8 minutes.
3. In a small bowl, whisk together the glaze ingredients with 1 tablespoon of water. Pour over the tofu and cook for 1–2 minutes, tossing to coat, until sticky and glossy.
4. In another bowl, whisk together all the dip ingredients until smooth and creamy.
5. Serve the tofu bites warm, topped with sliced spring onion and sesame seeds, with the tahini-lime dip on the side.

➔ NUTRIENTS MORE THAN 15% RDA
Folate, iron, magnesium, zinc, vitamin B1.

➔ NUTRIENTS MORE THAN 30% RDA
Calcium, phosphorus.

➔ PROTEIN BOOSTER
Add extra tofu, serve with steamed edamame beans on the side or add slightly mashed black or aduki beans to the glaze when cooking the tofu.

➔ NUTRIENT BOOSTER
Serve with shredded salad (carrot, cabbage and cucumber) dressed with a little of the dip.

➔ TAKE TO WORK
Yes – take with a salad and pack the dip separately to use as a dressing.

Smashed Edamame, Pea and Goat's Cheese Toast

Packed with plant protein and fibre from the edamame, peas and rye bread, this topped toast is both light and sustaining. The goat's cheese adds calcium and a creamy texture, while lemon zest brings freshness to balance the richness. It's a simple way to support muscle health and provide steady energy in a small, appetite-friendly portion.

- 2 tsp extra virgin olive oil
- 100g frozen edamame beans, defrosted
- 50g frozen peas, defrosted
- 50g baby spinach
- 50g soft goat's cheese
- Zest of ½ lemon
- 2 small slices of seeded rye bread
- Sea salt and black pepper

1. Heat the olive oil in a non-stick frying pan over a medium heat. Add the edamame, peas and baby spinach and cook for 2–3 minutes, stirring, until the spinach wilts and everything is heated through.
2. Tip the mixture into a bowl. Add the goat's cheese, lemon zest, a pinch of salt and some black pepper. Mash roughly with a fork, leaving some texture.
3. Toast the bread slices. Pile the warm smash on top and serve.

➔ NUTRIENTS MORE THAN 15% RDA
Calcium, iron, magnesium, potassium, zinc, vitamins B2, B6.

➔ NUTRIENTS MORE THAN 30% RDA
Folate, phosphorus, vitamins A, B1, B12, C, K.

➔ PROTEIN BOOSTER
Sprinkle over pumpkin or hemp seeds.

➔ NUTRIENT BOOSTER
Stir in ground flaxseed or fresh herbs like chives or dill.

➔ TAKE TO WORK
Not suitable.

➔ NOTE
If you find goat's cheese too rich then switch to ricotta or blended silken tofu.

SERVES 2

320 KCAL

19G PROTEIN

5.5G FIBRE

Smashed White Beans with Soft Egg and Herbs

This dish is simple but nourishing, combining creamy white beans, soft-boiled egg and fresh herbs for a protein-rich meal that's gentle and satisfying. A spoonful of yoghurt adds lightness, while feta brings a salty edge. As well as being quick to prepare and ideal for a smaller appetite, it's rich in folate, calcium and phosphorus to support energy and bone health.

- 2 medium eggs
- 250g jarred white beans, rinsed and drained
- 2 tsp extra virgin olive oil
- 1 tbsp natural Greek yoghurt
- Small squeeze of lemon juice
- 1 small garlic clove, grated
- 1 tbsp chopped dill, plus a few fronds to garnish
- 1 tbsp finely chopped flat-leaf parsley
- 40g feta cheese
- Pinch of chilli flakes (optional)
- Sea salt and black pepper

1. Bring a small saucepan of water to the boil. Gently lower in the eggs and simmer for 6 minutes for soft yolks.
2. Transfer the eggs to a bowl of cold water to stop them cooking further. Once cool enough to handle, peel, halve and set aside.
3. In a medium-sized bowl, mash the beans with the olive oil, yoghurt, lemon juice, garlic, dill and parsley until creamy but still textured. Season with salt and pepper, then tip into the pan you boiled the eggs in and place over a low heat to gently warm through.
4. Divide the mash between 2 small bowls. Sprinkle over the feta and chilli flakes (if using), then top each bowl with two egg halves.
5. Finish with a sprinkle of extra dill fronds.

➔ NUTRIENTS MORE THAN 15% RDA
Calcium, iodine, magnesium, potassium, zinc, vitamins A, B1, B2, B3, B6.

➔ NUTRIENTS MORE THAN 30% RDA
Folate, phosphorus, vitamins B12, K.

➔ PROTEIN BOOSTER
Serve with a couple of tinned mackerel fillets on the side or mash into the beans. Sprinkle over some toasted seed mix (see page 199).

➔ NUTRIENT BOOSTER
Add finely chopped sun-dried tomatoes to the mashed beans.

➔ TAKE TO WORK
Yes – you may want to cook the egg for longer for a hard yolk.

➔ NOTES
You can use tinned cannellini beans but cook them in water or stock for about 8 minutes to soften the skins before mashing. I use Bold Bean Co for jarred beans as they are much softer and flavoursome.

SERVES 2

300 KCAL

12.5G PROTEIN

6.8G FIBRE

Spiced Grains with Peas, Baby Spinach and Soft-yolk Egg

This is a great option for those who don't eat meat or fish, as the combination of grains, peas and egg provides a useful source of protein and fibre. The grains you often find in mixed pouches can include wheatberries, barley and quinoa, which are naturally rich in complex carbohydrates and offer varying levels of protein – useful if you're trying to get more protein from plants.

---

1 large egg
2 tsp extra virgin olive oil
½ small red onion, finely chopped
1 tsp ground cumin
1 tsp ground coriander
½ tsp ground turmeric
180g mixed cooked grains from a pouch
350ml vegetable stock
100g frozen peas
Small handful of baby spinach
Sea salt

1. Bring a small saucepan of water to the boil. Add the egg and cook for 7 minutes. Run the pan under cold water to cool the egg, then peel and set aside.
2. Heat the olive oil in a separate pan over a medium heat. Add the onion and cook for 3–5 minutes until softened. Stir in the cumin, coriander and turmeric and cook for 30 seconds until fragrant.
3. Break up the grains then add them to the pan. Stir to coat in the spices and pour in the stock. Bring to the boil, then reduce heat and simmer for 10 minutes.
4. Stir in the peas and cook for 3–4 minutes, then fold in the baby spinach until just wilted. Season with salt to taste.
5. Divide between 2 bowls, top each with half a soft-yolk egg and serve.

➔ NUTRIENTS MORE THAN 15% RDA
Chromium, iron, magnesium, potassium, zinc, vitamins B2, B3, B6.

➔ NUTRIENTS MORE THAN 30% RDA
Folate, phosphorus, vitamins A, B1, B12, C, K.

➔ PROTEIN BOOSTER
Add another egg. Swap half the peas for edamame beans. Add a dollop of Greek yoghurt or skyr.

➔ NUTRIENT BOOSTER
Add grated carrot or finely diced red pepper to the onions when cooking.

➔ TAKE TO WORK
Not suitable.

➔ NOTES
Cooking the grains in stock softens them, which may make them a little easier to digest. If you are reheating the grains then add a little more stock as they can dry out in the fridge.

SERVES 2

340 KCAL

17G PROTEIN

8G FIBRE

Baked Eggs with Spiced Chickpeas and Garlic Yoghurt

This dish is all about comfort without the heaviness. Baked eggs are a simple, satisfying source of quality protein, and the spiced chickpeas add fibre and flavour. It's also a good way to use up half a tin of leftover chopped tomatoes. The garlic yoghurt brings everything together with a creamy, tangy flavour and dose of friendly bacteria. Ideal for a quick lunch, light dinner or a savoury weekend breakfast.

2 tsp extra virgin olive oil
½ small onion, finely chopped
1 garlic clove, grated
½ tsp ground cumin
½ tsp smoked paprika
Small handful of baby spinach, chopped
180g tinned chickpeas, rinsed and drained
200g tinned chopped tomatoes
2 medium eggs
Sea salt and black pepper

For the garlic yoghurt
2 tbsp natural yoghurt
½ small garlic clove, crushed
Small squeeze of lemon juice

1. Preheat the oven to 200°C/180°C fan/Gas 6.
2. Heat the olive oil in a small ovenproof frying pan, add the onion and sauté for 3–5 minutes until soft. Add the garlic, cumin and paprika and cook for 1 minute.
3. Stir in the spinach, chickpeas and tomatoes and 1 tablespoon of water. Season well and simmer gently or 5–7 minutes until thickened.
4. Make two wells in the mixture and crack an egg into each one. Transfer the pan to the oven and bake for 8–10 minutes until the whites are set and the yolks still soft.
5. Meanwhile, mix the garlic yoghurt ingredients in a small bowl and season with salt and pepper.
6. Serve the baked eggs hot, drizzled with garlic yoghurt.

➔ NUTRIENTS MORE THAN 15% RDA
Calcium, magnesium, potassium, zinc, vitamins A, B1, B2, B3, B6.

➔ NUTRIENTS MORE THAN 30% RDA
Folate, phosphorus, vitamins A, B12, C.

➔ PROTEIN BOOSTER
Add extra chickpeas or peas or sprinkle over some toasted pumpkin seeds.

➔ NUTRIENT BOOSTER
Serve with a small slice of wholegrain bread or a mini wholemeal wrap.

➔ TAKE TO WORK
Not suitable.

➔ NOTE
You can swap chickpeas for black beans or add a pinch of dried chillies for a little heat.

SERVES 2

Crab and Brown Rice Stir Fry

310 KCAL

21G PROTEIN

4G FIBRE

This is a lighter take on fried rice that still ticks all the boxes when it comes to comfort. Using eggs, brown rice and sweet vegetables like peas and corn, it's filling without being too heavy. Crab might sound fancy, but you don't need to splash out as tinned white crab meat is much more affordable than fresh and still delivers a good hit of protein. It's quick, warm and full of flavour.

- 1 tsp extra virgin olive oil
- 1 garlic clove, finely chopped
- 1cm piece of fresh ginger, peeled and grated
- ½ green chilli, thinly sliced (optional)
- 120g cooked short-grain brown rice
- 2 large eggs, lightly beaten
- 60g frozen peas, defrosted
- 60g sweetcorn (tinned or frozen and defrosted)
- 100g white crab meat (fresh or tinned)
- 1 tsp fish sauce
- 1 tsp sesame oil
- 2 spring onions, thinly sliced
- 1 tbsp chopped coriander or Thai basil

1. Heat the olive oil in a non-stick wok or pan over a medium heat. Add the garlic, ginger and green chilli (if using) and cook for 1 minute until fragrant.
2. Add the cooked rice and stir-fry for 2–3 minutes to heat through.
3. Push the rice to one side and pour the eggs into the other side of the pan. Scramble gently until just set, then fold into the rice.
4. Add the peas, sweetcorn, crab meat and fish sauce. Stir everything together and cook for another 2 minutes until warmed through.
5. Drizzle with sesame oil and top with spring onions and chopped coriander or Thai basil. Serve warm.

➔ NUTRIENTS MORE THAN 15% RDA
Chromium, iodine, iron, magnesium, potassium, selenium, zinc, vitamins B1, B2, B3, B6.

➔ NUTRIENTS MORE THAN 30% RDA
Folate, phosphorus, vitamins A, B12, K.

➔ PROTEIN BOOSTER
Add extra crab meat or another egg.

➔ NUTRIENT BOOSTER
Add sliced white mushrooms or grated carrot.

➔ TAKE TO WORK
Yes – let the rice cool completely before transferring to an airtight container. Reheat thoroughly at work.

➔ NOTE
I use short-grain brown rice in these recipes because it's softer and less husky than long grain varieties, making it easier to digest. To cook from scratch, you will need 40g dried rice to get 120g cooked.

Warm Lentil Salad with Roasted Beetroot, Walnuts and Coconut Yoghurt

This warm lentil salad is earthy, tangy and satisfying. It's a bit bulkier than other dishes, so if you can't manage a full portion, keep the rest in the fridge for later. It also works well in smaller servings alongside extra protein like grilled fish. The beetroot, feta and toasted walnuts add flavour and texture, while the zesty yoghurt dressing brings everything together for a warm, balanced bowl.

½ small red onion, thinly sliced
Juice of ¼ lemon
180g cooked puy lentils
2 tsp extra virgin olive oil
1 tsp dried thyme
2 vacuum-packed beetroots, peeled and diced
1 tbsp walnuts, roughly chopped
1 tbsp coconut yoghurt
1 tbsp natural yoghurt
Juice of ½ lime
30g feta cheese
10g rocket
Sea salt and black pepper

1. Place the red onion in a small dish with the lemon juice and leave to soak for 5 minutes.
2. Heat the lentils through, then place them in a bowl with the olive oil, thyme and beetroots and set aside.
3. Meanwhile, toast the walnuts in a dry pan for 3–4 minutes until fragrant and lightly golden.
4. In a small bowl, mix together the coconut yoghurt, yoghurt and lime juice with a pinch of salt.
5. Drain the red onion then add to the bowl with the lentils and beetroot. Add the walnuts, feta and rocket to the bowl and toss. Season to taste.
6. Serve with the coconut yoghurt dressing spooned over the top.

➔ NUTRIENTS MORE THAN 15% RDA
Calcium, chromium, iron, magnesium, potassium, zinc, vitamins B1, B2, B3, B6, B12.

➔ NUTRIENTS MORE THAN 30% RDA
Folate, phosphorus, vitamins A, C, K.

➔ PROTEIN BOOSTER
Add extra feta cheese, walnuts or pumpkin seeds.

➔ NUTRIENT BOOSTER
Add frozen peas (defrosted), pomegranate seeds or leftover roasted vegetables.

➔ TAKE TO WORK
Yes – serve cold or at room temperature.

➔ NOTES
Soaking the sliced onion in water first makes it less pungent and easier to digest. You can use a pouch of ready-cooked lentils or cook them from scratch: 60g dried puy lentils will give you 180g cooked.

Turmeric Poached Egg Bowl with Quinoa, Greens and Smoky Tomato Sauce

This recipe features beautifully bright yellow eggs; they not only look stunning but add a rich, creamy texture. It's a simple yet satisfying dish that feels wholesome and comforting, perfect when you want something easy but full of flavour, and ideal any time of day. Egg yolks are also one of the few natural sources of vitamin D.

2 tsp extra virgin olive oil
1 garlic clove, finely chopped
150g mixed greens (spinach, kale, chard)
Juice of ¼ lemon
1 tsp ground turmeric
4 medium eggs
150g cooked tri-colour quinoa
1 tbsp pumpkin seeds
Sea salt and black pepper

For the smoky tomato sauce
4 tbsp passata
1 tsp extra virgin olive oil
½ tsp smoked paprika or ground cumin
Small squeeze of lemon juice

1. Heat the olive oil in a non-stick frying pan over a medium-high heat. Cook the garlic for 1 minute, then add the greens and sauté for 3–4 minutes until wilted. Season with lemon juice, salt and pepper. Set aside.
2. Bring a saucepan of water to a gentle simmer. Add the turmeric, then crack in the eggs and poach for 3–4 minutes until the whites are set and the yolks remain runny. Remove the eggs with a slotted spoon and drain on some kitchen paper. Rinse the pan, dry it, and set back on the heat, ready to make the sauce.
3. Pour the passata into the pan with the olive oil, smoked paprika or cumin and lemon juice and warm through for 1–2 minutes to make the sauce. Season with salt and pepper.
4. To serve, spread the smoky tomato sauce over the base of 2 bowls. Add the quinoa, then the sautéed greens followed by two poached eggs in each bowl. Finish by sprinkling with pumpkin seeds.

➔ NUTRIENTS MORE THAN 15% RDA
Calcium, iron, magnesium, potassium, selenium, zinc, vitamins B1, B3, B6, D, E.

➔ NUTRIENTS MORE THAN 30% RDA
Folate, phosphorus, vitamins A, B12, C, K.

➔ PROTEIN BOOSTER
Stir Greek yoghurt or skyr through the greens or serve with a dollop of hummus on the side.

➔ NUTRIENT BOOSTER
Add finely chopped sun-dried tomatoes and sliced green olives to the quinoa.

➔ TAKE TO WORK
Not suitable.

➔ NOTES
You can replace the egg with roasted extra firm tofu marinated in olive oil, garlic, lemon juice and a sprinkle of turmeric or smoked paprika. If you are cooking the quinoa from scratch, 50g dry quinoa will give you 150g cooked; alternatively use a pouch of ready-cooked quinoa.

Mashed Sweet Potato with Crispy Chickpeas and Tahini-Yoghurt Drizzle

This is a small, nourishing bowl that is more of a mini meal than a full plate. It might sound a little bit strange, but it's surprisingly tasty: the combination of creamy mash, crunchy chickpeas and sharp tahini drizzle really works, while the crunch of seeds really lifts the whole thing.

½ x 400g tin chickpeas, rinsed and drained
1 tsp extra virgin olive oil
¼ tsp ground cumin
350g sweet potatoes
50g cottage cheese
Splash of milk or water (optional)
1 tbsp tahini
1 tbsp natural yoghurt
Juice of ¼ lemon
1 tbsp sunflower seeds
1 tbsp toasted sesame seeds
Sea salt and black pepper

1. Preheat the oven to 220°C/200°C fan/Gas 7.
2. Pat the chickpeas dry with kitchen paper, then toss with the olive oil, cumin and a pinch of salt and pepper.
3. Halve the sweet potatoes (leave the skin on) and place them cut side down on a non-stick baking tray. Add the chickpeas to the tray and roast for 25–30 minutes, stirring the chickpeas halfway through. If the chickpeas are crisp but the sweet potato isn't fully soft, remove the chickpeas with a spatula and return the sweet potato to the oven until tender.
4. Scoop the sweet potato flesh into a bowl and season to taste. Add the cottage cheese and blitz with a stick blender until smooth. Loosen with a splash of milk or water if needed.
5. In a small bowl, whisk together the tahini, yoghurt, lemon juice, a splash of water and a pinch of salt until smooth and pourable.
6. Divide the mash between 2 bowls. Top with the crispy chickpeas, sunflower seeds and toasted sesame seeds. Drizzle over the tahini-yoghurt sauce and serve warm.

➔ NUTRIENTS MORE THAN 15% RDA
Calcium, chromium, potassium, zinc, vitamins B1, B2, B3, B6, B12, E.

➔ NUTRIENTS MORE THAN 30% RDA
Folate, iron, magnesium, phosphorus, vitamins A, C, K.

➔ PROTEIN BOOSTER
Add more cottage cheese (you can switch to high-protein cottage cheese) or serve with a small protein side such as chicken.

➔ NUTRIENT BOOSTER
Serve the mash on top of wilted baby spinach.

➔ TAKE TO WORK
Not suitable.

➔ NOTE
Some people may find the sweetness and puréed texture harder to tolerate in this recipe.

High-protein Cauliflower and White Bean Soup with Toasted Seeds

This is a light, fresh-tasting soup with a lovely lemony tang and plenty of fibre to help you feel satisfied without feeling too full. The cauliflower and white beans give it a creamy texture, but it's the cottage cheese that really boosts the protein content without adding heaviness. Topped with toasted seeds for crunch and extra nutrition, this one's ideal for lunch or a nourishing mini meal any time of day.

---

1 tsp extra virgin olive oil
½ small onion, finely chopped
1 garlic clove, finely chopped
¼ tsp smoked paprika, plus extra for dusting
200g cauliflower, chopped
½ x 400g tin cannellini beans, rinsed and drained
350ml vegetable stock
½ tsp Dijon mustard
Juice of ¼ lemon
75g cottage cheese
1 tbsp toasted pumpkin seeds
Sea salt and black pepper

1. Heat the olive oil in a saucepan and gently cook the onion and garlic for 4–5 minutes until softened. Add the smoked paprika and cook for 30 seconds until it all becomes fragrant.
2. Add the cauliflower and cook for 2 more minutes.
3. Stir in the beans and stock, bring to a simmer and cook for 15–20 minutes until the cauliflower is very soft.
4. Stir in the mustard, lemon juice and cottage cheese, then blend until smooth. Season to taste.
5. Ladle into bowls and top with toasted pumpkin seeds and a sprinkle of smoked paprika just before serving, either on its own or with a small slice of seeded rye bread.

➔ NUTRIENTS MORE THAN 15% RDA
Iron, magnesium, potassium, zinc, vitamins B1, B2, B6, B12, K.

➔ NUTRIENTS MORE THAN 30% RDA
Chromium, folate, phosphorus, selenium, vitamin C.

➔ PROTEIN BOOSTER
Add unflavoured plant-based protein powder or silken tofu. Sprinkle over more seeds or switch to high-protein cottage cheese.

➔ STORAGE
You can keep this in the fridge for 3 days and freeze for up to 3 months.

➔ NUTRIENT BOOSTER
Add baby spinach, shredded kale leaves or leftover roasted vegetable like carrots or butternut squash (both will change the colour of your soup).

➔ TAKE TO WORK
Yes.

➔ NOTE
Blending the beans and cauliflower makes this soup easier to digest than you might expect, but if you're very sensitive to fibre or prone to bloating, try a smaller portion first.

Creamy Beans and Greens

Creamy beans and greens is proper comfort food – warming, nourishing and satisfying without being too heavy. The cannellini beans and kale simmer into a soft, flavourful base, while cottage cheese and Parmesan give it richness and a protein boost. Served with garlicky rye toast, it's the kind of bowl that feels both indulgent and restorative. This dish is ideal for days when your appetite needs a gentle nudge, but you still want something wholesome.

- 1 tsp extra virgin olive oil
- 1 garlic clove, grated, plus 1 for the toast (optional)
- ½ tsp dried thyme
- ½ x 400g tin cannellini beans, rinsed and drained
- 80g kale, tough stems removed, and finely chopped
- 100ml vegetable stock
- 1 tbsp crème fraîche or Greek yoghurt
- 100g cottage cheese
- 2 tsp grated Parmesan cheese
- Zest of ¼ lemon
- 2 small slices of seeded rye bread
- Sea salt

1. Heat the olive oil in a saucepan over a medium heat. Add the garlic and dried thyme and cook for 1 minute until fragrant.
2. Stir in the drained beans, chopped kale and vegetable stock. Bring to a simmer, cover and cook for 10 minutes until the kale is tender.
3. Remove from the heat and stir in the crème fraîche, cottage cheese, Parmesan and lemon zest. Season with salt to taste.
4. Toast the bread and rub lightly with a garlic clove if you like.
5. Serve the creamy beans and greens in a warm bowl with the toast on the side.

➔ NUTRIENTS MORE THAN 15% RDA
Chromium, iodine, iron, potassium, selenium, zinc, vitamins B1, B3, B6.

➔ NUTRIENTS MORE THAN 30% RDA
Calcium, folate, phosphorus, vitamins A, B2, B12, C, K.

➔ PROTEIN BOOSTER
Add more beans or cottage cheese (you can also switch to high-protein cottage cheese).

➔ NUTRIENT BOOSTER
Add frozen peas or baby spinach, or fresh herbs like chives or flat-leaf parsley.

➔ TAKE TO WORK
Yes – add a splash of water and reheat at work.

➔ NOTE
This works best when the beans are soft and creamy – try Napoli, Biona or Suma varieties.

DINNER

LIGHT & ENERGISING 142

PROTEIN PACKED 154

EASY TO DIGEST 168

COMFORTING & WARMING 177

Za'atar Chicken with Roasted Roots and Tahini Drizzle

Traybakes are the easiest way to put a meal together. This dish combines bold Middle Eastern spices with the natural sweetness of roasted carrots and beetroot. Cooking the chicken on top lets the flavours mingle and caramelise really well while the tangy tahini drizzle adds creaminess and freshness to balance the earthy vegetables. A satisfying, high-protein meal that's perfect for days when you want something warm.

200g (2 medium) skinless and boneless chicken thighs, fat trimmed

1 tbsp za'atar spice blend

2 tsp extra virgin olive oil

2 medium carrots (about 120g), peeled and cut on a diagonal about 3cm thick

1 large or 2 medium beetroot (about 150g), peeled and cut into 8 wedges

Sea salt and black pepper

For the tahini drizzle

2 tbsp runny tahini

Juice of ½ lemon

2 tbsp warm water

Pinch of ground cumin

1. Preheat the oven to 200°C/180°C fan/Gas 6.
2. Put the chicken thighs in a bowl and add the za'atar, 1 teaspoon of the olive oil and some salt and pepper and combine well so all the chicken is fully coated.
3. Arrange the carrots and beetroot on a parchment-lined baking tray and coat with the remaining olive oil. Place the chicken on top of the vegetables.
4. Roast for 30–35 minutes, turning once, until the vegetables are tender and caramelised and the chicken is cooked through.
5. Meanwhile, whisk together the tahini drizzle ingredients until smooth and pourable. You may have to add more water to get to the consistency of single cream.
6. Once cooked, slice the chicken and serve it over the roasted roots. Drizzle with the tahini sauce.

➔ NUTRIENTS MORE THAN 15% RDA
Calcium, chromium, iron, magnesium, potassium, selenium, zinc, vitamins B1, B2.

➔ NUTRIENTS MORE THAN 30% RDA
Folate, phosphorus, vitamins A, B3, B6, B12, C, K.

➔ PROTEIN BOOSTER
Add extra chicken or chickpeas to the roasting tin with the vegetables and chicken. Sprinkle over some toasted seed mix or dukkah (see pages 199 and 198) just before serving.

➔ NUTRIENT BOOSTER
Add 1 small red onion (cut into 8 and roasted with the veg) or a handful of pomegranate seeds just before serving.

➔ TAKE TO WORK
Yes – enjoy cold or heat up at work. Keep the tahini drizzle separate.

➔ NOTE
Keep any leftover tahini drizzle in the fridge and use for salad dressings. It will last for up to 5 days.

Aubergine and Tofu Stew with Coconut, Edamame and Lime

This aubergine and tofu stew has creamy coconut and warming spices that soothe and satisfy. It's one of the more filling dishes in the book, offering a generous hit of plant-based protein along with key nutrients like folate, calcium and magnesium. Packed with nourishing ingredients like tofu, edamame and lime, it's perfect for when you want something filling but gentle, with just the right balance of rich and fresh flavours.

- 2 tsp extra virgin olive oil
- ½ small onion, thinly sliced
- 1 garlic clove, grated
- 2cm piece of fresh ginger, peeled and grated
- 1 tsp ground cumin
- ½ tsp ground turmeric
- 1 tsp soy sauce
- 1 small aubergine (200g), cut into small 1cm cubes
- 200g firm tofu, cubed
- 150ml coconut milk
- 200ml vegetable stock
- 80g frozen edamame beans, defrosted
- Juice of ½ lime
- ½ tsp garam masala
- Fresh coriander leaves (optional)
- Sea salt

1. Heat the oil in a non-stick saucepan set over a medium heat. Add the onion and sauté for 3–4 minutes until softened.
2. Stir in the garlic and ginger and cook for 1 minute until fragrant.
3. Add the cumin, turmeric and soy sauce, then stir in the aubergine and tofu and cook for 5–6 minutes, stirring occasionally, until the aubergine begins to soften, and the tofu is lightly golden.
4. Pour in the coconut milk and vegetable stock, followed by the edamame beans and lime juice. Bring to the boil, then reduce to a simmer and cook gently for 25 minutes until the aubergine is very soft and the broth has reduced slightly. Check the seasoning.
5. Stir in the garam masala and let the stew sit for 1 minute off the heat to infuse.
6. Divide between 2 small bowls and top each one with a scattering of coriander, if using.

➔ NUTRIENTS MORE THAN 15% RDA
Calcium, iron, magnesium, potassium, selenium, zinc, vitamins B1, B2, B3, B6.

➔ NUTRIENTS MORE THAN 30% RDA
Folate, phosphorus, vitamins A, K.

➔ PROTEIN BOOSTER
Add extra tofu. Stir nut butter into the broth when cooking.

➔ STORAGE
This will keep for up to 4 days in the fridge and 2 months in the freezer, stored in an airtight container.

➔ NUTRIENT BOOSTER
Add a handful of spinach into the broth.

➔ TAKE TO WORK
Yes.

➔ NOTES
You can serve this on its own or with brown rice, quinoa or a small flatbread. It also works well with a little chopped green chilli scattered over at the end, if you like a bit of heat.

Turmeric-spiced Prawns with Coconut Lentil Brown Rice and Peas

This is one of my favourite recipes. It's seriously good. The prawns are cooked in warming spices until golden and juicy, then served on top of rice that has been simmered with coconut milk and water and finished with black beans and peas for a hit of fibre and plant protein. It's totally satisfying but still light and fresh. You can use lighter coconut milk if you prefer.

150g raw peeled king prawns, defrosted if frozen
1 tsp coconut oil
½ tsp ground turmeric
½ tsp ground cumin
1 tsp garam masala
2cm piece of fresh ginger, peeled and grated
Pinch of chilli flakes
Juice of ½ lime
Sea salt and black pepper

For the rice

60g short-grain brown rice
90ml coconut milk
90ml water
100g tinned black beans, rinsed and drained
50g frozen peas

1. Start with the rice. Rinse the rice well, then place in a saucepan with the coconut milk, water and a pinch of salt. Bring to the boil, then reduce to a simmer, cover and cook for 30–35 minutes until tender. Stir in the black beans and peas for the last 5 minutes of cooking. If there's still liquid at the end, remove the lid to let it absorb. Let the rice sit off the heat for 5 minutes before serving.
2. While the rice cooks, toss the prawns with the coconut oil, turmeric, cumin, garam masala, ginger, chilli flakes, a pinch of sea salt and some black pepper.
3. Place a non-stick frying pan over a medium heat and cook the prawns for 2–3 minutes on each side until pink and cooked through. Squeeze over the lime juice and stir to deglaze the pan and coat the prawns in the spiced oil.
4. Spoon the rice onto plates and top with the warm turmeric prawns. Serve immediately.

➔ NUTRIENTS MORE THAN 15% RDA
Folate, iodine, magnesium, phosphorus, vitamin B12.

➔ NUTRIENTS MORE THAN 30% RDA
Iron, selenium, zinc, vitamins B3, B6, K.

➔ PROTEIN BOOSTER
Add extra prawns, beans or peas.

➔ NUTRIENT BOOSTER
Add sliced spinach with the peas and beans. Add a spoonful of sauerkraut or a side salad of grated carrot, ginger and coriander.

➔ TAKE TO WORK
Yes – warm through before serving.

SERVES 2

300 KCAL

19G PROTEIN

4.4G FIBRE

Courgetti with Tomato, Prawns and Chilli

This light, energising dish is ideal when you want something fresh without the heaviness of pasta. Courgetti keeps it simple and soft, while prawns offer a good source of protein and zinc, which is good for immunity. It's quick to make, easy to digest and a useful go-to when your appetite isn't at its best.

- 1 tbsp extra virgin olive oil
- ½ small red onion, finely diced
- 2 garlic cloves, thinly sliced
- 4 ripe vine tomatoes, chopped
- ½ red chilli, thinly sliced (optional)
- 150g raw peeled king prawns, defrosted if frozen
- Small handful of picked basil leaves, torn
- 1 large courgette (300g), spiralised or peeled with a julienne peeler (makes about 250g)
- 2 tbsp toasted pine nuts
- Sea salt

1. Heat the olive oil in a pan and add the onion, garlic, tomatoes and chilli (if using). Cook for about 5 minutes until the tomatoes have softened.
2. Add the prawns and cook for 4 minutes, or until pink and cooked through.
3. Stir in the basil leaves and season with a little sea salt.
4. Add the courgette and stir gently for 2–3 minutes until just softened.
5. Scatter with toasted pine nuts and serve immediately.

➔ NUTRIENTS MORE THAN 15% RDA
Chromium, iron, zinc, vitamins B1, E.

➔ NUTRIENTS MORE THAN 30% RDA
Folate, iodine, phosphorus, vitamins A, B2, B3, B6, B12, C, K.

➔ PROTEIN BOOSTER
Add extra prawns, pumpkin seeds or stir natural yoghurt through the sauce.

➔ NUTRIENT BOOSTER
Serve with more courgetti or stir in defrosted frozen peas.

➔ TAKE TO WORK
Not suitable.

➔ NOTES
You can swap the courgetti here for spiralised butternut squash or use a bed of lightly cooked shredded cabbage.

Smoky Prawn and Black Bean Tacos with Sour Cream

These tacos are full of flavour and texture without being too heavy, making them ideal for a light main meal. Mini wholemeal wraps are a great base for layering nutrient-dense toppings like prawns, beans, veg and seeds. You can swap the prawns in this recipe for salmon or tofu if you prefer or have any leftover in the fridge.

- 150g raw peeled king prawns, defrosted if frozen
- 1 tsp extra virgin olive oil
- ¼ tsp smoked paprika
- ½ tsp ground cumin
- ¼ tsp ground coriander
- ½ small garlic clove, grated
- 2 mini wholemeal tortillas
- 50g tinned black beans, rinsed and drained
- 2 tbsp sour cream or natural yoghurt
- 30g red cabbage, shredded
- 30g carrot, grated
- 1 spring onion, thinly sliced
- 2 tsp pumpkin seeds
- Juice of ½ lime
- Coriander, leaves picked (optional)
- Sea salt and black pepper

1. Toss the prawns with the olive oil, smoked paprika, cumin, coriander, garlic and a pinch of salt.
2. Set a non-stick frying pan over a medium heat. Add the tortilla wraps and warm on either side, then transfer to a plate.
3. Add the prawns to the pan with the beans and cook for 2–3 minutes per side until pink.
4. Spread the sour cream over the wraps then top with cabbage, carrot, spring onion and pumpkin seeds.
5. Top with the prawns, squeeze over the lime juice and sprinkle with coriander (if using). Serve immediately.

➔ NUTRIENTS MORE THAN 15% RDA
Calcium, chromium, folate, iron, magnesium, zinc, vitamins A, B6, C, E.

➔ NUTRIENTS MORE THAN 30% RDA
Iodine, phosphorus, selenium, vitamins B12, K.

➔ PROTEIN BOOSTER
Add extra prawns or beans.

➔ NUTRIENT BOOSTER
Add avocado or sweetcorn.

➔ TAKE TO WORK
Not suitable.

➔ NOTE
You can swap black beans for any type of bean, lentil or chickpea if you have leftovers.

Sesame-crusted Tuna Steak with Edamame and Avocado Salad

Tuna and edamame pack in the protein in this dish, making it a brilliant option if you're after something light but satisfying. The Asian flavours of sesame, lime and soy keep it fresh and vibrant, while the mix of colourful whole foods adds a serious nutrient boost. You're getting good fats from avocado and seeds, a load of B vitamins, plus key minerals like magnesium, zinc and phosphorus.

200g fresh tuna steak, halved
1 tsp light soy sauce, plus a drizzle to serve
2 tbsp sesame seeds
1 tsp sesame oil

For the salad

100g frozen edamame beans, defrosted
6cm piece of cucumber, deseeded and diced
1 spring onion, thinly sliced on the diagonal
½ small avocado, diced
2 tsp pumpkin seeds
1 tsp sesame oil
Juice of ½ lime
Sea salt and black pepper

1. Rub the tuna steaks with soy sauce and press each side into the sesame seeds to coat.
2. Heat the sesame oil in a non-stick frying pan over a medium-high heat. Wait for the pan to get really hot, then sear the tuna for 1–2 minutes per side, depending on your preference. Remove from the heat and let rest briefly before slicing.
3. In a bowl, combine the edamame, cucumber, spring onion, diced avocado, pumpkin seeds, sesame oil and lime juice. Season with salt and pepper, then toss to combine – keep going until the avocado starts to break up and coat the other ingredients.
4. Divide the salad between 2 plates and top with the sliced tuna with a little extra soy sauce.

➔ NUTRIENTS MORE THAN 15% RDA
Iron, potassium, zinc, vitamins B2, C, D, E, K.

➔ NUTRIENTS MORE THAN 30% RDA
Folate, magnesium, phosphorus, selenium, vitamins B1, B3, B6, B12. Contains omega-3.

➔ PROTEIN BOOSTER
Add extra tuna or edamame beans.

➔ NUTRIENT BOOSTER
Add diced red pepper, rocket or lentil sprouts to the salad.

➔ TAKE TO WORK
Not suitable.

➔ NOTE
You can make a vegan version of this using firm tofu.

SERVES 2

330 KCAL

26G PROTEIN

6.5G FIBRE

Poached Cod with Miso Broth, Wilted Greens and Brown Rice

This seriously comforting dish combines a fragrant miso broth with tender poached cod and finely shredded cabbage for warmth and gentle texture. It's soft, nourishing and easy to digest – I use short-grain brown rice as it has a softer texture than other more husky varieties. This is a great option for smaller appetites or when you want a bowl of something soothing and restorative.

- 1 tsp extra virgin olive oil
- 1 garlic clove, thinly sliced
- 2cm piece of fresh ginger, peeled and grated
- 500ml fresh vegetable stock
- 1 tbsp white miso paste
- 2 tsp light soy sauce
- 200g raw skinless cod fillet, sliced in half
- 200g Savoy cabbage, very thinly sliced
- 150g cooked short-grain brown rice
- 2 spring onions, thinly sliced
- Juice of ½ lime
- 1 tbsp sesame seeds
- 1 tbsp chopped coriander
- 1 tsp sesame oil

1. Heat the olive oil in a non-stick saucepan set over a medium heat. Gently cook the garlic and ginger for 1 minute until fragrant.
2. Stir in the vegetable stock, miso paste and soy sauce and bring to a gentle simmer, then lower in the cod fillets and poach for about 8 minutes, or until just cooked through. Add the cabbage for the final 3 minutes of cooking, gently pushing it down into the broth to wilt until tender.
3. Divide the cooked brown rice between 2 bowls. Carefully lift the cod and cabbage into the bowls. Ladle the broth over the top.
4. Finish with spring onion slices, a squeeze of lime juice, sesame seeds, coriander and a drizzle of sesame oil.

➔ NUTRIENTS MORE THAN 15% RDA
Calcium, iron, magnesium, potassium, zinc, vitamins A, B1, B2, B6, D.

➔ NUTRIENTS MORE THAN 30% RDA
Folate, iodine, phosphorus, selenium, vitamins B3, B12, C, K.

➔ PROTEIN BOOSTER
Add extra cod or a few prawns if you have any left over from another recipe or use defrosted frozen prawns. Switch the rice for cooked quinoa.

➔ NUTRIENT BOOSTER
Grate in a little raw carrot. Sprinkle with torn seaweed thins or toasted pumpkin seeds. Add extra rice.

➔ TAKE TO WORK
Yes – this will keep in the fridge for up to 2 days but keep the rice separate.

➔ NOTES
Try using fresh stock to the broth is nice and clear. Use ready-cooked rice from a pouch or cook from scratch: 50g dried brown rice will give you 150g cooked.

Prawn and Cauliflower Curry with Quinoa

This light, brothy curry is packed with flavour and perfect if you're on GLP-1 medication, as thicker sauces can sometimes feel too heavy. Curry leaves aren't essential, but they really do lift the dish with a subtle citrusy note, so are well worth seeking out. You can buy them fresh and freeze what you don't use, so nothing goes to waste. A nourishing, protein-rich meal that's gentle yet satisfying.

---

2 tsp extra virgin olive oil or coconut oil
½ small onion, finely chopped
1 small garlic clove, grated
2cm piece of fresh ginger, peeled and grated
4 curry leaves
1 tsp curry powder
¼ tsp ground ginger
150ml vegetable stock
150g cauliflower, cut into small florets
150g raw peeled king prawns, defrosted if frozen
100ml coconut milk
Small handful of baby spinach
Juice of ¼ lime
Sea salt
180g cooked quinoa, to serve
Coriander leaves (optional), to garnish

1. Heat the oil in a saucepan set over a medium heat. Add the onion and cook for 2–3 minutes until softened.
2. Stir in the garlic, fresh ginger and curry leaves and cook for another 2 minutes, then add the curry powder and ground ginger and cook for 1 minute until fragrant.
3. Pour in the vegetable stock and bring to a gentle simmer. Add the cauliflower and cook for 10 minutes until tender, stirring occasionally (don't be tempted to put any more stock into the pan).
4. Stir in the prawns and cook for about 3 minutes until they are pink and cooked through. Then add coconut milk and cook for another 1 minute. Take the pan off the heat and stir through the baby spinach until wilted, then add the lime juice and little salt to taste.
5. Serve over the cooked quinoa and sprinkle over a few coriander leaves (if using).

➔ NUTRIENTS MORE THAN 15% RDA
Iodine, iron, zinc, vitamin B6.

➔ NUTRIENTS MORE THAN 30% RDA
Folate, magnesium, phosphorus, selenium, vitamins B12, C, K.

➔ PROTEIN BOOSTER
Add extra prawns or a small handful of chickpeas.

➔ STORAGE
This will keep in the fridge in an airtight container for a day or two.

➔ NUTRIENT BOOSTER
Serve with extra quinoa or add thinly sliced yellow pepper.

➔ TAKE TO WORK
Yes – warm the curry and quinoa separately.

➔ NOTES
Swap the quinoa for brown rice or serve with a wholemeal mini wrap. Use a pouch of ready-cooked quinoa to save time or cook it from scratch: 60g dried quinoa will give you 180g cooked.

Harissa-spiced Turkey Skewers with Lentil, Olive and Sun-dried Tomato Salad

This is a simple, flavour-packed recipe that works well when you need something light but still protein-rich and satisfying. The lentil salad delivers fibre and a hit of umami from olives and sun-dried tomatoes. Perfect for those days when your appetite is low, but you still want to eat well and get plenty of nutrients in.

1 tbsp harissa paste
1 tsp extra virgin olive oil
Juice of ¼ lemon
200g turkey breast, cut into bite-sized cubes
1 small courgette, sliced into 8 rounds, each about 1cm thick
Sea salt and black pepper

For the salad

150g cooked green lentils (tinned works fine)
4 sun-dried tomatoes in oil, patted dry and finely chopped
1 tsp oil from the sun-dried tomato jar
6 black olives, chopped
½ garlic clove, finely chopped
¼ small red onion, finely chopped
1 tbsp chopped parsley
Squeeze of lemon juice

1. Preheat the oven to 200°C/180°C fan/Gas 6.
2. Mix the harissa, olive oil, lemon juice, salt and pepper in a bowl. Add the turkey and courgette and toss to coat. Marinate for 10–15 minutes, or overnight if preparing ahead.
3. In a separate bowl, combine all the salad ingredients together. Mix well and season to taste with salt and pepper.
4. Thread the turkey and courgette onto 2 skewers, then place on a baking sheet. Roast in the oven for about 20 minutes, turning halfway through, until the turkey is cooked through and golden.
5. Serve the skewers warm with the lentil salad on the side.

➔ NUTRIENTS MORE THAN 15% RDA
Calcium, iodine, iron, magnesium, potassium, selenium, zinc, vitamins B1, B2.

➔ NUTRIENTS MORE THAN 30% RDA
Folate, phosphorus, vitamins A, B3, B6, B12, C, K.

➔ PROTEIN BOOSTER
Add extra turkey or crumble feta cheese into the salad.

➔ NUTRIENT BOOSTER
Add sliced baby spinach or a roasted red pepper from a jar.

➔ TAKE TO WORK
Yes – the skewers can be warmed up or enjoyed at room temperature.

➔ NOTE
Raw onion may be an issue for GLP-1 users. You can gently sauté the onion in a splash of oil, soak in a little lemon juice or swap for chives.

Lentil, Chicken and Roast Carrot Protein Bowl

This high-protein bowl is a balanced, satisfying meal that's ideal for lunch or dinner. Lentils provide a good source of plant protein and fibre, helping to support gut health and keep you feeling fuller for longer. Paired with colourful fruit and veggies it's a great way to tick off several nutrition boxes in one dish. You can also swap the chicken for grilled halloumi, salmon or tofu, making this recipe a flexible option.

200g carrots, peeled and cut diagonally into 1cm slices
2 tsp extra virgin olive oil
½ small red onion, finely chopped
½ tsp cumin seeds
120g cooked puy lentils
30g baby spinach, shredded
150g cooked chicken breast, sliced
2 tbsp Greek-style yoghurt
Small squeeze of lemon juice
Chopped coriander or mint
2 tbsp pomegranate seeds
Sea salt and black pepper

1. Preheat the oven to 200°C/180°C fan/Gas 6. Toss the carrots with 1 teaspoon of the olive oil and some salt and pepper. Roast for 20–25 minutes until tender and slightly golden.
2. When the carrots are cooked, heat the remaining oil in a non-stick frying pan and cook the onion with the cumin seeds for 2–3 minutes until soft and fragrant.
3. Add the lentils, roasted carrots and baby spinach and cook for 2 minutes until the baby spinach has wilted. Add the chicken and a splash of water, then cook for another 2 minutes.
4. Mix the yoghurt with the lemon juice and a pinch of salt.
5. Serve the lentil salad warm, topped with the yoghurt drizzle, and fresh herbs and pomegranate seeds.

➔ NUTRIENTS MORE THAN 15% RDA
Iron, potassium, zinc, vitamin C.

➔ NUTRIENTS MORE THAN 30% RDA
Folate, phosphorus, selenium, vitamins A, B3, B6, K.

➔ PROTEIN BOOSTER
Add extra chicken, lentils or yoghurt.

➔ STORAGE
This will keep in the fridge for 3 days.

➔ NUTRIENT BOOSTER
Add defrosted frozen peas or pumpkin seeds.

➔ TAKE TO WORK
Yes – serve warm or cold.

➔ NOTES
You can use tinned green lentils to save time; to cook from scratch 60g dried puy lentils will give you 180g cooked. If you don't have leftover cooked chicken, roast or poach 200g raw chicken to get 150g cooked.

Baked Chicken with Creamy Coconut Brown Rice, Peas and Spinach

This creamy baked chicken dish is warm, satisfying and gentle on digestion – ideal for smaller appetites. The rice is cooked in coconut milk with lime for a subtle Thai-inspired flavour, then stirred through with spinach and peas for extra fibre and colour. Peas are a handy source of plant protein and help boost the nutritional value of this simple one-pan meal.

1 tsp extra virgin olive oil
¼ tsp ground turmeric
¼ tsp smoked paprika
1 small garlic clove, grated
1 tsp soy sauce
200g skinless chicken breast
70g short-grain brown rice, rinsed
100ml coconut milk
Zest and juice of ½ lime
75g frozen peas, defrosted
Small handful of spinach, shredded
Sea salt and black pepper

1. Preheat the oven to 200°C/180°C fan/Gas 6.
2. Mix the olive oil, turmeric, paprika, garlic, soy sauce and some salt and pepper in a bowl. Rub over the chicken.
3. Place the chicken in a small baking dish and roast for about 20 minutes, or until golden and cooked through.
4. Meanwhile, combine the rice, coconut milk, 100ml water, lime zest and juice in a saucepan with a pinch of salt. Bring to a simmer, then cover and cook gently for about 25 minutes, or until the liquid is absorbed and the rice is tender. Add more water if needed.
5. Add the peas and spinach, cover and steam off the heat for 5 minutes. Fluff with a fork and check the seasoning.
6. Slice the chicken and serve over the warm coconut rice.

➔ NUTRIENTS MORE THAN 15% RDA
Magnesium, zinc, vitamins A, B1, B12, C, K.

➔ NUTRIENTS MORE THAN 30% RDA
Folate, phosphorus, selenium, vitamins B3, B6.

➔ PROTEIN BOOSTER
Add extra chicken. Swap the peas for edamame beans.

➔ NUTRIENT BOOSTER
Serve with a dollop of kimchi or a sprinkle of pumpkin seeds.

➔ TAKE TO WORK
Yes – enjoy warmed up.

➔ NOTE
I prefer using short-grain brown rice as it is less husky than other types.

SERVES 2

400 KCAL

29G PROTEIN

6.3G FIBRE

Turkey Keema Curry with Wholemeal Pitta

This turkey keema is a quick, protein-packed dinner that delivers bold flavour with minimal effort. It's a lighter take on a traditional curry, using lean turkey mince, but choose the thigh as it is much more succulent than the breast. The pitta makes it easy to scoop and eat, while flaked almonds add crunch and richness. Feel free to scatter over some chopped green chillies before serving if you can take a bit of heat.

---

2 tsp extra virgin olive oil
200g turkey thigh mince (8% fat)
½ small onion, finely chopped
1 garlic clove, finely chopped
2cm piece of fresh ginger, peeled and grated
Pinch of sea salt
2 tsp ground cumin
2 tsp ground coriander
1 tsp ground turmeric
200ml chicken stock
125g frozen peas
Small handful of spinach
Juice of ¼ lemon
1 tbsp chopped coriander
1 tbsp toasted flaked almonds
1 wholemeal pitta bread, halved

1. Heat the oil in a non-stick saucepan pan over a medium heat. Add the turkey and cook for 5 minutes, breaking it up with a spoon, until browned.
2. Reduce the heat and add the onion, garlic and ginger and salt. Cook for another 2 minutes, then add the ground spices. Cook for another minute, stirring frequently.
3. Pour in the chicken stock and simmer gently for 15 minutes.
4. Add the peas and spinach and cook for a final 5 minutes, stirring occasionally to help the spinach to wilt.
5. Stir in the lemon juice and coriander before serving warm, topped with flaked almonds and with ½ wholemeal pitta on the side.

➔ NUTRIENTS MORE THAN 15% RDA
Iodine, iron, magnesium, potassium, vitamins A, B1, B2, C.

➔ NUTRIENTS MORE THAN 30% RDA
Folate, phosphorus, selenium, zinc, vitamins B3, B6, B12, K.

➔ PROTEIN BOOSTER
Add a dollop of skyr or Greek yoghurt. Add leftover cooked puy lentils.

➔ STORAGE
This will last for up to 3 days in the fridge and 3 months in the freezer stored in an airtight container.

➔ NUTRIENT BOOSTER
Add more spinach or a finely diced green pepper when cooking the onions. Serve with a chopped salad of tomato, cucumber and red onion.

➔ TAKE TO WORK
Yes – it can be warmed up or eaten cold.

➔ NOTE
You can also serve this with brown rice, quinoa, cauliflower rice or in baby gem lettuce cups.

Tandoori Salmon with Cucumber, Chickpea and Mint Salad

This dish combines protein-rich salmon with fibre-packed chickpeas and crisp vegetables, making it both satisfying and light. The yoghurt-based tandoori marinade adds flavour without heaviness, while the fresh mint and lemon keep the salad refreshing. It's a balanced option that delivers over 25g of protein in a modest portion, supporting muscle health while being gentle on the appetite.

1 tbsp Greek-style yoghurt
Juice of ½ lemon
1 tsp tandoori spice mix (or 1 tsp garam masala + ½ tsp smoked paprika)
200g skinless salmon fillets
6cm piece of cucumber, diced
1 small carrot, grated
3 radishes, thinly sliced
120g tinned chickpeas, rinsed and drained
1 tbsp chopped mint
1 tbsp chopped coriander
1 tsp extra virgin olive oil
½ tsp cumin seeds
Sea salt

For the dressing
2 tbsp Greek-style yoghurt
Squeeze of lemon juice
1 tbsp chopped mint

1. Preheat the grill to medium-high.
2. In a small bowl, mix the yoghurt, half the lemon juice, the tandoori spice (or garam masala and smoked paprika) and a pinch of salt. Rub over the salmon fillets and set aside to marinate for 10–15 minutes (or up to 2 hours in the fridge).
3. Place the salmon on a foil-lined tray and grill for 8–10 minutes, or until lightly charred and just cooked through.
4. Meanwhile, combine the cucumber, carrot, radishes, chickpeas, mint, coriander, olive oil and remaining lemon juice in a bowl. Toss to mix. Toast the cumin seeds in a dry pan for 1 minute and sprinkle over the salad.
5. In a separate bowl, mix all the dressing ingredients together with a pinch of salt.
6. Serve the salmon with the salad and a spoon of yoghurt dressing.

➔ NUTRIENTS MORE THAN 15% RDA
Iron, magnesium, potassium, zinc, vitamins A, B1, C, K.

➔ NUTRIENTS MORE THAN 30% RDA
Folate, iodine, phosphorus, selenium, vitamins B3, B6, B12, D. Contains omega-3.

➔ PROTEIN BOOSTER
Add extra salmon or swap half the chickpeas for edamame beans, or sprinkle over some mixed seeds at the end.

➔ STORAGE
The salad will keep in the fridge for up to 3 days in an airtight container and works well with any type of protein.

➔ NUTRIENT BOOSTER
Serve with a spoon of sauerkraut or red onions soaked in lemon juice. Add defrosted frozen peas to the salad.

➔ TAKE TO WORK
Yes.

➔ NOTE
Try using mackerel or trout instead of salmon.

Brown Rice Bowl with Teriyaki Turkey and Greens

This high-protein lunch bowl is a simple yet nourishing option, ideal for batch-cooking or taking to work. Lean turkey mince delivers a generous hit of protein, while the rice and edamame provide slow-releasing energy and fibre. Pak choi brings vitamin K and folate, and adding extra wilted greens like spinach or kale can easily boost the nutrient content.

- 1 tsp sesame oil
- 1 garlic clove, grated
- 2cm piece of fresh ginger, peeled and grated
- 200g turkey thigh mince (8% fat)
- 1 tbsp soy sauce, plus extra for drizzling
- 1 tsp honey
- 1 tsp rice vinegar
- 50g carrot, grated
- 50g shelled edamame beans (fresh or frozen)
- 2 small heads of pak choi, halved lengthways
- 180g cooked short-grain brown rice
- 1 tbsp sesame seeds
- 1 spring onion, thinly sliced

1. Heat the sesame oil in a saucepan over a medium heat. Add the garlic and ginger and sauté for 1 minute, then add the turkey mince and cook for 5 minutes until browned, breaking it up as it cooks.
2. Stir in the soy sauce, honey, rice vinegar and 1 teaspoon of water (leave out if your pan already has enough liquid). Cook, uncovered, for 3–4 minutes until thickened and slightly sticky. Add the grated carrot and edamame and warm through for 2 minutes.
3. Place a lidded frying pan over a medium heat then add the pak choi, cut sides down. Add a big splash of water or chicken stock, then cover and steam for 2–3 minutes. Drizzle with a little soy sauce when cooked.
4. Heat the rice in the microwave or pour over some boiling water.
5. Serve the turkey over the brown rice with pak choi on the side. Top with sesame seeds and spring onion slices.

➔ NUTRIENTS MORE THAN 15% RDA
Iron, potassium, vitamins A, B1, B2, C.

➔ NUTRIENTS MORE THAN 30% RDA
Folate, magnesium, phosphorus, selenium, zinc, vitamins B3, B6, B12, K.

➔ PROTEIN BOOSTER
Add extra turkey mince or sprinkle with pumpkin seeds.

➔ STORAGE
The turkey will keep in the fridge for 3 days and in the freezer for up to 2 months in an airtight container.

➔ NUTRIENT BOOSTER
Add spinach or kale (trimmed from the stalk) to the pan with the pak choi. Add brown rice.

➔ TAKE TO WORK
Yes.

➔ NOTES
If you are using a 500g pack of turkey mince then scale the quantities up to make a bigger batch and freeze the rest for later. If you are cooking your rice from scratch, 60g dried rice will give you 180g cooked.

Mini Turkey and Courgette Meatballs with Red Pepper Sauce and Courgetti

These light, protein-packed meatballs are ideal if you're working with a smaller appetite. The addition of ground almonds not only helps bind the mixture but also boosts the nutrient density with fibre, healthy fats and vitamin E. Served with a fresh red pepper sauce and soft courgetti, it's a simple, nourishing meal.

200g turkey thigh mince (less than 8% fat)
100g courgette, grated and squeezed in kitchen paper to remove excess water
1 small garlic clove, grated
2 tbsp ground almonds
½ tsp dried oregano
1½ tsp extra virgin olive oil
1 small red pepper, finely chopped
150ml passata
Small squeeze of lemon juice
½ tsp honey
Few basil leaves, torn
Sea salt and black pepper
300g courgette, spiralised or peeled with a julienne peeler, to serve

1. In a bowl, mix the turkey mince with the grated courgette, garlic, ground almonds, oregano, salt and pepper. Mix very well then form into 8 meatballs using about a tablespoon of mixture for each one.
2. Heat ½ teaspoon of olive oil in a small non-stick frying pan over a medium heat and cook the meatballs for 6–8 minutes, turning often until golden and cooked through. Transfer the meatballs to a plate lined with kitchen paper. Wipe the pan clean.
3. Heat the remaining teaspoon of olive oil in the pan, then add the chopped red pepper and sauté for 3–5 minutes. Add the passata, lemon juice, honey and torn basil, then season. Simmer for 5 minutes then add the meatballs back to the pan and cook for another 2 minutes to warm them through.
4. To prepare the courgetti, place the spiralised courgette in a bowl and pour over just-boiled water from a kettle. Let it sit for 1–2 minutes to soften, then drain and pat dry.
5. Serve the meatballs over the warm courgetti.

➔ NUTRIENTS MORE THAN 15% RDA
Potassium, vitamins E, K.

➔ NUTRIENTS MORE THAN 30% RDA
Folate, phosphorus, zinc, vitamins A, B3, B6, B12, C.

➔ PROTEIN BOOSTER
Add extra turkey to make extra meatballs. Serve with quinoa instead of courgetti.

➔ STORAGE
The meatballs will last up to 3 days in the fridge in an airtight container.

➔ NUTRIENT BOOSTER
Add extra vegetables to the sauce such as spinach, chopped cherry tomatoes or diced aubergine.

➔ TAKE TO WORK
Yes – reheat before eating.

➔ NOTES
Go for a good-quality passata brand (I like Mutti). You can also serve this with brown rice or just a wholemeal pitta or mini wrap.

Stuffed Courgettes with Harissa Lamb, Feta and Tomato Sauce

This light, flavour-packed dish shows how stuffed vegetables can be a satisfying alternative to heavier options like rice or pasta. Courgettes make a great base for a gently spiced lamb filling, balanced with the sweetness of tomato and a touch of feta. It's a nourishing meal that's rich in taste but light on the stomach – perfect when you want something wholesome without feeling overly full.

2 large courgettes (500g)
1 tsp extra virgin olive oil
200g lean lamb mince (10% fat)
1 large garlic clove, finely chopped
1 tsp ground cumin
2 tsp rose harissa (or use regular harissa)
1 x 400g tin chopped tomatoes
1 tbsp flaked almonds
20g feta cheese, crumbled
1 tbsp chopped flat-leaf parsley
Sea salt

1. Preheat the oven to 200°C/180°C fan/Gas 6. Halve the courgettes lengthways and scoop out the soft inner flesh, leaving a ½cm shell. Finely chop the scooped-out flesh and set aside.
2. Heat the olive oil in a non-stick saucepan over a medium heat. Add the lamb mince and chopped courgette flesh and cook for 5–6 minutes, breaking it up with a spoon, until lightly browned.
3. Stir in the garlic, cumin and 1 teaspoon of the harissa. Cook for another 2 minutes.
4. Pour the chopped tomatoes into a baking dish and stir in the remaining teaspoon of harissa. Nestle the courgette shells into the sauce and fill each one with the lamb mixture.
5. Cover the dish loosely with foil and bake for 20 minutes. Remove the foil and roast uncovered for another 20–25 minutes, or until the courgettes are tender and the sauce has thickened.
6. While the courgettes finish roasting, toast the flaked almonds in a dry pan over a medium heat for 2–3 minutes until golden.
7. Just before serving, scatter the feta, parsley and toasted almonds over the stuffed courgettes. Serve with a small mixed salad.

➔ NUTRIENTS MORE THAN 15% RDA
Folate, phosphorus, vitamins A, B2, B3, B12, C, K.

➔ NUTRIENTS MORE THAN 30% RDA
Calcium, iron, magnesium, potassium, zinc, vitamins B1, B6, E.

➔ PROTEIN BOOSTER
Add a dollop of skyr or Greek yoghurt or a few tablespoons of cooked quinoa to the lamb mixture.

➔ STORAGE
The mince can be kept in the fridge for up to 3 days and frozen for up to 3 months in an airtight container.

➔ NUTRIENT BOOSTER
Add finely chopped red pepper or sliced spinach to the chopped tomatoes. Top with pumpkin seeds.

➔ TAKE TO WORK
Yes – the dish can be warmed up at work or the mince can be served warm with rice or in a small wholemeal wrap.

➔ NOTE
If you are using a 500g pack of mince, scale the recipe up and freeze.

Seared Mackerel with Spiced Chickpeas and Parsley

Don't be put off by fresh mackerel: it's a budget-friendly oily fish that's packed with nutrients such as omega-3 and far milder in flavour than the tinned variety. When cooked fresh, it's light, tender and really easy to prepare. This recipe pairs crispy-skinned mackerel with warming spiced chickpeas and a zesty parsley drizzle for a dish that's simple, satisfying and full of goodness.

3 tsp extra virgin olive oil
1 tsp finely chopped parsley
Wedge of lemon
½ red small onion, finely chopped
1 garlic clove, finely chopped
1 tsp smoked paprika
80g tinned chickpeas, rinsed and drained
1 x 225g tin chopped tomatoes
1 tbsp tomato purée
200g fresh mackerel fillets, skin scored
Sea salt

1. In a small bowl, combine 2 teaspoons of the olive oil with the chopped parsley, a squeeze of lemon juice and a pinch of salt to make a simple drizzle. Set aside.
2. Heat the remaining teaspoon of olive oil in a non-stick saucepan over a medium heat. Sauté the onion and garlic for 2–3 minutes until soft.
3. Add the smoked paprika and cook for another 20 seconds. Then add the chickpeas, chopped tomatoes and tomato purée. Simmer for 7–8 minutes until thickened. Season with salt and a squeeze of lemon juice.
4. Meanwhile, place a non-stick frying pan over a medium-high heat. Cook the mackerel fillets skin side down for 3–4 minutes until crispy, then flip and cook for 1–2 minutes more.
5. Spoon the warm chickpeas onto plates, top with the mackerel and finish with the parsley drizzle.

➔ NUTRIENTS MORE THAN 15% RDA
Folate, iodine, vitamins C, K.

➔ NUTRIENTS MORE THAN 30% RDA
Phosphorus, selenium, vitamins A, B6, B12, D. Contains omega-3.

➔ PROTEIN BOOSTER
Add extra mackerel or stir yoghurt through the chickpeas.

➔ STORAGE
The chickpeas will last for 3 days in the fridge in an airtight container.

➔ NUTRIENT BOOSTER
Add sliced baby spinach or defrosted frozen peas to the chickpeas.

➔ TAKE TO WORK
Yes – reheat.

➔ NOTE
You can swap mackerel for any type of fish, such as salmon or cod.

SERVES 2

395 KCAL

28.3G PROTEIN

8.3G FIBRE

Chilli and Fennel Pork Stew with Tahini Drizzle

This gently spiced stew is full of flavour and comfort without being too heavy. Lean pork mince is a healthy, high-protein alternative to beef, and pairs beautifully with fennel, sweet red pepper and creamy beans. Tahini adds a small boost of calcium and protein, making it a useful addition to this satisfying, spoonable meal.

2 tsp extra virgin olive oil
120g fennel, finely diced (save the fronds)
1 garlic clove, grated
1 tsp fennel seeds
½ tsp chilli flakes (or to taste)
200g lean pork mince (5% fat)
120g chopped tinned tomatoes
120g tinned cannellini beans, rinsed and drained
100g red pepper, thinly sliced
150ml vegetable stock
Zest of ½ lemon
4 tsp tahini
Sea salt and black pepper

1. Heat the olive oil in a non-stick saucepan over a medium heat. Add the fennel and cook for 5 minutes until softened. Stir in the garlic, fennel seeds and chilli flakes and cook for 1 minute more until fragrant.
2. Add the pork mince and cook for 5 minutes, breaking it up with a spoon until browned.
3. Stir in the chopped tomatoes, cannellini beans, red pepper and stock and simmer, uncovered, for 15 minutes until the stew has thickened.
4. Stir in the lemon zest and season with salt and pepper.
5. In a small bowl, whisk the tahini with a splash of warm water to create a drizzle consistency.
6. Divide the stew between 2 bowls and spoon over the tahini drizzle. Garnish with the reserved fennel fronds.

➔ NUTRIENTS MORE THAN 15% RDA
Folate, phosphorus, potassium, zinc, vitamins A, B1, B12, C, K.

➔ NUTRIENTS MORE THAN 30% RDA
Calcium, chromium, iron, magnesium, selenium, vitamins B1, B2, B6.

➔ PROTEIN BOOSTER
Add extra beans or a dollop of skyr or Greek yoghurt.

➔ STORAGE
This will keep for up to 3 days in the fridge or 2 months in the freezer stored in an airtight container.

➔ NUTRIENT BOOSTER
Serve with short-grain brown rice or quinoa. Add grated carrot to cook with the fennel.

➔ TAKE TO WORK
Yes – keep the tahini separate. Reheat before eating.

➔ NOTE
You can swap the chilli flakes for 'nduja or harissa paste.

Marinated Tofu and Sweet Potato Skewers with Lemon Yoghurt Dip

These skewers are a light and nourishing option that you can enjoy on their own, with a side of rice or stuffed into a wholemeal wrap. Tofu is more than just a protein source, it also provides calcium, iron and healthy fats, while sweet potato adds natural sweetness, fibre and slow-releasing carbs to help keep you full. The roasted red pepper marinade brings smoky depth and umami.

For the skewers

150g sweet potato, peeled and chopped into 2–3cm pieces

1 tsp extra virgin olive oil

150g firm tofu, pressed and cut into chunks

For the marinade

1 large jarred roasted red pepper (about 100g drained weight)

1 tsp harissa paste

Small squeeze of lemon juice

1 tbsp chopped coriander

Sea salt and black pepper

For the lemon yoghurt dip

2 tbsp natural yoghurt or fortified soya yoghurt

Small squeeze of lemon juice

1. Preheat the oven to 200°C/180°C fan/Gas 6 and line a baking tray with parchment paper.
2. Toss the sweet potato in half the olive oil and a pinch of salt. Spread onto the tray and roast for 10 minutes.
3. Meanwhile, blend the red pepper, harissa, lemon juice, coriander and a pinch of salt and pepper into a thick marinade. Place the tofu chunks in a bowl, pour over the marinade and toss gently to coat.
4. Once the sweet potato has roasted for 10 minutes, remove the tray from the oven and allow the sweet potato to cool slightly. Add it to the bowl with the tofu and gently toss again.
5. When cool enough to handle, thread the tofu and sweet potato onto skewers. Place back on the tray, drizzle with the remaining ½ teaspoon of olive oil and roast for another 15–20 minutes, turning once, until golden and slightly crisp.
6. While the skewers roast, mix the yoghurt with the lemon juice and a pinch of salt to make the dipping sauce.
7. Serve 2 skewers per person with the lemon yoghurt on the side.

➔ NUTRIENTS MORE THAN 15% RDA
Calcium, iron, potassium, vitamins B2, B3, B6, E.

➔ NUTRIENTS MORE THAN 30% RDA
Folate, phosphorus, vitamins A, C.

➔ PROTEIN BOOSTER
Add extra tofu or serve with a salad containing edamame beans and seeds.

➔ NUTRIENT BOOSTER
Add red pepper to the skewer or serve on a small bed of short-grain brown rice.

➔ TAKE TO WORK
Not suitable.

➔ NOTE
If 2 skewers feels overwhelming for your appetite, just serve one.

Sweetcorn and Potato Chowder with Cod, Paprika and Cumin

This nourishing chowder is gently spiced and naturally thickened with potato, making it feel satisfying even in a smaller portion. Sweetcorn adds sweetness, while soft flakes of cod bring lean protein to the dish. Fish and seafood are also a good source of iodine, a mineral that supports healthy thyroid function and energy metabolism. A sprinkle of chilli flakes on top works beautifully. You can use any white fish.

- 2 tsp extra virgin olive oil
- ½ small onion, finely chopped
- 1 garlic clove, grated
- 200g Maris Piper potatoes, peeled and diced into small cubes
- 150g sweetcorn (tinned or frozen and defrosted)
- 1 tsp smoked paprika
- ½ tsp ground cumin
- 300ml vegetable stock
- 200g skinless cod fillet, cut into chunks (fresh or frozen and defrosted)
- 50ml milk
- 1 tbsp chopped flat-leaf parsley, plus extra to garnish
- Chilli flakes (optional)
- Sea salt and black pepper

1. Heat the olive oil in a non-stick saucepan over a medium heat. Add the onion and garlic and sauté for 3–5 minutes until softened and fragrant.
2. Stir in the potatoes, sweetcorn, smoked paprika and cumin. Pour in the stock and bring to a boil, then reduce the heat and simmer for 10 minutes, before adding the cod pieces. Simmer gently for another 8–10 minutes until the fish is cooked through and the potatoes are soft.
3. Lightly mash with a potato masher to create a chunky texture.
4. Stir in the milk and parsley then season with salt and black pepper. Add a splash more stock or water if you prefer a thinner consistency.
5. Serve warm, garnished with chopped parsley and chilli flakes (if using).

➔ NUTRIENTS MORE THAN 15% RDA
Calcium, iron, magnesium, niacin, potassium, zinc, vitamins B1, B2, B6.

➔ NUTRIENTS MORE THAN 30% RDA
Folate, iodine, phosphorus, selenium, vitamins A, B12, C, K.

➔ PROTEIN BOOSTER
Add extra cod. Add a dollop of skyr or Greek yoghurt. Switch to high-protein milk.

➔ STORAGE
This will keep for up to 2 days in the fridge or 2 months in the freezer stored in an airtight container.

➔ NUTRIENT BOOSTER
Stir in leftover cannellini beans, spinach or cooked short-grain brown rice. Serve with small slices of seeded wholemeal bread.

➔ TAKE TO WORK
Yes.

➔ NOTES
High-protein milks like Arla and Supernutrio contain nearly twice the protein of regular milk. They're made by filtering out some of the water and sugar (lactose), which naturally concentrates the protein.

Quick Chicken and Carrot Broth with Spelt

This simple one-pot broth is warm, comforting and full of goodness, ideal for days when your appetite is low, but you still want something satisfying. It's made with quick-cook spelt, a high-fibre wholegrain that softens quickly while adding texture and slow-release energy. Everything cooks together in one pan, making it a low-effort meal that still feels balanced and nourishing.

- 90g quick-cook spelt
- 2 tsp extra virgin olive oil
- 1 small red onion, finely chopped
- 1 garlic clove, grated
- ½ tsp ground coriander
- 2 large skinless and boneless chicken thighs (200g)
- 2 medium carrots (240g), peeled and thinly sliced diagonally
- 1 bay leaf
- 500ml chicken stock
- Small handful of flat-leaf parsley, chopped
- Sea salt and black pepper

1. Place the spelt in a bowl, cover with water and soak for 10 minutes while you prep the rest of the ingredients.
2. Heat the olive oil in a saucepan over a medium heat. Sauté the onion and garlic until soft, about 2 minutes, then add the ground coriander and cook for another 1 minute.
3. Drain the spelt and add it to the pan with chicken, carrots, bay leaf and chicken stock. Bring to the boil, then reduce the heat and simmer gently. Cook for about 30 minutes, or until the spelt is very tender and chicken is cooked through. Season to taste with salt and pepper.
4. Place a cooked chicken thigh into each bowl, then ladle over the broth and spelt and scatter over the chopped parsley. Eat straight away as the spelt will continue to absorb the broth.

➔ NUTRIENTS MORE THAN 15% RDA
Calcium, iron, magnesium, potassium, selenium, zinc, vitamins B1, B2, B6, B12.

➔ NUTRIENTS MORE THAN 30% RDA
Folate, phosphorus, vitamins A, B3, C, K.

➔ PROTEIN BOOSTER
Add extra chicken or a dollop of skyr or Greek yoghurt. You can also mash soft white beans and stir them through the dish at the end.

➔ NUTRIENT BOOSTER
Add very finely shredded cabbage just before broth is cooked.

➔ TAKE TO WORK
Yes – serve warmed up but remember that the spelt will continue to absorb liquid and swell so it will be thicker.

➔ NOTE
Make sure you use quick-cook spelt for this recipe.

Creamy Millet, Pea and Leek Bowl with Poached Haddock

This comforting bowl is a great alternative to mashed potato or rice-based dishes. Millet cooks to a naturally creamy texture and is a high-fibre grain that's easy to digest and ideal when your appetite is low. The mellow base pairs well with sweet leeks, peas and gently smoked haddock, while a mustard yoghurt adds a sharp lift. This recipe also works well with any white fish or even smoked mackerel for a boost of omega-3.

50g millet
200ml vegetable stock
200ml milk
200g undyed skinless smoked haddock fillets
1 tbsp extra virgin olive oil
1 large leek, halved lengthways and thinly sliced
50g frozen peas, defrosted
Zest of ½ lemon
1 tbsp finely chopped dill or flat-leaf parsley
Sea salt and black pepper

For the mustard yoghurt
1 tbsp natural yoghurt
1 tsp Dijon mustard
Squeeze of lemon juice

1. Rinse the millet, then add it to a saucepan with the vegetable stock and 50ml of the milk. Bring to a gentle simmer over a medium heat, cover with a lid, and cook for 20–25 minutes, stirring occasionally, until creamy and tender. Add a splash of water if needed. Once cooked, cover and set aside to keep warm.
2. Rinse out the pan, then add the remaining milk and 150ml water. Bring to a gentle simmer, then add the haddock and poach for 5–7 minutes, or until the fish flakes easily.
3. Meanwhile, heat the olive oil in a non-stick frying pan over a low heat. Add the sliced leek and cook for 10–12 minutes until soft and sweet.
4. Stir the cooked leeks into the millet along with the peas, lemon zest and chopped herbs. Season to taste with salt and pepper, then cover and set aside.
5. In a small bowl, mix together the yoghurt, Dijon mustard and a squeeze of lemon juice.
6. To serve, spoon the millet into bowls, top with the poached fish and finish with the mustard yoghurt.

➔ NUTRIENTS MORE THAN 15% RDA
Calcium, iron, magnesium, potassium, zinc, vitamins B1, B2, B3, B6, D.

➔ NUTRIENTS MORE THAN 30% RDA
Iodine, phosphorus, selenium, vitamins A, B12, C, K.

➔ PROTEIN BOOSTER
Add extra haddock. Add more yoghurt or switch to high-protein milk.

➔ NUTRIENT BOOSTER
Serve with a mixed salad.

➔ TAKE TO WORK
Not suitable.

➔ NOTE
Millet isn't always stocked in supermarkets, but you can usually find it in health food shops or online.

Kitchari-style Lentil and Rice Bowl with Coconut, Lime and Pumpkin Seeds

This dish is a bit like a dhal – warm, soft and gently spiced with turmeric, cumin and mustard seeds. While it's not as high in protein as some of the other recipes in this book, it's a good option when you're after something nourishing and nurturing. This bowl is the ultimate comfort food: easy to eat, soothing on the stomach and full of feel-good ingredients.

- 40g basmati rice
- 60g dried red lentils
- 2 tsp extra virgin olive oil
- ½ tsp mustard seeds
- ½ small onion, finely chopped
- 1 garlic clove, grated
- 2cm piece of fresh ginger, peeled and grated
- ½ tsp ground cumin
- ½ tsp ground turmeric
- 450ml vegetable stock
- 2 tbsp coconut cream
- Juice of ½ lime
- Small handful of coriander leaves, chopped
- 2 tbsp pumpkin seeds
- Sea salt and black pepper

1. Rinse the rice and lentils thoroughly in a sieve under cold water.
2. Heat the olive oil in a non-stick saucepan set over a medium heat. Add the mustard seeds and cook until they start to pop, then add the onion, garlic and ginger and cook gently for 2–3 minutes until softened. Add the cumin and turmeric and cook for another 1 minute.
3. Stir in the rinsed rice and lentils, then pour in the stock. Bring to the boil, reduce the heat and simmer gently, partially covered, for 20–25 minutes, stirring occasionally until the mixture is soft and porridge-like.
4. Stir in the coconut cream, lime juice and coriander and season well with salt and pepper.
5. Spoon into bowls and top with pumpkin seeds.

➔ NUTRIENTS MORE THAN 15% RDA
Calcium, potassium, vitamins A, B1.

➔ NUTRIENTS MORE THAN 30% RDA
Folate, iron, magnesium, phosphorus, zinc, vitamin B6.

➔ PROTEIN BOOSTER
Add chickpeas with the rice and lentils. You can also top with leftover cooked chicken or prawns.

➔ STORAGE
This keeps for 3 days in the fridge and 2 months in the freezer stored in an airtight container.

➔ NUTRIENT BOOSTER
Stir in baby spinach when you add the coconut cream. Add more pumpkin seeds.

➔ TAKE TO WORK
Yes.

➔ NOTES
This recipe does not work as well with brown rice.

Creamy Parmesan Orzo with Wilted Greens, Beans and Lemon

Sometimes, you just need a bowl of something warm, creamy and deeply comforting – and that's where this simple orzo dish comes in, although its rich, cheesy texture may feel a little heavy for some people on GLP-1 medications. However, pasta can be the ultimate soothing food, especially when your appetite is low and you're looking for something to gently tempt you back into eating.

---

1 tsp extra virgin olive oil
6 cherry tomatoes
1 small garlic clove, finely chopped
75g orzo
300ml vegetable stock, warmed
Large handful of baby spinach or Swiss chard/kale, hard stalks cut off, leaves shredded
60g tinned cannellini beans, rinsed and drained
40g grated Parmesan cheese
Zest of ½ large lemon, plus juice of ¼
2 tbsp Greek yoghurt
Sea salt and black pepper

1. Heat the olive oil in a non-stick saucepan over a medium heat. Add the cherry tomatoes and garlic and cook gently for 2 minutes.
2. Add in the orzo and cook for 1 minute, stirring to coat in the garlicky oil.
3. Gradually add the warm stock, stirring frequently, and cook for about 12 minutes until the orzo is tender and most of the liquid is absorbed. Squash the tomatoes if they haven't burst.
4. Add the greens and cannellini beans to the pan and cook for a final 2 minutes to allow the beans to soften and the greens to wilt.
5. Remove from the heat and stir in the Parmesan, lemon zest, lemon juice and Greek yoghurt.
6. Season to taste with salt and pepper and serve warm.

➔ NUTRIENTS MORE THAN 15% RDA
Magnesium, potassium, selenium, vitamins B1, B2, B3, B6, B12.

➔ NUTRIENTS MORE THAN 30% RDA
Calcium, folate, phosphorus, vitamins A, C, K.

➔ PROTEIN BOOSTER
Top with a soft-boiled egg, swap the yoghurt for skyr or stir in a spoonful of blended/mashed silken tofu.

➔ NUTRIENT BOOSTER
Add a handful of defrosted frozen peas.

➔ TAKE TO WORK
Yes – can be eaten at room temperature or reheated.

➔ NOTES
You can use quick-cook spelt in place of orzo, but you may need to add more stock while it cooks.

Comforting Bowl with Spelt and Egg

This comforting bowl is simple, satisfying and packed with umami thanks to mushrooms, miso and Parmesan. It's a great example of how you can eat well with minimal effort. While eggs are often praised for their protein, they also provide a source of at least 10 essential nutrients, including choline and vitamins A and B12. The spelt adds substance and is naturally higher in protein than many common grains like rice or couscous, along with fibre, magnesium and B vitamins, making this dish both nourishing and delicious.

- 2 tsp extra virgin olive oil
- 1 garlic clove, grated
- 120g chestnut mushrooms, finely chopped
- 100g quick-cook pearled spelt
- 300ml vegetable stock
- 1 tsp white miso paste
- 1 tbsp Greek yoghurt or skyr
- 1 tsp grated Parmesan cheese
- 2 poached eggs
- Chopped chives (optional)
- Black pepper

1. Heat the olive oil in a saucepan over a medium heat. Add the garlic and mushrooms and cook for 5–6 minutes until softened and reduced.
2. Stir in the spelt and cook for 1 minute to toast slightly.
3. Add the stock, bring to a simmer and cook, uncovered, for about 20 minutes, giving it a good stir occasionally, until the spelt is tender and most of the liquid has been absorbed. Add a few more tablespoons of water if it dries out. It should still have some bite.
4. Stir in the miso paste, yoghurt and Parmesan and season with black pepper.
5. Serve warm in shallow bowls topped with a poached egg and scattered with chives (if using).

➔ NUTRIENTS MORE THAN 15% RDA
Calcium, iron, magnesium, selenium, vitamins A, B2, B6.

➔ NUTRIENTS MORE THAN 30% RDA
Folate, phosphorus, vitamins B12, K.

➔ PROTEIN BOOSTER
Add an extra egg or more Greek yoghurt or stir through defrosted frozen peas.

➔ NUTRIENT BOOSTER
Add thinly sliced leeks to the pan with the mushrooms. Serve with a side of wilted spinach.

➔ TAKE TO WORK
Not suitable.

➔ NOTE
Make sure you use quick-cook spelt.

SERVES 2

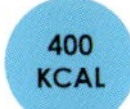
400 KCAL

17G PROTEIN

10G FIBRE

Soft Lentil and Nut Patties with Creamy Avocado Drizzle

These soft, savoury patties are a great way to get more plant protein and fibre into your day without making a heavy meal. Lentils, nuts and a little tahini bring a nutty richness, while the creamy avocado dressing adds freshness and healthy fats. These plant foods are a good way to get fibre into your diet if you don't eat meat. It works well for smaller appetites thanks to the soft texture and vibrant flavours.

---

2 tsp extra virgin olive oil
½ small onion, finely chopped
1 garlic clove, grated
150g mushrooms, finely chopped
150g tinned green or brown lentils, rinsed and drained
30g ground almonds
4 walnuts, finely chopped
1 tsp tahini
1 egg, lightly beaten
½ tsp dried thyme
Sea salt and black pepper

For the avocado dressing
½ ripe avocado
Juice of ½ lemon
2 tbsp natural yoghurt

1. Heat the olive oil in a non-stick frying pan over a medium heat. Add the onion, garlic and mushrooms and cook for 6–8 minutes until softened and most of the moisture has evaporated.
2. Lightly mash the lentils in a bowl. Add the cooked mushroom mixture, ground almonds, chopped walnuts, tahini, egg, thyme and a good pinch of salt and pepper. Mix thoroughly until well combined. The mixture will be quite moist. Shape into 4 small patties.
3. Wipe the pan clean and add a little more oil if needed. Fry the patties over a medium-high heat for 3–4 minutes on each side until golden brown.
4. Blend the avocado, lemon juice, yoghurt and 1 tablespoon of water until smooth. Add a little more water to loosen if needed and season with salt.
5. Gently lift the patties out of the pan and serve on small plates with a generous spoonful of the avocado dressing.

➔ NUTRIENTS MORE THAN 15% RDA
Calcium, iron, magnesium, potassium, zinc, vitamins A, B1, B2, B3, B6, B12, E.

➔ NUTRIENTS MORE THAN 30% RDA
Folate, phosphorus, vitamins C, K.

➔ PROTEIN BOOSTER
Swap the yoghurt for silken tofu in the dressing or add cooked quinoa to the mushroom patty.

➔ NUTRIENT BOOSTER
Add sesame seeds or nutritional yeast to the patty. Serve with some salad leaves on the side or a salad of grated beetroot and carrot.

➔ TAKE TO WORK
Not suitable.

➔ NOTE
These patties are quite soft so be gentle when flipping and removing from the pan.

Spelt and Roasted Cauliflower and Chickpea Bowl with Creamy Tahini Drizzle

This bowl combines nutty spelt with caramelised roasted cauliflower and a creamy tahini drizzle. Spelt offers more protein than most common grains like rice or barley, making it a smart choice for those looking to increase their intake through whole foods. Balanced, nourishing and full of flavour, this is a perfect lunch or light dinner option.

250g cauliflower, cut into small florets
2 tbsp tinned chickpeas
1 tbsp extra virgin olive oil, plus 1 tsp for the spelt
½ tsp smoked paprika
½ tsp ground coriander
Juice of ½ lemon
80g quick-cook spelt
Sea salt

For the tahini dressing
1½ tbsp runny tahini
1½ tbsp natural yoghurt
1 tsp lemon juice
½ tsp maple syrup or honey
¼ small garlic clove, grated

1. Preheat the oven to 220°C/200°C fan/Gas 7.
2. Tip the cauliflower and chickpeas into a bowl with the tablespoon of olive oil, smoked paprika, ground coriander, half the lemon juice and a pinch of sea salt. Toss to combine, then spread out on a baking tray and roast for about 20 minutes until the cauliflower is golden and tender, turning once during cooking.
3. Meanwhile, cook the spelt in lightly salted water for about 15–20 minutes until soft. Drain, then stir through the teaspoon of olive oil and remaining lemon juice with a pinch of salt.
4. Whisk together the tahini, yoghurt, lemon juice, maple syrup or honey and garlic with a tablespoon of warm water and a pinch of salt until smooth and creamy.
5. To serve, divide the spelt between two bowls, top with roasted cauliflower and chickpeas and drizzle generously with the tahini dressing.

➔ NUTRIENTS MORE THAN 15% RDA
Calcium, iron, magnesium, potassium, selenium, zinc, vitamins A, B1, B2, B3.

➔ NUTRIENTS MORE THAN 30% RDA
Folate, phosphorus, vitamins C, K.

➔ PROTEIN BOOSTER
Sprinkle over pumpkin seeds or add extra chickpeas.

➔ NUTRIENT BOOSTER
Serve with a handful of salad leaves and a sprinkle of pomegranate seeds.

➔ TAKE TO WORK
Not suitable.

➔ NOTES
You can find small 215g tins of chickpeas in large supermarkets or buy them in a jar that you can store in the fridge. Cauliflower can be a little bloating for some people, so keep the portion size small to start if you're sensitive.

Buckwheat, Mushroom and Pea Pilaf with Feta

This dish may feel a little bulky for some people, but it's still light, easy to digest and full of nourishing ingredients. The mild flavours make it ideal for days when your appetite is low, and it's a great way to get fibre, magnesium and B vitamins onto your plate. It also works really well as a base or side to a portion of protein, such as grilled fish, chicken, eggs or tofu, helping you build a balanced, nutrient-dense meal with minimal effort.

- 100g buckwheat
- 2 tsp extra virgin olive oil
- ½ small onion, finely chopped
- 1 garlic clove, grated
- 100g mushrooms, chopped
- 1 tsp dried thyme
- Zest and juice of ¼ lemon
- 250ml vegetable stock
- 50g frozen peas, defrosted
- 30g feta cheese
- Small handful of chopped flat-leaf parsley
- Sea salt and black pepper

1. Rinse the buckwheat under cold water and set aside.
2. Heat the olive oil in a non-stick saucepan over a medium heat, then add the onion and garlic and sauté for 2–3 minutes until softened.
3. Add the mushrooms and cook for another 5 minutes until tender.
4. Stir in the buckwheat, thyme, lemon zest and juice and vegetable stock. Bring to the boil, then reduce the heat, cover and simmer for about 12 minutes. Add the peas and cook for another 3 minutes; by this time the buckwheat should be tender and all the liquid absorbed. Let it sit for 5 minutes before fluffing with a fork, then season with salt and pepper.
5. Crumble over the feta and chopped parsley before serving in small bowls.

➔ NUTRIENTS MORE THAN 15% RDA
Folate, zinc, vitamins B2, B3, C.

➔ NUTRIENTS MORE THAN 30% RDA
Magnesium, phosphorus.

➔ PROTEIN BOOSTER
Add extra feta cheese or peas. You can also stir through a little yoghurt.

➔ STORAGE
This will keep in the fridge for 3 days in an airtight container.

➔ NUTRIENT BOOSTER
Add sweetcorn, finely diced peppers or serve with fermented vegetables like sauerkraut.

➔ TAKE TO WORK
Yes.

➔ NOTE
You can find buckwheat in the grains section of most large supermarkets.

Saffron-spiced Prawn Rice with Peas and Baby Spinach

This light and fragrant rice dish is packed with protein from prawns, which are naturally low in fat and rich in important nutrients like selenium, vitamin B12, iodine and zinc. The addition of peas brings sweetness and a gentle boost of fibre, along with folate and vitamin C to support energy and immune health. Using white basmati rice keeps the texture soft and digestible.

Small pinch of saffron threads
2 tsp extra virgin olive oil
½ small onion, finely chopped
1 small garlic clove, grated
½ tsp ground coriander
¼ tsp sweet paprika
80g basmati rice
200ml vegetable stock
100g frozen peas
50g baby spinach, chopped
150g raw peeled king prawns, defrosted if frozen
Zest and juice of ¼ lemon
Sea salt and black pepper

1. Soak the saffron threads in 2 tablespoons of hot water and set aside.
2. Heat the oil in a non-stick pan set over a medium heat, then add the onion and garlic and sauté for 2–3 minutes until softened. Add the ground coriander and paprika and cook for 1 minute until fragrant.
3. Add the rice and stir to coat. Pour in the saffron and its soaking water and vegetable stock and bring to the boil, then reduce the heat and simmer, covered, for 12 minutes.
4. Add the peas, baby spinach and prawns. Stir gently, cover and cook for another 4–5 minutes until the prawns are pink and cooked through and the rice is tender.
5. Remove from the heat, stir in the lemon zest and juice and season to taste. Serve warm.

➔ NUTRIENTS MORE THAN 15% RDA
Magnesium, vitamin A.

➔ NUTRIENTS MORE THAN 30% RDA
Folate, iodine, phosphorus, selenium, vitamins B12, C, K.

➔ PROTEIN BOOSTER
Add more prawns or swap the peas for roughly chopped edamame beans.

➔ STORAGE
This will keep in the fridge for 2 days in an airtight container.

➔ NUTRIENT BOOSTER
Add diced red pepper with the onion and garlic or serve with salad.

➔ TAKE TO WORK
Yes.

➔ NOTES
This dish will also work with small chunks of white fish such as cod or haddock.

Golden Paneer Curry with Spinach and Peas

This vibrant curry may look like it has a long list of ingredients, but it's surprisingly easy to make as most of the flavour comes from a quick sauce that's blitzed together in seconds. Paneer is a great source of protein when you're not in the mood for meat, and it holds its shape really well in the pan. Look for ripe, sweet tomatoes as they form the base of the sauce and really lift the overall flavour.

1 tsp ground turmeric
1 tsp ground cumin
1 tsp ground coriander
Pinch of cayenne pepper (optional)
150g paneer, cut into 1cm cubes
1 small onion, roughly chopped
3 garlic cloves, roughly chopped
2cm piece of fresh ginger, peeled and roughly chopped
2 ripe vine or plum tomatoes (200g), roughly chopped
2 tsp extra virgin olive oil
½ green pepper, thinly sliced
6 curry leaves (optional)
Large handful of spinach
50g frozen peas
Juice of ¼ lemon
Sea salt

1. In a bowl, mix the turmeric, cumin, coriander and cayenne (if using). Toss the paneer cubes in the spice mix to coat.
2. Put the onion, garlic, ginger and tomatoes into a jug and blitz with a stick blender until smooth.
3. Heat 1½ teaspoons of the olive oil in a saucepan over a medium heat. Fry the paneer for 4–5 minutes until golden and crisp. Remove from the pan and set aside.
4. Add the remaining oil to the same pan. Add the blended tomato mixture, sliced green pepper and curry leaves (if using). Cook for 8–10 minutes until thickened and soft.
5. Return the paneer to the pan. Add the spinach, peas and 100ml water and bring to a simmer, then cook for 5 minutes until the spinach is wilted and the peas are tender.
6. Season with sea salt and finish with a squeeze of lemon juice.

➔ NUTRIENTS MORE THAN 15% RDA
Iron, potassium, vitamins B1, B2, B3, B6, B12.

➔ NUTRIENTS MORE THAN 30% RDA
Calcium, folate, phosphorus, vitamins A, C, K.

➔ PROTEIN BOOSTER
Add extra paneer, cooked lentils or a dollop of skyr or Greek yoghurt.

➔ STORAGE
This will keep for up to 3 days in the fridge or 2 months in the freezer stored in an airtight container.

➔ NUTRIENT BOOSTER
Add chickpeas to the pan with the tomato sauce or sprinkle over chopped toasted cashews. You can also serve with a little brown rice or wholemeal flatbread or roti.

➔ TAKE TO WORK
Yes – reheat before eating.

➔ NOTES
You can often find curry leaves in large supermarkets. Freeze what you don't use for future dishes.

Cauliflower Parmigiana with Mozzarella and Parmesan Crust

If you love aubergine parmigiana but fancy a twist, this cauliflower version makes a lighter, equally satisfying alternative. Roasting thick cauliflower steaks brings out their natural sweetness and gives them a tender, golden finish. Cauliflower is also an excellent source of vitamin C needed for immunity and collagen production in the body.

1 medium cauliflower
2 tbsp extra virgin olive oil
1 garlic clove, finely chopped
200ml passata or chopped tomatoes
1 tbsp tomato purée
½ tsp dried oregano
2 tbsp wholemeal breadcrumbs
20g grated Parmesan cheese
40g grated mozzarella
Few basil leaves
Sea salt and black pepper

1. Preheat the oven to 200°C/180°C fan/Gas 6. Trim the cauliflower and slice 2 thick steaks from the centre (about 2cm thick each). Reserve the remaining florets for another use.
2. Brush both sides of the cauliflower steaks with 1 tablespoon of the olive oil, season with salt and pepper and place on a lined baking tray. Roast for 20–25 minutes, turning halfway, until golden and tender.
3. While the cauliflower is roasting, heat 1 teaspoon of olive oil in a small saucepan. Add the garlic and cook for 1 minute, then stir in the passata, tomato purée, oregano and some salt and pepper. Simmer gently for 10 minutes until slightly thickened.
4. In a small bowl, mix the breadcrumbs, Parmesan, remaining olive oil and a pinch more oregano.
5. Once the cauliflower is roasted, spoon the tomato sauce evenly over each steak. Top with grated mozzarella, then scatter over the breadcrumb mixture.
6. Return to the oven for 10–12 minutes, or until the cheese is melted, golden and bubbling.
7. Serve hot, scattered with fresh basil leaves.

➔ NUTRIENTS MORE THAN 15% RDA
Folate, magnesium, potassium, vitamins B1, B6, E.

➔ NUTRIENTS MORE THAN 30% RDA
Calcium, phosphorus, vitamins A, B2, B12, C, K.

➔ PROTEIN BOOSTER
Sprinkle over toasted pine nuts or a small drizzle of sour cream. Serve with a small portion of chicken, salmon or grilled halloumi.

➔ NUTRIENT BOOSTER
Serve with a small mixed leaf salad with added leftover beans or quinoa. Add chopped black olives or sun-dried tomatoes to the tomato sauce.

➔ TAKE TO WORK
Yes – reheat at work.

➔ NOTE
Keep leftover florets and roast them to use in soups, salads, as a side vegetable, or as a healthy snack with tahini as a dip.

Thai Red Cod and Prawn Curry with Brown Rice

I absolutely love a good Thai curry and there is no reason you can't enjoy this as a smaller serving. This is a no-fuss recipe where all the main ingredients get added at once to save you time. It's light, warming and full of bright flavours, with a creamy coconut base and tender seafood. The prawns and cod provide lean protein, while the veg and brown rice help round out the dish with fibre and essential nutrients.

- 1 tsp extra virgin olive oil
- 2 spring onions, thinly sliced (save some greens for garnish)
- Small handful of coriander, leaves and stalks chopped separately
- 1–2 tsp Thai red curry paste
- 200ml coconut milk
- 80g fine green beans, halved
- Small head of pak choi, roughly chopped
- 125g cod fillet, cut into chunks
- 75g raw peeled king prawns, defrosted if frozen
- Juice of ¼ lime
- 1 tsp fish sauce
- ½ tsp brown sugar
- 180g cooked short-grain brown rice, to serve

1. Heat the olive oil in a non-stick saucepan set over a medium heat. Sauté the spring onions and chopped coriander stalks for 2 minutes.
2. Stir in the curry paste, add the coconut milk and bring to a simmer.
3. Add the green beans, pak choi, cod and prawns. Cover and simmer gently for about 5 minutes until the seafood is cooked through. For a less brothy curry, cook with the lid off.
4. Stir in the lime juice, fish sauce and brown sugar.
5. Serve with the brown rice, topped with the reserved spring onion greens and coriander leaves.

➔ NUTRIENTS MORE THAN 15% RDA
Iron, magnesium, potassium, zinc, vitamins A, B1, B6, C, K.

➔ NUTRIENTS MORE THAN 30% RDA
Folate, iodine, phosphorus, selenium, vitamins B3, B12.

➔ PROTEIN BOOSTER
Add extra cod or prawns or swap brown rice for quinoa. Add edamame beans.

➔ STORAGE
This will last for up to 2 days in the fridge and 1 month in the freezer stored in an airtight container.

➔ NUTRIENT BOOSTER
Add edamame beans or spinach to the curry. Add extra brown rice.

➔ TAKE TO WORK
Yes.

➔ NOTES
This recipe works with chicken or firm tofu in place of the fish and seafood. You can use ready-cooked rice from a pouch or, if cooking from scratch, 60g dried rice will give you 180g cooked.

Spiced Sardine and Lentil Traybake with Tahini Drizzle

This traybake is a quick, affordable way to get oily fish into your diet, with fibre-rich lentils, roasted veg and a creamy tahini drizzle to pull it all together. Go for a good-quality tin of sardines if your budget allows (brands like Ortiz make a difference). If you find sardines in oil a bit rich, swap for tinned mackerel in brine.

- ½ large red pepper, chopped
- 1 small courgette (120g), sliced into rounds
- ½ small red onion, sliced
- 1 small garlic clove, whole
- 2 tsp extra virgin olive oil
- ½ tsp ground cumin
- ½ tsp smoked paprika
- 180g cooked green lentils (tinned is fine)
- Zest and juice of ¼ lemon
- 1 tbsp chopped flat-leaf parsley
- 2 tsp tahini
- 1 x 125g tin sardines in olive oil, drained well and patted dry
- Sea salt and black pepper

1. Preheat the oven to 200°C/180°C fan/Gas 6. Toss the chopped pepper, courgette, red onion and garlic with 1 teaspoon of the olive oil, cumin and smoked paprika. Roast on a tray for 20–25 minutes until golden and soft.
2. In a bowl, combine the cooked lentils with the roasted vegetables and mash in the garlic flesh, then add the lemon zest and juice, parsley and remaining teaspoon of olive oil. Season with salt and pepper.
3. In a small bowl, whisk the tahini with some warm water, adding a teaspoon at a time to create a light drizzle. Season with a pinch of salt.
4. Divide the lentil mixture between 2 plates, drizzle with the tahini, then top with the sardines.

➔ NUTRIENTS MORE THAN 15% RDA
Iron, zinc, vitamins A, B1, K.

➔ NUTRIENTS MORE THAN 30% RDA
Phosphorus, selenium, vitamins B6, B12, C, D. Contains omega-3.

➔ PROTEIN BOOSTER
Add more lentils, tinned sardines or combine the tahini with yoghurt.

➔ STORAGE
This will keep in the fridge for 3 days in an airtight container.

➔ NUTRIENT BOOSTER
Increase the roasted vegetables and add cherry tomatoes.

➔ TAKE TO WORK
Yes.

➔ NOTES
This recipe also works with puy lentils or chickpeas if you have leftovers. If you are cooking lentils from scratch, 60g dried lentils will give you 180g cooked.

Middle Eastern Chickpea and Aubergine One-pot

This warmly spiced one-pot is on the lighter side, making it ideal for days when your appetite is small, but you still want something nourishing and full of flavour. It's fibre-rich and gently satisfying thanks to the chickpeas and aubergine, but you can easily build it into a more substantial meal. It also batch-cooks well and keeps in the fridge or freezer.

---

2 tsp extra virgin olive oil
1 small onion, finely chopped
1 garlic clove, grated
1 small aubergine (about 200g), cut into 1cm cubes
1 tsp ground cumin
½ tsp smoked paprika
¼ tsp ground cinnamon (optional)
1 tbsp tomato purée
200ml passata
150g tinned chickpeas, rinsed and drained
1 tbsp sultanas
150ml vegetable stock
Juice of ½ lemon
Small handful of flat-leaf parsley, chopped
Sea salt and black pepper

1. Heat the oil in a non-stick saucepan set over a medium heat. Add the onion and garlic and sauté for 2–3 minutes.
2. Add the aubergine and cook for 5 minutes until softened.
3. Stir in the cumin, paprika, cinnamon (if using) and tomato purée. Cook for 1 minute.
4. Add the passata, chickpeas, sultanas and stock and bring to the boil, then reduce the heat and simmer gently, uncovered, for 25–30 minutes until thick and the aubergine is very soft, stirring occasionally.
5. Stir in the lemon juice and parsley and season before serving in small bowls.

➔ NUTRIENTS MORE THAN 15% RDA
Calcium, iron, magnesium, potassium, vitamins B3, B6, E, K.

➔ NUTRIENTS MORE THAN 30% RDA
Folate, phosphorus, vitamins A, C.

➔ PROTEIN BOOSTER
Add Greek yoghurt or skyr or fortified soya yoghurt or leftover lentils or chickpeas.

➔ STORAGE
This will keep in the fridge for 3 days and the freezer for 3 months in an airtight container.

➔ NUTRIENT BOOSTER
Add frozen peas, chopped fresh tomatoes or red pepper.

➔ TAKE TO WORK
Yes.

➔ NOTE
This is best to serve on days when your protein intake is already on target.

NUTRIENT BOOSTERS

Nordic Seed Loaf

This loaf is an easy and delicious way to boost your intake of protein, fibre and healthy fats. Packed with a variety of seeds, it provides valuable nutrients including omega-3 fatty acids and key minerals like magnesium, iron and zinc. It's simple to make, keeps brilliantly and improves in texture as it stays moist over time. Enjoy it alongside soups, stews or salads or serve it on its own as a mini meal topped with something protein-rich like smoked salmon, hummus or a sliced boiled egg.

100g sunflower seeds
100g pumpkin seeds
50g flaxseeds (linseeds)
50g sesame seeds
50g chia seeds
100g rolled oats
50g hazelnuts or almonds, chopped
2 tbsp psyllium husk
1 tsp fine sea salt
350ml water
1 tbsp maple syrup or honey
3 tbsp extra virgin olive oil

1. In a large bowl, combine the sunflower seeds, pumpkin seeds, flaxseeds, sesame seeds, chia seeds, oats, chopped nuts, psyllium husk and salt.
2. In a jug, mix the water, maple syrup or honey and olive oil.
3. Pour the wet mixture into the dry ingredients and stir thoroughly until it forms a thick, porridge-like consistency.
4. Spoon into a lined 20 x 10cm loaf tin, pressing down firmly and smoothing the top.
5. Let the loaf rest for at least 2 hours at room temperature or overnight in the fridge, to allow the chia and psyllium to absorb the liquid and bind the loaf.
6. Preheat the oven to 200°C/180°C fan/Gas 6.
7. Bake the loaf in the tin for 25 minutes. Remove the loaf from the tin and return to the oven, placed directly on the oven rack. Bake for a further 20–25 minutes until firm and golden.
8. Cool completely on a wire rack before slicing. The loaf will firm up further as it cools.

➔ NUTRIENTS MORE THAN 15% RDA
Calcium, folate, iron, zinc, vitamins B1, B6, E.

➔ NUTRIENTS MORE THAN 30% RDA
Magnesium, phosphorus. Contains omega-3.

➔ PROTEIN BOOSTER
Top with smoked salmon, sliced hard-boiled egg, tinned sardines, soft cheese and chopped herbs or mashed jarred white beans.

➔ STORAGE
Keeps for 5 days in the fridge in an airtight container. Slice and freeze for up to 2 months. Defrost or toast from frozen.

➔ NUTRIENT BOOSTER
Spread with a dip like hummus or mashed avocado (see page 201).

➔ TAKE TO WORK
Yes – add a protein topping.

➔ NOTE
The ingredients for this loaf can be costly, so look out for deals on nuts and seeds in health food shops or buy in bulk online to save money.

A: Nordic seed loaf
B: Cottage cheese bread
C: Beetroot and seed wholemeal loaf

Beetroot and Seed Wholemeal Loaf

This is another nourishing loaf that's rich in both protein and fibre, with just one slice giving you around a sixth of your daily intake. While the ingredient list may look long, it's simple to make: just mix the dry and wet ingredients together and bake. The grated beetroot not only boosts the nutritional value but also adds a gentle natural sweetness balanced by the subtle aniseed flavour of caraway seeds. Enjoy it toasted for breakfast or alongside soup or salad.

250g wholemeal flour
100g rolled oats
2 tbsp sunflower seeds
2 tbsp pumpkin seeds
2 tbsp chia seeds
2 tsp caraway seeds
2 tsp baking powder
½ tsp bicarbonate of soda
1 tsp fine sea salt
2 large eggs
75ml milk or unsweetened fortified soya milk
75g sour cream
3 tbsp extra virgin olive oil
1 tbsp apple cider vinegar or lemon juice
1 tbsp maple syrup or honey (optional)
300g cooked beetroot (vacuum-packed is fine), grated
1 tbsp mixed seeds, for topping (optional)

1. Preheat the oven to 200°C/180°C fan/Gas 6. Grease and line a medium loaf tin with parchment paper.
2. In a large bowl, combine the wholemeal flour, oats, sunflower seeds, pumpkin seeds, chia seeds, caraway seeds, baking powder, bicarbonate of soda and salt.
3. In a separate bowl, whisk together the eggs, milk, sour cream, olive oil, vinegar or lemon juice and maple syrup or honey (if using). Stir in the grated beetroot until evenly combined.
4. Add the wet ingredients to the dry and fold gently until just mixed. The batter will be thick.
5. Spoon the mixture into the prepared tin and smooth the top. Sprinkle with extra seeds if desired.
6. Bake for 40 minutes, then cover loosely with foil and bake for another 20 minutes until a skewer inserted into the centre comes out mostly clean.
7. Let the loaf cool in the tin for 5–10 minutes, then transfer to a wire rack to cool completely. Slice only once fully cooled.

➔ NUTRIENTS MORE THAN 15% RDA
Calcium, chromium, iron, magnesium, zinc, vitamins A, B1, B2, B3, B6, D, E.

➔ NUTRIENTS MORE THAN 30% RDA
Folate, phosphorus, vitamins B12, K.

➔ PROTEIN BOOSTER
Spread with cottage cheese, Greek yoghurt and a small squeeze of maple syrup or honey, coconut yoghurt or hummus. Toast, top with scrambled egg or tofu.

➔ STORAGE
Keeps for 5 days in the fridge in an airtight container. Slice and freeze for up to 2 months.

➔ NUTRIENT BOOSTER
Spread with avocado. Top with sliced tomatoes or jarred roasted peppers.

➔ TAKE TO WORK
Yes – add a protein topping.

➔ NOTE
If you're freezing it, separate slices with parchment paper to make it easier to toast straight from frozen.

Cottage Cheese Bread

This clever cottage cheese bread became a big trend on social media – and for good reason. It's incredibly easy to make, high in protein and surprisingly satisfying for such a light loaf. Serve it as part of a meal or enjoy a slice on its own when your appetite is particularly low. It also works brilliantly as a savoury, protein-rich snack. I highly recommend the sun-dried tomato and black olive version.

220g full-fat cottage cheese
2 large eggs
150g oat flour (see Note)
1 tsp baking powder
¼ tsp bicarbonate of soda
¼ tsp sea salt

Optional additions

1 tbsp extra virgin olive oil

1 tbsp chopped herbs, like chives

1 tbsp dill and zest of ½ lemon

4 sun-dried tomatoes (finely chopped) and 6 black olives, sliced

1. Preheat the oven to 180°C/160°C fan/Gas 4 and line a 900g loaf tin with parchment paper.
2. Add the cottage cheese and eggs to a blender or food processor and blend until smooth.
3. In a separate bowl, combine the oat flour, baking powder, bicarbonate of soda and salt.
4. Stir the blended mixture into the dry ingredients until just combined. Fold in any optional additions (if using), then pour the mixture into the lined tin and level the top.
5. Bake for 30–35 minutes, or until the top is golden brown, the loaf is pulling slightly away from the sides, and it springs back when gently pressed in the centre. To test doneness, insert a toothpick or skewer into the centre; if it comes out clean or with a few dry crumbs, it's ready. If it's wet or sticky, bake for another 5–10 minutes and test again.
6. Cool the loaf completely in the tin before slicing.

➔ NUTRIENTS MORE THAN 15% RDA
Calcium, vitamins B1, B2, B12.

➔ NUTRIENTS MORE THAN 30% RDA
Phosphorus.

➔ STORAGE
This will keep for 5 days in the fridge stored in an airtight container or sliced and frozen for up to 2 months. Defrost as needed or toast.

➔ TAKE TO WORK
Yes.

➔ NOTE
To make oat flour, add rolled oats to a food processor or high-speed blender and blitz until fine and powdery.

1 SERVING = 1TBSP

Dukkah

This savoury, Egyptian-inspired seed and nut blend is a brilliant way to add an extra boost of minerals to almost any meal. Just a spoonful can provide meaningful amounts of magnesium, iron, zinc and vitamin E – all from a crunchy, flavour-packed mix. It's endlessly versatile and can be sprinkled over roasted vegetables, salads, soups, hummus, or avocado toast. Keep a jar on the counter or in the fridge so it's always ready to add texture, taste and valuable nutrients.

70g hazelnuts (or almonds/ pistachios)
2 tbsp sesame seeds
1 tbsp coriander seeds
1 tbsp cumin seeds
1 tsp fennel seeds
½ tsp black peppercorns
½ tsp sea salt flakes
Pinch of chilli flakes (optional)

1. Toast the nuts in a dry frying pan over a medium heat until golden, then set aside.
2. Toast the sesame seeds separately until lightly browned. Do the same with the coriander, cumin and fennel seeds and peppercorns until fragrant, around 1 minute.
3. Let everything cool, then add to a spice grinder or food processor with the salt and chilli flakes (if using) and blitz to a coarse mix. Don't over-blend as it should be crunchy, not powdery.

➔ NUTRIENTS MORE THAN 15% RDA
Iron, magnesium, phosphorus, vitamin E.

➔ STORAGE
Keeps for up to 3 weeks in an airtight jar at room temperature and up to 6 weeks if stored in the fridge.

1 SERVING = 1 TBSP

Toasted Seed Mix

This simple toasted seed mix is a great way to boost the mineral content of your meals – especially magnesium – while also adding a little fibre, protein and omega-3 from the flaxseeds. I always keep a jar on the kitchen counter so I can sprinkle it on everything from soups to salads, eggs, or even porridge as an easy nutrient booster. It's quick to make, easy to store and adds crunch, flavour and valuable nutrition to just about anything.

70g sunflower seeds
70g pumpkin seeds
50g sesame seeds
20g golden linseeds (flaxseeds)
10g nigella seeds (optional)
½ tsp sea salt

Optional flavour boost

½ tsp smoked paprika or ground cumin

or

2 tsp soy sauce (don't add salt to soy version)

1. Place all the seeds in a dry frying pan over a medium heat. Toast for 6–8 minutes, stirring often, until golden and fragrant.
2. In the last minute, stir in the salt and any spices.
3. Let cool completely, then transfer to an airtight jar.

NUTRIENTS MORE THAN 15% RDA

Calcium, magnesium, phosphorus, vitamins B1, E. Contains omega-3.

STORAGE

Store in an airtight jar for up to 2 weeks or 1 month if you store in the fridge.

NOTES

Keeps for up to 3 weeks in an airtight jar. Use within 7–10 days if adding soy sauce.

Super Seeded Crackers

1 SERVING = 2 CRACKERS

These crunchy seeded crackers are a great way to nudge up your daily fibre and protein intake, especially if you're struggling with appetite. They're naturally gluten-free and incredibly versatile – serve them with dips, soups, salads, or any meal that needs a bit of texture and nourishment on the side. With a good dose of healthy fats and essential minerals, they're a smart staple to keep in the cupboard.

100g sunflower seeds
50g sesame seeds
50g pumpkin seeds
50g chia seeds
2 tbsp psyllium husk
½ tsp sea salt
250ml warm water
1 tbsp extra virgin olive oil, plus extra for brushing

Optional additions

½ tsp garlic powder or smoked paprika
1 tsp dried rosemary or thyme
Flaky sea salt, cracked black pepper, or chilli flakes for topping

1. Preheat the oven to 180°C/160°C fan/Gas 4 and line 2 baking trays with parchment paper.
2. In a large bowl, combine all the dry ingredients, including any optional herbs or spices.
3. Stir in the warm water and olive oil until a thick, gel-like dough forms. Let sit for 10 minutes to absorb the liquid.
4. Place the dough between two sheets of parchment paper and roll out evenly to a thickness of 3–4mm. Remove the top sheet of paper.
5. Use a 5cm round cutter to cut out crackers, then transfer them carefully to the trays using a greased spatula. Reroll and repeat as needed.
6. If liked, brush the tops with olive oil and sprinkle with flaky salt, cracked black pepper or chilli flakes.
7. Bake for 25–30 minutes, rotating the trays halfway through, until dry, golden and crisp.
8. Cool completely on a wire rack before storing in an airtight jar or tin.

➔ NUTRIENTS MORE THAN 15% RDA
Magnesium, phosphorus, vitamins B1, E. Contains omega-3.

➔ STORAGE
These will keep for up to 3 weeks in an airtight jar or up to 6 weeks in the fridge.

Avocado Smash with Toasted Nuts and Seeds

This creamy, savoury dip is rich in healthy fats, plant-based protein and fibre – ideal for adding extra nourishment and energy content to a small meal or snack. The toasted nuts and seeds bring crunch and a boost of key nutrients like magnesium, vitamin E and zinc. Enjoy it with seeded bread or crackers (see pages 194 and 200), raw vegetable sticks, or serve it alongside any other recipe in the book.

20g cashew nuts
20g hazelnuts
1 tsp sunflower seeds
1 tsp white sesame seeds
1 tsp black sesame seeds
2 small ripe avocados (120g each)
Juice of ½ lemon
2 tbsp finely chopped chives or spring onion
Few coriander leaves (optional)
Sea salt and black pepper

1. Preheat the oven to 200°C/180°C fan/Gas 6. Spread the nuts and seeds out on a baking tray and toast for 8 minutes until golden. Cool slightly, then crush lightly using a pestle and mortar or chop roughly.
2. Halve and stone the avocados. Scoop the flesh into a bowl and mash with lemon juice, chives and salt and pepper until chunky but spreadable.
3. Stir in most of the crushed nuts and seeds.
4. Spoon into a small bowl, sprinkle over the remaining nuts and seeds and top with coriander leaves (if using).

➔ NUTRIENTS MORE THAN 15% RDA
Magnesium, vitamins B6, C, E.

➔ STORAGE
Best eaten within 24 hours. Store any leftovers in an airtight container with cling film pressed directly onto the surface to minimise browning.

➔ TAKE TO WORK
Yes – pack with dippers in a sealed container and eat the same day.

Whipped Cottage Cheese

1 SERVING = 50G (2 HEAPED TBSP)

This smooth, whipped cottage cheese is a simple way to add a little extra protein to your meals. It has a light, fluffy texture that works well served on the side or dolloped onto salads, grain bowls, or spread over wholegrain toast. You can also enjoy it sweet with fresh berries, stewed fruit or baked oats for a creamy, high-protein twist.

250g full-fat cottage cheese
1 tbsp natural yoghurt
Pinch of salt (optional)

1. Place the cottage cheese in a food processor and blend for 30–60 seconds until completely smooth, light and fluffy. Alternatively, use a stick blender.
2. Add the yoghurt to loosen the consistency, using a little more if needed.
3. Season lightly with salt, if desired, or leave plain for a more adaptable base.

➔ NUTRIENTS MORE THAN 15% RDA
Phosphorus, vitamin B12.

➔ NOTES
You can add herbs, spices or a little honey to this whipped cottage cheese. You can also use high-protein cottage cheese.

Cashew Nut Cream

SERVES 6

96 KCAL

2.6G PROTEIN

0.5G FIBRE

1 SERVING = 50G

Cashew nuts are naturally rich in magnesium – more so than most other nuts. Magnesium plays a vital role in supporting muscle function, reducing fatigue and maintaining steady energy levels. This simple cashew cream is not only deliciously smooth but is also a great way to give meals a nutrient boost. You can drizzle it over almost any dish or add to wraps in place of mayo or butter.

100g raw cashew nuts
200ml water

1. Soak the cashew nuts in hot water for 30 minutes (or overnight in cold water), then drain and rinse.
2. Blend with 200ml fresh water in a high-powered blender until smooth and creamy.
3. Add a splash more water, if needed, to reach the consistency of double cream. It should be thick, pourable and smooth.

➔ NUTRIENTS MORE THAN 15% RDA
Magnesium, phosphorus.

➔ STORAGE
This keeps in the fridge for up to 4 days.

➔ NOTES
Try giving this a Mediterranean twist by blending in 30g sun-dried tomatoes (about 3–4 pieces from a jar) and 1 small garlic clove. Add a pinch of smoked paprika to taste.

JUICES, SMOOTHIES & WARMING DRINKS

Coconut and Mango Lassi

100g ripe mango (fresh or defrosted from frozen)
100ml fortified coconut milk drink
1 tbsp natural skyr or Greek yoghurt or fortified soya yoghurt
Small squeeze of lime juice
Pinch of ground cardamom
Ice cubes, to blend

1. Blend all the ingredients until smooth and creamy.

Blueberry and Almond Butter Smoothie

80g frozen blueberries
100ml unsweetened almond milk (or use oat milk for extra creaminess)
1 tbsp almond butter
1 tbsp natural skyr or Greek yoghurt
¼ tsp ground cinnamon (optional)

1. Blend everything until smooth. Add a splash more milk if needed for blending.

Warm Honey and Cinnamon Almond Milk

180ml unsweetened fortified almond milk
½ tsp honey or maple syrup
¼ tsp ground cinnamon
Tiny pinch of ground turmeric or ginger

1. Gently warm the almond milk in a small pan, then stir in the honey or maple syrup, cinnamon and turmeric or ginger. Whisk briefly or froth for a creamier texture.

Carrot and Ginger Juice

2 medium carrots

½ apple

1cm piece of fresh ginger, peeled and grated (add more for an increased ginger hit)

Juice of ½ lemon

50–100ml cold water

1. Blitz everything in a high-speed blender until smooth, then strain through muslin. Alternatively, use a juicer.

Tummy Tea for Bloating

This herbal tea blends fennel, caraway and mint, which are all ingredients traditionally used to ease bloating by relaxing the muscles of the stomach and intestines, helping gas pass more easily. It's a gentle option after meals, especially when digestion feels sluggish. Sip slowly, but avoid if you're prone to heartburn, as mint can relax the valve between the stomach and oesophagus.

1 tsp fennel seeds

½ tsp caraway seeds

A few mint leaves

200ml freshly boiled water

➔ NOTE
Do not drink this for heartburn. Just bloating.

1. Crush the fennel and caraway seeds lightly with a spoon or pestle to release their oils. Place in a teapot or mug with the mint leaves. Pour over the freshly boiled water, cover and let steep for 10 minutes. You can serve through a tea strainer if you like.

Refreshing Mixed Berry Protein Shake

200ml unsweetened fortified almond milk (or any milk)

80g frozen mixed berries

1 scoop of unsweetened plain protein powder (whey or plant-based)

2 tbsp Greek-style yoghurt or fortified soya yoghurt

1. Blend all the ingredients until smooth. Add extra cold water or ice to loosen if too thick. Serve immediately.

A: Tummy tea for bloating
B: Refreshing mixed berry protein shake
C: Carrot and ginger juice
D: Blueberry and almond butter smoothie
E: Coconut and mango lassi
F: Warm honey and cinnamon almond milk
B
C
A

E
F
D

PRE- AND POST-WORKOUT SNACKS

PRE-WORKOUT SNACKS
212

POST-WORKOUT SNACKS
218

Spiced Almond and Date Energy Balls

These naturally sweet energy balls are made with whole ingredients and contain no added sugar, just the goodness of dates, almonds and chia seeds. They're perfect as a small snack between meals or as a quick boost before the gym when you need a little energy without feeling too full. Lightly spiced with cinnamon and ginger, they're satisfying and nutrient-rich, as well as being freezer-friendly.

100g almonds
100g pitted dates (soaked in warm water for 10 minutes if dry)
1 tbsp chia seeds
½ tsp ground cinnamon
¼ tsp ground ginger
Pinch of sea salt
1 tbsp water (if needed)

1. Put the almonds, dates, chia seeds, cinnamon, ginger and salt into a food processor. Blitz to crush the almonds, then keep blending until the mixture forms a sticky, dough-like consistency. Add a splash of water if needed to help it blend.
2. Roll the mixture into 8–10 small balls (about 1 tablespoon per ball).
3. Store in an airtight container in the fridge for up to 1 week or freeze for longer.

➔ NUTRIENTS MORE THAN 15% RDA
Chromium, folate, magnesium, phosphorus, vitamin E.

➔ PROTEIN BOOSTER
Add an additional 1–2 tablespoons of hemp seeds or protein powder (you may need to add a splash more water).

➔ STORAGE
Freeze until solid on a lined baking tray then transfer to an airtight container for up to 3 months.

➔ NUTRIENT BOOSTER
Serve with juice or a smoothie.

➔ TAKE TO WORK
Yes.

➔ NOTES
Experiment with different spices or unsweetened cocoa powder. You can also eat these straight from the freezer if you like a chewy toffee texture.

Tahini and Pistachio Energy Balls

These energy balls are rich, nutty and packed with healthy fats and plant protein to keep you going. They're ideal before exercise or as a nutrient-dense snack when your appetite is low. Make a bigger batch and store in the fridge or freezer for an easy grab-and-go option.

100g unsalted shelled pistachios, roughly chopped
100g tahini
2 tsp honey or maple syrup
1 tbsp chia seeds
Pinch of sea salt

1. In a food processor, combine the pistachios, tahini, honey or maple syrup, chia seeds and a pinch of salt.
2. Blend until the mixture comes together into a sticky dough. Add a little water, 1 tablespoon at a time, if needed.
3. Roll into 10 small balls using your hands.
4. Store in an airtight container in the fridge for up to a week.

➔ NUTRIENTS MORE THAN 15% RDA
Phosphorus, vitamins B1, B6.

➔ PROTEIN BOOSTER
Add 1 tablespoon hemp seeds.

➔ STORAGE
They can be stored in the fridge for 1 week or the freezer for 3 months in an airtight container.

➔ NUTRIENT BOOSTER
Add a few chopped dried apricots.

➔ TAKE TO WORK
Yes.

➔ NOTES
This is a compact, nutrient-rich option. One ball is usually well tolerated on GLP-1 medication, but eat slowly and see how your body responds.

A
B

A: Tahini and pistachio energy balls
B: Quinoa and almond energy bites
C: Spiced almond and date energy balls
D: Coconut, oat and banana bites

Quinoa and Almond Energy Bites

These light and energising snacks are designed to fuel your body before exercise, but because dates aren't used in many of these types of bites, they won't feel too heavy or sweet. The focus is on quick energy, a little protein and easy digestion – ideal when your appetite is low. This recipe works best when you use freshly cooked quinoa over ready-cooked from a pouch, but they are also a great way to use up leftover cooked quinoa.

100g cooked quinoa, cooled
80g almonds, roughly chopped
2 tbsp almond butter (or use peanut butter)
2 tsp maple syrup or honey
1 tbsp chia seeds
½ tsp ground cinnamon
Pinch of sea salt

1. Combine all the ingredients in a large bowl. Mix well until everything is evenly incorporated, pressing the mixture firmly in the bowl with a spatula.
2. If the mixture is too dry, add some water, 1 tablespoon at a time, until a dough-like consistency forms, making it easy to roll.
3. Roll the mixture into small balls (1 generous tablespoon of dough per ball).
4. Place the energy bites on a lined baking tray or plate and refrigerate for at least 30 minutes to set.

➔ NUTRIENTS MORE THAN 15% RDA
Magnesium, phosphorus, vitamin B2.

➔ NUTRIENTS MORE THAN 30% RDA
Vitamin E.

➔ PROTEIN BOOSTER
Add more chia seeds.

➔ STORAGE
They last up to 5 days in the fridge and 3 months in the freezer stored in an airtight container.

➔ NUTRIENT BOOSTER
Add more chia seeds.

➔ TAKE TO WORK
Yes.

➔ NOTE
These work best if you use freshly cooked quinoa (rather than a pouch of ready-cooked) – 35g dried quinoa will give you 100g cooked.

Coconut, Oat and Banana Bites

These soft, naturally sweet bites are perfect before exercise or as a quick energy boost. They contain vitamin B6, which helps your body convert food into fuel, along with fibre-rich oats and flaxseed to support digestion.

1 small ripe banana
30g rolled oats
1 tbsp desiccated coconut
½ tbsp ground flaxseed
Pinch of sea salt

1. Mash the banana thoroughly in a bowl until smooth, then add the oats, coconut, flaxseed and sea salt and mix well to combine.
2. Use your hands to shape the mixture into 6 small bite-sized balls.
3. Place in the fridge for 30 minutes to firm up.

➔ NUTRIENTS MORE THAN 15% RDA
Phosphorus, vitamins B6, C.

➔ STORAGE
They will keep in the fridge for 3 days in an airtight container.

➔ TAKE TO WORK
Yes.

Coconut Berry Protein Shake

A protein shake is a useful way to top up your intake if you've struggled to eat enough during the day, especially when managing a smaller appetite. It's also a great quick breakfast when you don't feel like eating much but want a nourishing start to the day.

100g frozen mixed berries
2 scoops of unflavoured plant-based protein powder
1 tbsp rolled oats
300ml chilled fortified coconut milk drink
½ tsp maple syrup or honey (optional)

1. Add the berries, protein powder, oats, coconut milk drink and maple syrup or honey (if using) to a blender. Blend until completely smooth.
2. Pour into 2 small glasses and serve immediately.

➔ NUTRIENTS MORE THAN 15% RDA
Phosphorus, vitamins B2, C.

➔ NUTRIENTS MORE THAN 30% RDA
Calcium, vitamins B12, D.

➔ NUTRIENT BOOSTER
Add a small handful of baby spinach or a teaspoon of ground flaxseed or unsweetened cocoa powder (it will change the colour slightly).

➔ TAKE TO WORK
Not suitable.

➔ NOTE
You can try this with other frozen fruits like mango and pineapple.

Refreshing Apple and Lime Overnight Oats

This light and refreshing overnight oats recipe is the perfect way to start your day, especially if you struggle with appetite in the morning. The zingy combination of apple and lime adds brightness, while the addition of protein powder helps boost your intake – useful if you're finding it hard to reach your daily protein goals. It's quick to prep, easy to digest, and ideal for after the gym or busy mornings.

40g rolled oats
1 tbsp chia seeds
1 scoop of unflavoured plant-based protein powder
100ml unsweetened apple juice
150ml milk or unsweetened fortified soya milk
Zest and juice of ½ lime
1 small apple, coarsely grated (with peel)
Pinch of ground cinnamon (or ground ginger)
Berries, toasted coconut flakes, mixed seeds or chopped nuts, to top
2 tbsp Greek yoghurt or skyr or fortified soya yoghurt

1. In a bowl mix the oats, chia seeds and protein powder.
2. Stir in the apple juice, milk and lime zest and juice, then lightly whisk to combine.
3. Add the grated apple and cinnamon – or ginger if you want more of a kick. Cover and refrigerate overnight.
4. In the morning, stir well and add more milk if needed to loosen the oats. Serve topped with your chosen topping, or on its own with yoghurt or skyr.

➔ NUTRIENTS MORE THAN 15% RDA
Calcium, iodine, magnesium.

➔ NUTRIENTS MORE THAN 30% RDA
Phosphorus, vitamin B12.

➔ PROTEIN BOOSTER
Add more yoghurt or skyr. Sprinkle over nuts and seeds.

➔ STORAGE
It will keep in the fridge for 3 days, but you will need to add more milk to loosen the oats.

➔ NUTRIENT BOOSTER
Add different types of fruit. Look for a fortified protein powder.

➔ TAKE TO WORK
Yes.

➔ NOTE
These oats also make a great breakfast or nourishing snack option across the day.

Edamame and Pomegranate Seeded Salad

This super fresh salad is packed with texture and colour, and edamame brings a decent hit of plant-based protein to the mix. It's not quite giving 20g like some of the other recipes in this post-workout section, but it's a great option if you want something lighter or if your appetite is small. Edamame beans are rich in fibre, folate and magnesium, making them a great all-round recovery food.

80g frozen edamame beans, defrosted
2 tbsp pomegranate seeds
2 tsp pumpkin seeds
1 tsp sunflower seeds
Squeeze of lime
Small pinch of salt
Few coriander leaves, to serve

1. Put the edamame beans into a bowl and toss with the pomegranate seeds, pumpkin seeds and sunflower seeds.
2. Add a squeeze of lime juice and a pinch of salt, then stir well to combine.
3. Sprinkle over a little fresh coriander just before serving.

➔ NUTRIENTS MORE THAN 15% RDA
Iron, zinc, vitamin B1.

➔ NUTRIENTS MORE THAN 30% RDA
Folate, magnesium, phosphorus, vitamins C, K.

➔ PROTEIN BOOSTER
Add more edamame beans.

➔ STORAGE
It will keep for 3 days in an airtight container.

➔ NUTRIENT BOOSTER
Serve as a side dish to cooked protein foods like chicken or fish.

➔ TAKE TO WORK
Yes.

➔ NOTE
You can turn this dish into a salad by adding salad leaves, cucumber, tomatoes and grated carrot.

Egg, Avocado and Sriracha Mini Wraps

This is a great option if you're looking for something quick and nourishing after training. The mix of protein and carbs makes it ideal for post-workout recovery, especially if you train early and need a solid breakfast or brunch to refuel. You can buy egg whites in a carton if you're adding more to up the protein content of this one.

---

1 tsp extra virgin olive oil
2 medium eggs
2 medium egg whites
½ ripe avocado, mashed
1 tbsp natural skyr or Greek yoghurt
2 small wholewheat mini wraps
1 tbsp sriracha sauce (or to taste)
1 tbsp chopped coriander (optional)
Sea salt and black pepper

1. Heat the olive oil in a small non-stick saucepan over a medium heat.
2. Crack the eggs into a bowl, add the egg whites and whisk well. Season with a little salt and pepper.
3. Pour the egg mixture into the pan and scramble gently until just set but still soft. Remove from the heat.
4. In a small bowl, mash the avocado with the skyr or Greek yoghurt and a pinch of salt.
5. Warm the wraps slightly in a dry pan or microwave, then spread the avocado-yoghurt mix evenly over each wrap.
6. Top with the scrambled egg, a drizzle of sriracha and scatter with coriander (if using). Roll up or fold and enjoy warm.

➔ NUTRIENTS MORE THAN 15% RDA
Calcium, chromium, folate, iodine, magnesium, selenium, zinc, vitamins B1, B3, B6, D, E.

➔ NUTRIENTS MORE THAN 30% RDA
Phosphorus, vitamins A, B2, B12, K.

➔ PROTEIN BOOSTER
Add another egg white or some cooked black beans to the scrambled egg.

➔ NUTRIENT BOOSTER
Add shredded red cabbage, carrot or lettuce or pumpkin seeds.

➔ TAKE TO WORK
Yes.

➔ NOTE
If you don't like sriracha try tomato relish, olive tapenade or tomato ketchup.

SERVES 2

250 KCAL

20G PROTEIN

4.5G FIBRE

Prawn and Avocado Cracker Stack with Grated Radish

This light, post-workout meal is ideal when you need protein but don't feel like eating much. It's really quick and easy to put together, with no cooking involved – you just layer and go. Prawns provide lean, high-quality protein to support recovery, while avocado adds healthy fats and a creamy texture.

1 small ripe avocado
1 tsp lemon juice
1 tbsp chopped coriander
1 tsp extra virgin olive oil
2 seeded rye crispbreads (like Ryvita)
4 radishes, finely grated
150g cooked peeled prawns
Black pepper

1. In a bowl, mash the avocado with the lemon juice, chopped coriander, olive oil and a pinch of black pepper.
2. Spoon the avocado mash onto the crackers and scatter the grated radish over the top.
3. Pile the prawns generously on top of the avocado.

➔ NUTRIENTS MORE THAN 15% RDA
Potassium.

➔ NUTRIENTS MORE THAN 30% RDA
Folate, iodine, phosphorus, selenium, vitamins B6, B12, C, E, K.

➔ PROTEIN BOOSTER
Add extra prawns or sprinkle pumpkin seeds over the avocado mash.

➔ NUTRIENT BOOSTER
Add extra avocado, herbs, finely shredded iceberg lettuce or chopped tomatoes to the mash mixture. You can also serve on small slices of toasted rye bread for something more substantial.

➔ TAKE TO WORK
Yes – assemble just before eating.

➔ NOTE
You can switch prawns for crumbled feta or cubes of grilled halloumi, but it will be lower in protein.

MEAL PLANS

Omnivore Menu Plan 1

This menu plan shows how the recipes in this book can work together across a week and you'll find a mix of meat, fish and plant-based meals. Each day includes the option to add snacks if you need extra energy or protein.

	Monday				Tuesday				Wednesday			
		Cals	Protein (g)	Fibre (g)		Cals	Protein (g)	Fibre (g)		Cals	Protein (g)	Fibre (g)
Breakfast	Coconut chia pudding with mango and toasted almonds	257	10.1	10	Gut-loving kefir breakfast shake *plus almonds*	391	16.3	7	Raspberry almond quinoa porridge	333	13.1	6.5
Lunch	Zesty tuna and brown rice nourish bowl	390	23	6	Carrot and lentil soup with coconut and lime *plus pumpkin seeds*	390	19	10.5	Smoked mackerel and avocado mash on rye	340	20	4
Dinner	Quick chicken and carrot broth with spelt	400	27	9	Turkey keema curry with wholemeal pitta	400	29	8.2	Chilli and fennel pork stew with tahini drizzle	395	28	8.3
Snacks (optional)	Spiced almond and date energy balls	102	2.8	2.7	Cashew nut cream *with red pepper slices*	80	2.3	3	Edamame, pomegranate seeded salad	200	14	6.5
	Refreshing mixed berry protein shake	187	27	3.8	Refreshing apple and lime overnight oats	251	20	5	Coconut, oat and banana bites	126	3	3
Totals		1336	89.9	31.5		1512	86.6	33.7		1394	78.1	28.3

Thursday				Friday				Saturday				Sunday			
	Cals	Protein (g)	Fibre (g)		Cals	Protein (g)	Fibre (g)		Cals	Protein (g)	Fibre (g)		Cals	Protein (g)	Fibre (g)
Nutty banana power pancakes *plus skyr and chia seeds*	373	25.2	7	Spiced apple and hazelnut chia skyr pot	255	17	7.5	Coconut chia pudding with mango and toasted almonds	257	10.1	10	Raspberry almond quinoa porridge	333	13.1	6.5
Herby lentils with whipped feta, cumin, carrots and toasted almonds	370	17	6.5	Baked eggs with spiced chickpeas and garlic yoghurt	340	17	8	Turmeric poached egg bowl with quinoa, greens and smoky tomato sauce	395	22	5.4	Lentil, chicken and roast carrot protein bowl	313	31	6.6
Poached cod with miso broth, wilted greens and brown rice	330	26	6.5	Spiced sardine and lentil traybake with tahini drizzle	325	22	7	Sesame-crusted tuna steak with edamame and avocado salad	387	38.1	5.5	Buckwheat, mushroom and pea pilaf with feta	331	13	9.3
Blueberry and almond butter smoothie *plus almonds*	253	9	6.8	Beetroot and seed wholemeal loaf *with* Cashew nut cream	279	9.5	5.3	Edamame and pomegranate seeded salad	200	14	6.5	Prawn and avocado cracker stack with grated radish	250	20	4.5
Quinoa and almond energy bites	110	3.7	2	Coconut berry protein shake	180	25	1.8	Whipped cottage cheese *with carrot sticks*	88	2.2	2.3	Coconut, oat and banana bites	126	3	3
	1436	80.9	28.8		1379	90.5	29.6		1327	86.4	29.7		1353	80.1	29.9

Omnivore Menu Plan 2

This second omnivore menu plan gives another look at how the recipes from this book can work in real life, this time alongside the kind of everyday meals you might naturally cook yourself (flagged with italics).

	Monday				Tuesday				Wednesday			
		Cals	Protein (g)	Fibre (g)		Cals	Protein (g)	Fibre (g)		Cals	Protein (g)	Fibre (g)
Breakfast	Raspberry almond quinoa porridge	333	13.1	6.5	Spiced apple and hazelnut chia skyr pot	279	12.7	6	Refreshing apple and lime overnight oats *plus chia seeds*	300	22	8.8
Lunch	*Shredded chicken, apple, celery and walnut with Greek yoghurt and rye crackers*	340	25	5.2	Soft egg and spinach dhal with coconut yoghurt *plus toasted pumpkin seeds*	420	27.5	7	*Tinned tuna and chickpea salad with lemon juice, olive oil and seeded crackers*	350	27.6	8.2
Dinner	Poached cod with miso broth, wilted green and brown rice	330	26	6.5	*Grilled chicken breast with mixed wholegrains, roasted courgette and pesto*	380	26	6	Aubergine and tofu stew with coconut, edamame and lime	400	20	6.5
Snacks (optional)	Edamame and pomegranate seeded salad	200	14	6.5	*Roasted almonds, cherry tomatoes and feta cubes*	215	7	3	*Turkey slices rolled with hummus and spinach leaves*	145	15	2.5
	Whipped cottage cheese with seeded crackers	181	5.8	3.7	*Edamame and cucumber with* Toasted seed mix, *lime juice and salt*	180	12	6	*Peanut butter on apple slices with sunflower seeds*	102	2.9	1.6
Totals		1384	83.9	28.4		1474	85.2	28		1297	87.5	27.6

Thursday				Friday				Saturday				Sunday			
	Cals	Protein (g)	Fibre (g)		Cals	Protein (g)	Fibre (g)		Cals	Protein (g)	Fibre (g)		Cals	Protein (g)	Fibre (g)
Scrambled egg in a mini wholemeal wrap with black beans and guacamole	265	14	5.6	*Porridge made with protein powder, milk, with stewed fruit and chia seeds*	380	28.6	8.6	Miso scrambled eggs with chives and pumpkin seeds	310	19	3	Baked oats with blueberries and honey plus *Greek yoghurt*	389	22.1	4.1
Herby salmon bowl with radish and pesto *plus lentils*	420	33.2	6.4	Smashed edamame, spinach and goat's cheese toast	300	17	7	Nordic seeded loaf *with smoked salmon and avocado*	378	17.4	7.4	*Falafel, hummus and wholewheat couscous with carrot and sultanas*	370	11	7.5
Saffron-spiced prawn rice with peas and baby spinach	325	21	4.3	*Salmon with cooked lentils, cherry tomatoes and tzatziki*	360	28.4	6	Sweetcorn and potato chowder with cod, paprika and cumin	300	24	6.9	Buckwheat, mushroom and pea pilaf with feta	331	13	9.3
Chickpeas mashed with tahini on rye crackers with sliced spring onion	185	7	6	*Hard-boiled egg with cherry tomatoes and olives*	107	6.5	2	Blueberry and almond butter smoothie *plus almonds*	253	9	6.8	*Boiled egg mashed with avocado on rye crispbread*	160	7	4.2
Greek yoghurt with chia seeds, almonds and berries	196	11.6	7	*Wholemeal wrap with almond butter and banana*	220	6	3.8	*Cottage cheese with fresh or tinned peach slices and chia seeds*	130	11	3	Refreshing mixed berry protein shake	187	27	3.8
	1391	86.8	29.3		1367	86.5	27.4		1371	80.4	27.1		1437	80.1	28.9

Plant-based Menu Plan

This third menu is completely plant-based, showing how you can meet protein, fibre and micronutrient needs on a smaller appetite without animal products or heavy reliance on substitutes.

	Monday				Tuesday				Wednesday			
		Cals	Protein (g)	Fibre (g)		Cals	Protein (g)	Fibre (g)		Cals	Protein (g)	Fibre (g)
Breakfast	Raspberry almond quinoa porridge	333	13.1	6.5	Nutty banana power pancakes *plus soya yoghurt (fortified)*	322	17.3	4	Baked oats with blueberries and honey *plus soya yoghurt (fortified)*	330	17.2	6.6
Lunch	Crunchy tofu wraps with peanut drizzle	350	20	4.5	Spinach dhal with coconut yoghurt *(no egg) plus mini wholemeal pitta*	330	16.8	8	Tofu scramble with baby spinach and sun-dried tomatoes *plus wholegrain toast*	320	23.4	6.5
Dinner	Kitchari-style lentil and rice bowl wth coconut, lime and pumpkin seeds	350	13	5	Aubergine and tofu stew with coconut, edamame and lime	400	20	6.5	*Quorn and veggie stir fry with wholemeal noodles and edamame*	300	22	6.5
Snacks (optional)	Edamame and pomegranate seeded salad	200	14	6.5	Refreshing apple and lime overnight oats	251	20	5	Nordic seeded loaf *with* Cashew nut cream	247	8	5.7
	Refreshing mixed berry protein shake	197	27	3.8	Roasted chickpeas	120	6	4.8	*Soya yoghurt (fortified) with berries, flaked almonds and chia seeds*	220	9.4	6.5
Totals		1430	87.1	26.3		1423	80.1	28.3		1417	80	31.8

Thursday				Friday				Saturday				Sunday			
	Cals	Protein (g)	Fibre (g)		Cals	Protein (g)	Fibre (g)		Cals	Protein (g)	Fibre (g)		Cals	Protein (g)	Fibre (g)
Tofu scramble with baby spinach and sun-dried tomatoes *plus mini wholemeal wrap*	250	14	4.5	Refreshing apple and lime overnight oats	251	20	5	Raspberry almond quinoa porridge	333	13.1	6.5	*Soya yoghurt (fortified) with granola (low sugar), berries and* Toasted seed mix	250	10.3	3.6
Warm lentil salad with roasted beetroot, walnuts and coconut yoghurt	320	15	5.8	Carrot and lentil soup with coconut and lime	390	19	8	Silken tofu and brown rice bowl with sesame, lime and avocado	350	16.5	6.5	Nordic seeded loaf *topped with mashed chickpeas, tahini, nutritional yeast and lemon juice*	400	18	12
Spelt and roasted cauliflower and chickpea bowl with creamy tahini drizzle	380	14	8.3	Marinated tofu and sweet potato skewers with lemon yoghurt dip *plus quinoa*	320	19	5	*Quorn and chickpea tagine with wholemeal couscous*	300	18.5	6.2	*Smokey bean and edamame chilli*	380	17	6.5
Edamame and cucumber with Toasted seed mix, *lime juice and salt*	180	12	6	Coconut chia pudding with mango and toasted almonds	257	10.1	10	*Wholemeal wrap with almond butter and banana*	220	6	3.8	Coconut berry protein shake *plus almonds*	270	29	1.8
Refreshing mixed berry protein shake *plus almonds*	287	30.2	5.7	Edamame and pomegranate seeded salad	200	14	6.5	Refreshing mixed berry protein shake *plus almonds*	287	30.2	5.7	Cashew nut cream *with seeded crackers and red pepper slices*	191	5.8	5.7
	1417	85.2	30.3		1418	82.1	34.5		1490	84.3	28.7		1491	80.1	29.6

APPENDIX 1

PORTION SIZE GUIDE FOR SMALL APPETITES

Why these portion sizes were chosen

There is no universal rule for how much food someone with a small appetite should eat. However, the best-studied model for appetite reduction comes from people taking GLP-1 receptor agonists (such as semaglutide or tirzepatide), who typically consume around 35 per cent fewer calories than those not taking the medication. This reduction is due to earlier satiety, slower gastric emptying and lower day-to-day appetite.

Because this is one of the few situations where appetite reduction has been clearly quantified, the portion sizes throughout this book are based on an average one-third reduction from standard UK adult servings. While developed with GLP-1 users in mind, this model also provides a helpful and realistic starting point for anyone navigating low appetite, from any cause. These portions are:

- Approximately one-third smaller than standard UK adult servings
- Designed to support nutrient density in smaller volumes
- Balanced to avoid overfilling the stomach while still delivering protein, fibre and key micronutrients
- Grounded in real-world dietetic practice, practical and flexible, not rigid or calorie-obsessed

How to use these portion tables

These tables are here to help you build meals, not dictate them. Each portion represents a suggested amount of a single ingredient, based on its role in a balanced meal, such as protein, grains, vegetables or fats. You can mix and match these portioned ingredients to create meals that are nutritionally balanced, enjoyable and well-tolerated, even when your appetite is small. Use them as:

- A guide when cooking from scratch
- A reference when reading recipes
- A way to build meals that feel manageable and satisfying

Portion size tables

These tables aim to help you meet your nutrition needs without waste, overwhelm or pressure to eat more than you feel comfortable with.

PROTEIN FOODS (COOKED OR READY-TO-EAT WEIGHTS)

Food	Normal Portion	Normal Protein	Reduced Portion (70%)	Reduced Protein (70%)
Chicken breast	90g	27g	65g	19.5g
Salmon fillet	140g	35.3g	100g	25.2g
Cod fillet	140g	33.5g	100g	23.9g
Tinned fish (average)	110g	27.4g	77g	19.2g
Beef mince (lean)	90g	19.6g	65g	14.2g
Pork (lean)	90g	24.3g	65g	17.6g
Lamb (lean)	90g	23.9g	65g	17.3g
Eggs	2 medium (120g)	16.9g	2 small (100g)	14.1g
Prawns	100g	16.2g	70g	11.3g
Tofu (firm)	100g	12g	70g	8.4g
Whey protein powder	30g	24g	–	–
Plant-based protein powder	30g	22g	–	–
Greek yoghurt	150g	8.5g	105g	5.7g
Soya yoghurt (fortified)	150g	5g	105g	3.3g
Skyr	150g	15.9g	105g	11.6g
Dairy milk	200ml	6.8g	140ml	4.8g
Soya milk (fortified)	200ml	4.8g	140ml	3.4g
Cheese	30g	7.5g	20g	5g
Cottage cheese	100g	9.4g	70g	6.6g
Nuts	30g	7.1g	–	–
Seeds	30g	7.3g	–	–

Note: The protein powders, nuts and seeds are not shown with a 30% reduction, as they are already used in smaller, practical amounts in recipes (e.g. 1–2 tbsp for nuts/seeds; portioned slices for the loaf).

A NOTE ON INDIVIDUAL VARIATION

Everyone's appetite is different, and it can fluctuate daily. These portion sizes are a starting point, not a rule. They're designed to reflect typical reductions seen in GLP-1 users, but they can also support people with other causes of low appetite.

Factors like age, sex, body size, energy needs and health status will influence how much food feels right for you. Always listen to your body and adjust accordingly, as the goal is to eat in a way that feels nourishing and sustainable for you.

LEGUMES (COOKED OR READY-TO-EAT WEIGHTS)

Food	Normal Portion	Normal Protein	Normal Fibre	Reduced Portion (70%)	Reduced Protein (70%)	Reduced Fibre (70%)
Chickpeas	150g	12.6g	7.1g	105g	8.8g	5g
Lentils (average)	150g	11.7g	5.7g	105g	8.2g	4g
Beans (average)	150g	11.2g	9.1g	105g	7.8g	6.4g
Edamame beans	150g	18g	8.7g	105g	12.6g	6.1g
Peas	80g	4.2g	3g	60g	3.2g	2.1g

CARBOHYDRATE FOODS

Food	Normal Portion	Normal Fibre	Reduced Portion (70%)	Reduced Fibre (70%)
Quinoa	150g cooked / 75g dry	3.5g	100g cooked / 55g dry	2.4g
Brown rice	150g cooked / 50g dry	1.4g	100g cooked / 35g dry	1g
Wholewheat pasta	150g cooked / 75g dry	6.6g	100g cooked / 50g dry	4.6g
Oats (porridge)	40g raw	2.9g	30g raw	2.2g
Wholemeal bread	35g (medium slice)	2.2g	25g (small slice)	1.5g
Wholemeal noodles	150g cooked / 60g dry	3.8g	100g cooked / 40g dry	2.7g
Millet	150g cooked / 60g dry	3g	100g cooked / 40g dry	2g

NON-STARCHY VEGETABLES

Veg Type	Normal Portion	Normal Fibre	Reduced Portion	Reduced Fibre
Leafy greens	80g	2.2g	40–80g	1.1g–2.2g
Cruciferous (e.g. broccoli, cauliflower)	80g	1.8g	40–80g	0.9g–1.8g
Colourful soft veg (e.g. red pepper, salad leaves, tomatoes)	80g	0.8g	40–80g	0.4g–0.8g

STARCHY AND MODERATELY STARCHY VEGETABLES

Food	Normal Portion	Normal Fibre	Reduced Portion (70%)	Reduced Fibre (70%)
Sweet potato (skin on)	180g	5.9g	100g	3.3g
Squash	80g	1.1g	60g	0.8g
Plantain	80g	1g	60g	0.7g
Sweetcorn	80g	2.4g	60g	1.7g
Peas	80g	3.2g	60g	2.2g
Beetroot	80g	1.5g	60g	1.1g
Carrots	80g	1.7g	60g	1.2g
Turnips	80g	1.5g	60g	1.1g
Celeriac	80g	2.5g	60g	1.8g
Okra	80g	2.9g	60g	2.0g

FRUIT, NUTS AND SEEDS

Fruit	Normal Portion	Normal Fibre	Reduced Portion	Reduced Fibre
Apple	80g	1g	40–80g	0.5g–1g
Banana	80g	0.6g	40–80g	0.3g–0.6g
Berries	80g	1.2g	40–80g	0.6g–1.2g
Orange	80g	1.4g	40–80g	0.7g–1.4g
Kiwi	80g	1.5g	40–80g	0.8g–1.5g
Melon	80g	0.5g	40–80g	0.3g–0.5g
Dried fruit	30g	2.3g	30g	2.3g
Mixed nuts	30g	1.9g	15g	0.9g
Seeds	30g	3g	15g	1.5g

Sources: British Dietetic Association (BDA) portion size guidance; McCance & Widdowson's Composition of Foods (CoFID) for nutrient values; Friedrichsen et al. (2021) study on appetite and energy intake in GLP-1 users.

APPENDIX 2

KEY VITAMINS AND MINERALS AND WHERE TO FIND THEM

Fat-soluble vitamins

Vitamin A: Needed for healthy skin, hair and teeth. Antioxidant that protects against infection, heart disease and cancer.

Retinol: liver, oily fish, eggs and dairy foods.

Beta-carotene: brightly coloured fruit and vegetables such as pumpkin, mangoes, tomatoes, peppers, carrots and dark green vegetables, including kale and broccoli.

Vitamin D: Required for the absorption of calcium, essential for maintaining strong bones. Also has a role in immune system and muscle function.

Sourced mainly from sunlight but found in eggs, oily fish, fortified margarines and shiitake mushrooms.

Vitamin E: Antioxidant required for healthy skin, heart and immune system.

Sunflower oil, avocados, papayas, broccoli, sunflower seeds, nuts (especially almonds), wholegrain foods, edamame beans and parsley.

Vitamin K: Essential for strong bones and proper blood clotting.

Eggs, oily fish, avocados and dark green leafy vegetables such as Brussels sprouts, kale, spinach and broccoli.

Water-soluble vitamins

Vitamin B1 (thiamin): Needed for energy production, digestion of carbohydrates and heart function.

Liver, wholegrain foods such as oats, rye and quinoa, pulses, kale, broccoli, avocados and spinach.

Vitamin B2 (riboflavin): Helps to convert food into energy and essential for healthy hair and nails.

Eggs, dairy foods, liver, asparagus, broccoli, chard, spinach and almonds.

Vitamin B3 (niacin): Helps to convert food into energy and promote normal growth.

Lean meat, poultry, eggs, mushrooms, asparagus, halibut, salmon, peanut butter and pulses such as red kidney beans and chickpeas.

Vitamin B5 (pantothenic acid): Helps to convert food into energy and supports the adrenal glands (these control stress response in the body) and a healthy immune system.

Wholegrain foods such as oats, brown rice and quinoa, nuts, chicken, eggs, liver, sunflower seeds, sweetcorn, broccoli and cauliflower.

Vitamin B6: Required for healthy immune and nervous systems.

Poultry and lean red meat, eggs, oily fish, tofu, potatoes, cabbage, leeks, spinach, peppers, white fish and bananas.

Vitamin B12: Needed for energy production. Essential for growth, digestion and nerves, and to ensure healthy blood cells and prevention of pernicious anaemia.

Meat, sardines, scallops, eggs, fortified soya milk, seaweed and spirulina.

Biotin: Required for energy production and healthy nails, hair and skin.

Swiss chard, brewer's yeast, brown rice, nuts, edamame beans and egg yolks.

Folic acid (folate): Prevents neural tube defects in unborn babies. Essential for a healthy immune system and preventing anaemia.

Eggs, carrots, apricots, squash, melon, spinach, broccoli, okra, cauliflower and pulses such as lentils, chickpeas and black-eyed beans.

Vitamin C: Antioxidant essential for a strong immune system, good skin and wound healing. Antioxidant properties linked to protection against cancer and heart disease.

Fruit and vegetables, especially berries, kiwi fruit, oranges, pomegranates, peppers, potatoes, squash and broccoli.

Minerals

Calcium: Essential for strong bones, teeth and heart. Also involved in muscle function and helps to maintain healthy blood pressure.

Calcium-enriched soya products, dark green leafy vegetables (except spinach and Swiss chard), small-boned fish such as sardines, tofu, almonds, sesame seeds (also tahini) and dried fruit.

Chromium: Enhances the activity of insulin in the body to help maintain normal blood glucose levels.

Broccoli, liver, eggs, shellfish, nuts, seeds, prunes and wholegrain foods such as brown rice and quinoa.

Iron: Required for proper growth and development, and essential for the production of red blood cells (prevents iron-deficiency anaemia).

Lean red meat, liver, eggs, lentils, oats, dried fruit, kale, avocados and dried herbs and spices.

Magnesium: Required to build healthy bones and helps the body to deal with stress. Associated with healthy muscle and nervous systems.

Dark green vegetables, cashew nuts, sunflower and other seeds, halibut, meat, dried fruit, tomatoes, aubergines and onions.

Potassium: Required for proper muscle and nerve function. Lowers blood pressure and eases fatigue and irritability.

Avocados, bananas, dried fruit and all vegetables (in particular chard and spinach).

Selenium: Antioxidant that is essential for a healthy immune system. Also helps to regulate thyroid hormone activity.

Brazil nuts, shellfish, bran, tomatoes and broccoli (found in most fruit and vegetables, depending on the soil they're grown in).

Zinc: Essential for a strong immune system. Also involved in sexual development, brain function and nervous system, beneficial for men's health.

Shellfish, lean red meat, turkey, wholegrain foods such as oats, brown rice, buckwheat and quinoa, eggs, cashew nuts, almonds, tahini, sesame seeds, lentils, miso, pumpkin seeds and pine nuts.

Phosphorus: Needed for strong bones and teeth. Also involved in energy production and the formation of cell membranes (as part of phospholipids).

Meat, poultry, fish, eggs, dairy foods, nuts, seeds, wholegrains, pulses and soya products.

Iodine: Essential for the production of thyroid hormones, which regulate metabolism, growth and development. Also supports brain development during pregnancy and infancy.

White fish, shellfish, seaweed, eggs, dairy foods and iodised salt (if used). Amounts in plant foods vary depending on soil levels.

REFERENCES

1 Johnson, B. *et al*. (2025) 'Investigating nutrient intake during use of glucagon-like peptide-1 receptor agonist: a cross-sectional study', *Frontiers in Nutrition*, 2025, *12*, 1566498. https://doi.org/10.3389/fnut.2025.1566498

2 McDonald, D. *et al*. (2018) 'American Gut: an Open Platform for Citizen Science Microbiome Research', *mSystems*, *3*(3), e00031-18. https://doi.org/10.1128/mSystems.00031-18

3 Look, M. *et al*. (2025) 'Body composition changes during weight reduction with tirzepatide in the SURMOUNT-1 study of adults with obesity or overweight', *Diabetes, Obesity and metabolism*, *27*(5), 2720–2729. https://doi.org/10.1111/dom.16275

4 Neeland, I. J., Linge, J. and Birkenfeld, A. L. (2024) 'Changes in lean body mass with glucagon-like peptide-1-based therapies and mitigation strategies', *Diabetes, Obesity and Metabolism*, *26 Suppl 4*, 16–27. https://doi.org/10.1111/dom.15728

5 Friedrichsen, M. *et al*. (2021) 'The effect of semaglutide 2.4 mg once weekly on energy intake, appetite, control of eating, and gastric emptying in adults with obesity', *Diabetes, Obesity and Metabolism*, 23(3), 754–762. https://doi.org/10.1111/dom.14280

ACKNOWLEDGEMENTS

Thanks to my agent, Dorie Simmonds, and the brilliant team at Thorsons for their unwavering support and dedication to this project. A special mention to the fabulous journalist Louise Atkinson for inspiring me to write this book, and my friend and dietitian Nichola Ludlum-Raine for her support. And, as always, to my friends and family a big thanks for putting up with me and for tolerating my endless agonising over tight deadlines and relentless recipe testing.

INDEX

almond butter: Blueberry and almond butter smoothie 206
Quinoa and almond energy bites 216
almond milk, Warm honey and cinnamon 206
almonds: Raspberry almond quinoa porridge 81
Spiced almond and date energy balls 212
apples: Refreshing apple and lime overnight oats 218
Spiced apple and hazelnut chia skyr pot 88
aubergines: Aubergine and tofu stew 144
Middle Eastern chickpea and aubergine one-pot 191
avocados 19, 65
Avocado smash 201
Creamy avocado drizzle 179
Dukkah-topped avocado and cottage cheese 98
Edamame and avocado salad 151
Egg, avocado and sriracha mini wraps 220
Prawn and avocado cracker stack 221
Silken tofu and brown rice bowl 118
Smoked mackerel and avocado mash on rye 99

bananas: Coconut, oat and banana bites 217
Nutty banana power pancakes 84
beans 19, 28, 52
Bean dip 68
Creamy beans and greens 138
Creamy Parmesan orzo 177
High-protein cauliflower and white bean soup 137
Sardine and white bean mash 102
Smashed white beans with soft egg 128
Tuna and white bean mash on seedy crackers 113
beetroot: Beetroot and seed wholemeal loaf 196
Smoked mackerel and beetroot toast 117
Warm lentil salad with roasted beetroot 133
berries: Coconut berry protein shake 217
Refreshing mixed berry protein shake 207
biotin 233
black beans: Smoky prawn and black bean tacos 148
blueberries: Baked oats with blueberries and honey 89
Blueberry and almond butter smoothie 206
bread: Beetroot and seed wholemeal loaf 196
Cottage cheese bread 197
Nordic seed loaf 194
Smashed edamame, pea and goat's cheese toast 126
Smoked mackerel and beetroot toast 117
broths: Poached cod with miso broth, wilted greens and brown rice 152
Quick chicken and carrot broth 172
Rice noodle and chicken broth 114
bubble and squeak, Crispy top 68
Buckwheat, mushroom and pea pilaf with feta 182

calcium 12, 14, 27, 43, 55, 233
carrots: Carrot and ginger juice 207
Carrot and lentil soup 123
Ginger carrot soup with silken tofu 116
Herby lentils with whipped feta, cumin and carrots 92
Lentil, chicken and roast carrot protein bowl 157
Quick chicken and carrot broth 172
cashews: Cashew nut cream 203
Thai prawn, grapefruit, cashew and toasted coconut bites 103
cauliflower: Cauliflower parmigiana 187
High-protein cauliflower and white bean soup 137
Prawn and cauliflower curry 153
Spelt and roasted cauliflower and chickpea bowl 180
cheese 52
Buckwheat, mushroom and pea pilaf with feta 182
Cauliflower parmigiana 187
Creamy Parmesan orzo 177
Herby lentils with whipped feta, cumin and carrots 92
Mini baby spinach, pea and Parmesan omelette 120
Mini egg muffins with spinach, sweetcorn and feta 86
Smashed edamame, pea and goat's cheese toast 126
Stuffed courgettes with harissa lamb, feta and tomato sauce 164
chia seeds: Coconut chia pudding with mango 82
Spiced apple and hazelnut chia skyr pot 88
chicken 19, 52, 67
Baked chicken with creamy coconut brown rice, peas and spinach 158
Crunchy chicken salad 104
Lentil, chicken and roast carrot protein bowl 157
Quick chicken and carrot broth 172
Rice noodle and chicken broth 114
Za'atar chicken with roasted roots 142

chickpeas: Baked eggs with spiced chickpeas 130
Cucumber, chickpea and mint salad 160
Mashed sweet potato with crispy chickpeas 136
Middle Eastern chickpea and aubergine one-pot 191
Savoury veg and chickpea mash 68
Seared mackerel with spiced chickpeas 167
Spelt and roasted cauliflower and chickpea bowl 180
chillies: Chilli and fennel pork stew 168
Courgetti with tomato, prawns and chilli 147
chowder, Sweetcorn and potato 170
chromium 233
coconut, desiccated: Coconut, oat and banana bites 217
Thai prawn, grapefruit, cashew and toasted coconut bites 103
coconut milk: Aubergine and tofu stew 144
Carrot and lentil soup 123
Coconut and mango lassi 206
Coconut berry protein shake 217
Coconut chia pudding with mango 82
Coconut lentil brown rice 146
Creamy coconut brown rice, peas and spinach 158
Comforting bowl with spelt and egg 178
cottage cheese 52
Cottage cheese and lentil stuffed peppers 108
Cottage cheese bread 197
Dukkah-topped avocado and cottage cheese 98
Whipped cottage cheese 202
courgettes: Courgetti with tomato, prawns and chilli 147
Mini turkey and courgette meatballs 163
Stuffed courgettes with harissa lamb, feta and tomato sauce 164
crab: Crab and brown rice stir fry 132
Crab, mango and noodle salad 100
crackers: Prawn and avocado cracker stack 221
Super seeded crackers 200
Tuna and white bean mash on seedy crackers 113
creatine 57–8
Cucumber, chickpea and mint salad 160
curry: Golden paneer curry 184
Prawn and cauliflower curry 153
Thai red cod and prawn curry 188
Turkey keema curry 159

dates: Spiced almond and date energy balls 212
dhal, Soft egg and spinach 124
dips: Avocado smash 201
Lemon yoghurt dip 169
Tahini and lime dip 125
drinks 44, 49, 60, 63
Blueberry and almond butter smoothie 206
Carrot and ginger juice 207
Coconut and mango lassi 206
Coconut berry protein shake 217
Gut-loving kefir breakfast shake 85
Refreshing mixed berry protein shake 207
Tummy tea for bloating 207
Warm honey and cinnamon almond milk 206
Dukkah 198
Dukkah-topped avocado and cottage cheese 98

edamame 19, 52
Aubergine and tofu stew 144
Edamame and avocado salad 151
Edamame and pomegranate seeded salad 219
Smashed edamame, pea and goat's cheese toast 126
Sticky soy salmon with edamame rice 110
eggs 19, 52
Baked eggs with spiced chickpeas 130
Comforting bowl with spelt and egg 178
Egg, avocado and sriracha mini wraps 220
Egg scramble with veg 68
Mini baby spinach, pea and Parmesan omelette 120
Mini egg muffins with spinach, sweetcorn and feta 86
Miso scrambled eggs 80
Roasted sweet potato and egg stack 78
Smashed white beans with soft egg 128
Soft egg and spinach dhal 124
Spiced grains with peas, baby spinach and soft-yolk egg 129
Turmeric poached egg bowl with quinoa, greens and smoky tomato sauce 134
energy balls: Coconut, oat and banana bites 217
Quinoa and almond energy bites 216
Spiced almond and date energy balls 212
Tahini and pistachio energy balls 213

fennel: Chilli and fennel pork stew 168
fibre 12, 14, 28–30, 43, 44, 48, 50–1, 57
fish 19, 52, 67
Creamy millet, pea and leek bowl with poached haddock 173
Herby salmon bowl 109
Poached cod with miso broth, wilted greens and brown rice 152
Sardine and white bean mash 102
Seared mackerel with spiced chickpeas 167
Sesame-crusted tuna steak with edamame and avocado salad 151
Smoked mackerel and avocado mash on rye 99
Smoked mackerel and beetroot toast 117

INDEX

Smoked salmon and quinoa bowl 107
Spiced sardine and lentil traybake 190
Sticky soy salmon with edamame rice 110
Sweetcorn and potato chowder with cod 170
Tandoori salmon with cucumber, chickpea and mint salad 160
Thai red cod and prawn curry 188
Tuna and white bean mash on seedy crackers 113
Zesty tuna and brown rice nourish bowl 95
folic acid (folate) 14, 233

Garlic yoghurt 130
Ginger carrot soup 116
GLP-1 medications 17, 20–1, 22, 40–9
Golden paneer curry 184
grains 28, 45, 51, 66
Spiced grains with peas, baby spinach and soft-yolk egg 129
grapefruit: Thai prawn, grapefruit, cashew and toasted coconut bites 103
greens 19
Brown rice bowl with teriyaki turkey and greens 162
Creamy beans and greens 138
Creamy Parmesan orzo with wilted greens 177
Poached cod with miso broth and wilted greens 152
Turmeric poached egg bowl with quinoa, greens and smoky tomato sauce 134
Gut-loving kefir breakfast shake 85

harissa: Cottage cheese and lentil stuffed peppers 108
Harissa-spiced turkey skewers 154
Stuffed courgettes with harissa lamb, feta and tomato sauce 164
hazelnuts: Dukkah 198
Spiced apple and hazelnut chia skyr pot 88
herbs 66
Herby lentils with whipped feta, cumin and carrots 92
Herby salmon bowl 109
honey: Baked oats with blueberries and honey 89
Warm honey and cinnamon almond milk 206
Hummus 68

ingredients 18–19, 33, 52, 71–3
iodine 234
iron 11, 12, 14, 43, 51, 55, 233

juice, Carrot and ginger 207

keema curry, Turkey 159
kefir: Gut-loving kefir breakfast shake 85
Kitchari-style lentil and rice bowl 174

lamb: Stuffed courgettes with harissa lamb, feta and tomato sauce 164
lassi, Coconut and mango 206
leeks: Creamy millet, pea and leek bowl with poached haddock 173
leftovers 65–8
Lemon yoghurt dip 169
lentils 19, 52
Carrot and lentil soup 123
Coconut lentil brown rice 146
Cottage cheese and lentil stuffed peppers 108
Herby lentils with whipped feta, cumin and carrots 92
Kitchari-style lentil and rice bowl 174
Lentil, chicken and roast carrot protein bowl 157
Lentil, olive and sun-dried tomato salad 154
Soft egg and spinach dhal 124
Soft lentil and nut patties 179
Spiced sardine and lentil traybake 190
Warm lentil salad with roasted beetroot 133
lettuce: Crunchy tofu wraps 96
leucine 21

magnesium 11, 12, 14, 27, 43, 51, 233
mango: Coconut and mango lassi 206
Coconut chia pudding with mango 82
Crab, mango and noodle salad 100
meatballs, Mini turkey and courgette 163
Middle Eastern chickpea and aubergine one-pot 191
millet: Creamy millet, pea and leek bowl with poached haddock 173
minerals 10, 11, 12–13, 233–4
miso: Miso scrambled eggs 80
Poached cod with miso broth 152
Sticky miso tofu bites 125
muffins: Mini egg muffins with spinach, sweetcorn and feta 86
mushrooms: Buckwheat, mushroom and pea pilaf 182

no-cook recipe ideas 74–5
noodles: Crab, mango and noodle salad 100
Rice noodle and chicken broth 114
Tofu noodles with peanut and sesame dressing 94
Nordic seed loaf 194
Nourishing Dozen 18–19, 33, 71
nut butter 19
Nutty banana power pancakes 84
nuts: Avocado smash with toasted nuts 201
Soft lentil and nut patties 179

oats 19
Baked oats with blueberries and honey 89
Coconut, oat and banana bites 217
Refreshing apple and lime overnight oats 218
olives: Lentil, olive and sun-dried tomato salad 154
omega-3 14, 55
omelette, Mini baby spinach, pea and Parmesan 120

one-pots: Middle Eastern chickpea and aubergine one-pot 191
One-pot nourish bowl 68
orzo, Creamy Parmesan 177

pancakes, Nutty banana power 84
paneer: Golden paneer curry 184
parmigiana, Cauliflower 187
patties: Soft lentil and nut patties 179
Vegetable patties 68
peas: Baked chicken with creamy coconut brown rice, peas and spinach 158
Buckwheat, mushroom and pea pilaf 182
Coconut lentil brown rice and peas 146
Creamy millet, pea and leek bowl 173
Golden paneer curry with spinach and peas 184
Mini baby spinach, pea and Parmesan omelette 120
Saffron-spiced prawn rice with peas and baby spinach 183
Smashed edamame, pea and goat's cheese toast 126
Spiced grains with peas, baby spinach and soft-yolk egg 129
peppers: Cottage cheese and lentil stuffed peppers 108
Mini turkey and courgette meatballs with red pepper sauce 163
pesto, Herby salmon bowl with radish and 109
phosphorous 234
pilaf, Buckwheat, mushroom and pea 182
pistachios: Tahini and pistachio energy balls 213
pomegranate seeds: Edamame and pomegranate seeded salad 219
pork: Chilli and fennel pork stew 168
porridge, Raspberry almond quinoa 81
potassium 12, 233
potatoes: Crispy top bubble and squeak 68
Sweetcorn and potato chowder 170
prawns: Courgetti with tomato, prawns and chilli 147
Prawn and avocado cracker stack 221
Prawn and cauliflower curry 153
Saffron-spiced prawn rice with peas and baby spinach 183
Smoky prawn and black bean tacos 148
Thai prawn, grapefruit, cashew and toasted coconut bites 103
Thai red cod and prawn curry 188
Turmeric-spiced prawns 146
pre- and probiotics 30
protein 12, 14, 20–7, 43, 45, 48, 50, 51, 53, 55, 57
protein shakes: Coconut berry protein shake 217
Refreshing mixed berry protein shake 207
pumpkin seeds, Miso scrambled eggs with 80

quinoa: Herby salmon bowl 109
Prawn and cauliflower curry 153
Quinoa and almond energy bites 216
Raspberry almond quinoa porridge 81
Smoked salmon and quinoa bowl 107
Turmeric poached egg bowl with quinoa, greens and smoky tomato sauce 134

radishes: Herby salmon bowl 109
Prawn and avocado cracker stack 221
Raspberry almond quinoa porridge 81
rice: Baked chicken with creamy coconut brown rice, peas and spinach 158
Brown rice bowl with teriyaki turkey and greens 162
Coconut lentil brown rice and peas 146
Crab and brown rice stir fry 132
Ginger carrot soup with silken tofu and brown rice 116
Kitchari-style lentil and rice bowl 174
Poached cod with miso broth, wilted greens and brown rice 152
Saffron-spiced prawn rice 183
Silken tofu and brown rice bowl 118
Sticky soy salmon with edamame rice 110
Thai red cod and prawn curry 188
Zesty tuna and brown rice nourish bowl 95
Rule of Four 51–2
Rule of Three 53–4

Saffron-spiced prawn rice 183
salads: Crab, mango and noodle salad 100
Crunchy chicken salad 104
Edamame and avocado salad 151
Edamame and pomegranate seeded salad 219
Lentil, olive and sun-dried tomato salad 154
Tandoori salmon with cucumber, chickpea and mint salad 160
Warm lentil salad with roasted beetroot and walnuts 133
seeds 19
Avocado smash with toasted seeds 201
Beetroot and seed wholemeal loaf 196
Dukkah 198
Edamame and pomegranate seeded salad 219
Nordic seed loaf 194
Super seeded crackers 200
Toasted seed mix 199
Tuna and white bean mash on seedy crackers 113
selenium 233
Sesame-crusted tuna steak with edamame and avocado salad 151
shakes: Coconut berry protein shake 217
Gut-loving kefir breakfast shake 85

Refreshing mixed berry protein shake 207
skewers: Harissa-spiced turkey skewers 154
Marinated tofu and sweet potato skewers 169
skyr: Spiced apple and hazelnut chia skyr pot 88
Smashed edamame, pea and goat's cheese toast 126
Smashed white beans with soft egg and herbs 128
Smoky prawn and black bean tacos 148
smoothie, Blueberry and almond butter 206
snacks 33–4, 57, 74–5, 210–21
soups: Carrot and lentil soup 123
Ginger carrot soup 116
High-protein cauliflower and white bean soup 137
Leftover veg soup shot 68
Quick chicken and carrot broth 172
Sweetcorn and potato chowder 170
spelt: Comforting bowl with spelt and egg 178
Quick chicken and carrot broth 172
Spelt and roasted cauliflower and chickpea bowl 180
spinach: Baked chicken with creamy coconut brown rice, peas and spinach 158
Golden paneer curry 184
Mini baby spinach, pea and Parmesan omelette 120
Mini egg muffins with spinach, sweetcorn and feta 86
Saffron-spiced prawn rice with peas and baby spinach 183
Soft egg and spinach dhal 124
Spiced grains with peas, baby spinach and soft-yolk egg 129
Tofu scramble with baby spinach and sun-dried tomatoes 121
sriracha: Egg, avocado and sriracha mini wraps 220
stews: Aubergine and tofu stew 144
Chilli and fennel pork stew 168
stir fry, Crab and brown rice 132
Super seeded crackers 200
sweet potatoes: Marinated tofu and sweet potato skewers 169
Mashed sweet potato with crispy chickpeas 136
Roasted sweet potato and egg stack 78
sweetcorn: Mini egg muffins with spinach, sweetcorn and feta 86
Sweetcorn and potato chowder 170

tacos, Smoky prawn and black bean 148
tahini: Tahini and lime dip 125
Tahini and pistachio energy balls 213
Tandoori salmon with cucumber, chickpea and mint salad 160
tea: herbal tea 49
Tummy tea for bloating 207
teriyaki turkey, Brown rice bowl with 162
Thai prawn, grapefruit, cashew and toasted coconut bites 103
Thai red cod and prawn curry 188
tofu 19, 52
Aubergine and tofu stew 144
Crunchy tofu wraps 96
Ginger carrot soup with silken tofu 116
Marinated tofu and sweet potato skewers 169
Silken tofu and brown rice bowl 118
Sticky miso tofu bites 125
Tofu noodles with peanut and sesame dressing 94
Tofu scramble with baby spinach and sun-dried tomatoes 121
tomatoes: Courgetti with tomato, prawns and chilli 147
Lentil, olive and sun-dried tomato salad 154
Smoky tomato sauce 134
Stuffed courgettes with harissa lamb, feta and tomato sauce 164
Tofu scramble with baby spinach and sun-dried tomatoes 121
traybake, Spiced sardine and lentil 190
Tummy tea for bloating 207
turkey 19, 52, 67
Brown rice bowl with teriyaki turkey and greens 162
Harissa-spiced turkey skewers 154
Mini turkey and courgette meatballs with red pepper sauce and courgetti 163
Turkey keema curry 159
turmeric: Turmeric poached egg bowl with quinoa, greens and smoky tomato sauce 134
Turmeric-spiced prawns with coconut lentil brown rice and peas 146

vegetables 12, 28, 45, 51, 66
leftover vegetables 68
Za'atar chicken with roasted roots 142
see also individual types of vegetable
vitamins 12–13, 232–3
deficiencies 10, 11, 12
vitamin A 12, 51, 232
vitamin B6 14, 45, 233
vitamin B12 11, 14, 43, 55, 233
vitamin C 12, 233
vitamin D 11, 12, 14, 27, 43, 51, 55, 232
vitamin E 12, 51, 232
vitamin K 27, 51, 232

walnuts, Warm lentil salad with roasted beetroot and 133
wraps: Crunchy tofu wraps 96
Egg, avocado and sriracha mini wraps 220

yoghurt 19, 52
Garlic yoghurt 130
Lemon yoghurt dip 169
Spiced apple and hazelnut chia skyr pot 88

Za'atar chicken with roasted roots 142
zinc 234

ABOUT THE AUTHOR

With a successful career spanning nearly two decades, Rob is an award-winning registered nutritionist known for his varied expertise in the field. At the heart of London, he founded RH Nutrition, a renowned consultancy that caters to a diverse clientele and is sought after by private clients and leading health and wellness brands. He's a frequent contributor to top-tier health magazines and is no stranger to the airwaves, making appearances on both radio and TV. Rob is the author of *The Detox Kitchen Bible, The Art of Sleeping*, *Unprocess Your Life* and *Unprocess Your Family Life*.

robhobson.co.uk   @robhobsonnutritionist

Thorsons
An imprint of HarperCollins*Publishers*
1 London Bridge Street
London SE1 9GF

www.harpercollins.co.uk

HarperCollins*Publishers*
Macken House,
39/40 Mayor Street Upper
Dublin 1, D01 C9W8, Ireland

First published by Thorsons 2025

1 3 5 7 9 10 8 6 4 2

A catalogue record of this book is available from the British Library

ISBN 978-0-00-878316-7

Food Stylist: Emily Jonzen
Prop Stylist: Faye Wears

Printed and bound by GPS in Bosnia & Herzegovina

This book is produced from FSC™ certified paper and other controlled sources to ensure responsible forest management.

For more information visit: www.harpercollins.co.uk/green

WHEN USING KITCHEN APPLIANCES PLEASE ALWAYS FOLLOW THE MANUFACTURER'S INSTRUCTIONS